WILL

BIG LEAGUE BASEBALL

SURVIVE?

LINCOLN A. MITCHELL

WILL

BIG LEAGUE BASEBALL

SURVIVE?

Globalization, the End of Television, Youth Sports,
and the Future of Major League Baseball

TEMPLE UNIVERSITY PRESS
Philadelphia · Rome · Tokyo

TEMPLE UNIVERSITY PRESS
Philadelphia, Pennsylvania 19122
www.temple.edu/tempress

Library of Congress Cataloging-in-Publication Data

Names: Mitchell, Lincoln Abraham, author.
Title: Will big league baseball survive? : globalization, the end of
  television, youth sports, and the future of major league baseball /
  Lincoln A. Mitchell.
Description: Philadelphia : Temple University Press, 2017. | Includes bibliographical
  references and index.
Identifiers: LCCN 2016022125 (print) | LCCN 2016037572 (ebook) |
  ISBN 9781439913789 (Cloth : alk. paper) | ISBN 9781439913796 (Paper : alk.
  paper) | ISBN 9781439913802 (E-book)
Subjects: LCSH: Baseball—United States. | Baseball—Social aspects—United
  States. | Major League Baseball (Organization)
Classification: LCC GV863.A1 M56 2017 (print) | LCC GV863.A1 (ebook) | DDC
  796.357/64—dc23
LC record available at https://lccn.loc.gov/2016022125

♾ The paper used in this publication meets the requirements
of the American National Standard for Information Sciences—
Permanence of Paper for Printed Library Materials, ANSI Z39.48-1992

Printed in the United States of America

9 8 7 6 5 4 3 2 1

In memory of my brother,

Jonathan Mitchell

CONTENTS

PREFACE

The Future of Big League Baseball

Major League Baseball has been part of the fabric of American life for more than a century. Although big league baseball has changed, it has also remained constant in many ways over the past 120 years or so. For example, of the thirty major league teams today, ten are the same teams playing in the same cities as they did in 1903, the year of the first World Series. Field dimensions, the ninety feet between bases and the sixty feet six inches from home plate to the pitcher's mound, have remained unchanged for well over a century. Baseball terms, such as "can of corn" for a soft fly ball or "iron man" for a player who shows unusual durability, are remnants from a very different America. For decades, "Take Me Out to the Ballgame" has been perhaps the most universally recognized secular American song.

Big league baseball is steeped in its past, creating a strong sense of continuity in the sport. Following the 2014 World Series, for example, in which San Francisco Giants ace Madison Bumgarner dominated, playing a huge role in carrying his team to victory, knowledgeable fans compared Bumgarner's feat not just to the pitching performances of Sandy Koufax, Bob Gibson, and other World Series greats of the postwar era but, indeed, to the 1905 accomplishments of another Giant, Christy Mathewson, who threw three shut-outs to help carry his team to victory in the second World Series.[1] In 2015, when Ichiro Suzuki's hit total for the United States and Japan reached 4,192, baseball fans recognized that, in some respects, he had tied the total number of hits by Ty Cobb, who played his last game in 1928. That record had been broken by Pete Rose in 1985. In 1995, the baseball world celebrated when Cal Ripken played in his 2,131st consecutive game, breaking a record Lou Gehrig had set in 1939.

Because of this continuity in big league baseball, it is easy to assume that its basic construct—highly paid ballplayers who are the best the world has to offer, who are drawn from everywhere baseball is played, and who play in front of large live audiences in games that are broadcast far and wide—has been in place for a long time and will stay that way for the foreseeable future. The truth, however, is a bit more complicated. For much of the twentieth century, the major leagues were only one of the forums where elite-level baseball involving the best players in the country was played. Moreover, during much of this time, there were competing leagues, some of which were more formally structured than others, inside and outside the United States, and ballplayers earned modest salaries while frequently playing in largely empty stadiums.

The primary question posed in this book—whether big league baseball will survive for more than another decade or two—asks specifically whether big league baseball will continue in its current form as a huge global and lucrative business offering a monopoly, in the United States and Canada, on the best baseball played any-where in the world. The questions of whether big league baseball will survive and whether baseball itself will survive are two dis-tinctly different issues. If big league baseball disappears or changes dramatically, professional baseball will still likely be played in the United States at a reasonably high level, but it may be organized very differently. Similarly, regardless of the fate of Major League Baseball, the game itself will not disappear from American culture more broadly. People will still watch it, and even play it, but the numbers of people who do that and the structures through which these activities occur will evolve.

Major League Baseball in its current form is a product of the economic, social, and media structures that have evolved in the United States over the past century or more. These structures are changing, and these changes may begin to have a more substantial impact on big league baseball. Thus far in the twenty-first century, baseball appears to be weathering these developments well, but the challenges are real.

Although the terms "Major League Baseball" and "big league baseball" are frequently used interchangeably, they do not have quite the same meaning. "Big league" is a general term that has long referred to baseball at its highest and most visible level. "Major League Baseball," usually shortened to MLB in recent years, is the brand that is associated with big league baseball. The term "big league" has long been part of colloquial American English, referring to a competitive and intense level in any field. Demanding and high-stakes workplaces and prestigious firms of all kinds are at times referred to as the big leagues, but almost never as the Major Leagues.

The survival of big league baseball in anything close to its early twenty-first-century iteration is inextricably connected to the survival of the MLB brand. But that may not have always been true. During the late nineteenth century and even into the early twentieth century, the National and the American Leagues did not yet have a monopoly on big league ball, even among white players in North America. Today, however, the fates of big league baseball and MLB are unavoidably linked.

This book examines how not only changes that are directly related to baseball (including how youth sports work in the United States today) and the increased globalization of the game but also broader societal trends (including developments in media consumption and the changing nature of celebrity) will affect big league baseball over the next few decades. The study also proposes several possible scenarios for what big league baseball might look like in its next iteration.

Analysis, Not Kvetchiness

The notion that baseball is dying has probably been around as long as baseball itself, but it has been particularly persistent since about 1960. During spring training or during the play-offs, and frequently during the times in between as well, it is easy to find articles, blogs, and reports purporting that baseball is no longer the leading American pastime and will soon be replaced by soccer, football, or something else. In 2015, Bret Smiley wrote, "Declaring that baseball is dying is as much an American pastime as the game of baseball itself."[2] A century earlier, a 1915 article in the *Pittsburg Press* argued, "Baseball[,] as the kingpin of national pastimes, is going to be crowded for honors in a very short time, if the tennis 'bug' keeps working at the speed it has shown for the past couple of years."[3] In 1991, Dorothy and Harold Seymour wrote that "ever since the game's rise to prominence and popular appeal in the latter half of the nineteenth century, assertions of its decline ha[ve] been made. In the 1870s gambling became the supposed culprit."[4]

In the first decade of the twentieth century, no less an American icon than Mark Twain explained why he found baseball boring and confusing:

> Nine men that had their calves clothed in red did strive against other nine that had blue hose upon their calves. Certain of those in blue stood at distances, one from another, stooping, each with his palms upon his knees, watching; these they called Basemen and Fielders—wherefore, God knoweth. It concerneth me not to know, neither to care. One with red legs stood wagging a club about his head, which from time to time he struck upon the ground, then wagged he it again.
>
> Behind him bent one with blue legs that did spit much upon his hands, and was called a Catcher. Beside him bent one called Umpire, clothed in the common fashion of the time, who marked upon the ground with a stick, yet accomplished nothing by it that I could make out. Saith this one, Low Ball. Whereat one with blue legs did deliver a ball with

vicious force straight at him that bore the club, but failed to bring him down, through some blemish of his aim.

At once did all that are called Basemen and Fielders spit upon their hands and stoop and watch again. He that bore the club did suffer the ball to be flung at him divers times, but did always bend in his body or bend it out and so save himself, whilst the others spat upon their hands. . . . Conceiving this to be the end, I did crave my father's leave to go, and got it, though all beside me did remain, to see the rest disabled. Yet I had seen a sufficiency, and shall visit this sport no more, forasmuch as the successful hits come too laggingly, wherefore the game doth lack excitement. Moreover was Jebel there, windy with scorn of these modern players, and boastful of certain mighty Nines he knew three hundred years gone by—dead, now, and rotten, praise God, who doeth all things well.[5]

In a 1977 episode of his weekly BBC radio broadcast *Letter from America*, Alistair Cooke, a keen observer of American culture, asserted, "The tone of the 1970s is now set by the most popular, the richest gamesman in America, not baseball players by a longshot. Baseball now ranks about fourth in popularity, behind, in ascending order, ice hockey, American football, and at the top basketball."[6] These articles and commentaries seem infinite and tend to peak in frequency around Opening Day and again during the World Series.

A related theme that has also been around for decades is that baseball today is not as good as it was a few decades ago. Such players as Mike Trout and Miguel Cabrera, so the argument goes, are not really as good as Willie Mays and Harmon Killebrew, who, in turn, were not nearly as good as Ty Cobb and Jimmie Foxx.

These arguments generally rely heavily on anecdotes as extensions of feelings rather than on data: "I saw Sandy Koufax, and there's no way Pedro Martínez or Randy Johnson was as good" or "I am kind of bored with baseball, so the country must be moving on to other things." Shortly after his 2009 Cooperstown induction, Hall of Famer Jim Rice gave a prototypical rant of the kind we frequently hear from former players and older writers:

You see a Manny Ramirez, you see an A-Rod, you see [a Derek] Jeter. . . . Guys that I played against and with, these guys you're talking about cannot compare. You have these baggy uniforms, you have the dreadlocks, that's not part of the game. It was a clean game, and now they're setting a bad example for the young guys. What you see right now is more individuals, it's not a team. Now you have guys coming in, they pick the days they want to play, they make big money. The first thing they see are dollar bills.[7]

Most of these articles and comments reflect the grumpiness of men—and it is mostly men who, getting older, write them—and their disbelief that anything could be better than it was when they were ten or fifteen years old, when baseball, in their view, was an innocent metaphor rather than an industry:

Ballparks aren't cathedrals any longer, either. Ballparks aren't churches. Ballparks are malls, built by merchants who worship not country or church, but cash. But baseball isn't America's perfect game anymore, is it? . . . Was it the juicing that did it in? Perhaps, that and the realization that games played for money are for entertainment and betting. Myths can't germinate on such hard ground.

A-Rod didn't kill baseball and turn it into a cousin of professional wrestling all by himself. He's had help over time, over years and years, when baseball got sick and turned to drugs. . . . Baseball knew it and baseball let it happen, because the lords of baseball wanted to sell tickets.[8]

Frequently, the writers of these pieces simply do not like baseball, so they just bring out old tropes about the game—it is too slow, there is not enough athleticism, too much time is spent standing around, and similar notions. Some critics argue that baseball is some kind of uniquely American phenomenon and that as the world becomes more globalized, the United States, too, will succumb to the superior appeal of soccer.[9]

This book is emphatically not written in that vein. I am a life-long baseball fan who believes the game is as exciting as ever. I also recognize that the talent and competition at the big league level today are almost certainly better than in any previous era. It is my view that anybody who cannot appreciate the all-around skills of Mike Trout, the extraordinary pitching of Clayton Kershaw, the defensive wizardry of Andrelton Simmons, the hitting skills of Miguel Cabrera, or the gruff genius of Bruce Bochy either does not like or does not understand baseball.

While I recognize that soccer is a beautiful sport adored by millions, I would still rather watch a midsummer game between the White Sox and the Rangers than the World Cup Final. And I believe that, given the growing global appeal of our national pastime, there is a scenario where baseball could supplant, or at least rival, soccer as the world's preeminent sport in fifty to a hundred years.

This book is therefore not a criticism of baseball; it is probably more accurately understood as a celebration of the game. It is also, however, an analysis of the structures that frame how baseball is played at its most competitive and lucrative levels and a discussion of whether those structures can remain in place, largely unchanged over the next decades. Baseball may, in fact, be eternal, but MLB in its current form may not be.

Analytical Approach

Few areas of American life are as rich in data as baseball, and the amount of data available to even a casual fan is increasing every year. But this book is not an advanced statistical analysis of the game. For the most part, the baseball statistics in this book are pretty conventional: home runs, batting average, wins, and earned run average (ERA). At times, however, more advanced statistics, such as Wins above Replacement (WAR) or adjusted on-base plus slugging (OPS+) are included, primarily to make comparisons across eras. These measures are explained as they are introduced.

Most of the quantitative data in this book do not concern on-the-field baseball performance. Instead, data largely concerning attendance, television revenues, television ratings, and other measures of either the financial aspect of baseball or of general trends in media consumption are cited.

This book also draws on interviews with people from various genres of baseball involvement. Some have been around youth baseball for decades; others have observed the game at the big league level for many years. These interviews add not only flavor but also sociological context to the book.

My Perspective

For several years, I coached Little League Baseball. During the season, I sent out a weekly e-mail to the parents, which included the time of the next game, the practice schedule, and other relevant information. I concluded every e-mail with a baseball trivia question. Most parents just ignored the trivia question, but on every team I coached, two or three parents would enjoy the trivia questions enough to try, with occasional success, to answer them.

Once when I was chatting with one of the fathers who had a pretty good familiarity with baseball trivia, he told me he was impressed with my knowledge of the game and wondered whether I had ever worked in baseball. I told him that I had not but that I had been a baseball fan my whole life and had spent thousands of dollars on tickets, memorabilia, books, baseball cards, caps, T-shirts, and the like, which was kind of the opposite of having a job in baseball. That is the perspective I take in this book. I am a reasonably knowledgeable fan, but I am looking at baseball from the outside. As a baseball outsider, I hope that my perspective helps inoculate me against the shared assumptions that come with being an insider in any industry.

Several years ago, my late brother and I met with my brother's longtime psychiatrist, a brilliant and dedicated man. He had been a refusenik from Latvia who had immigrated to the United States in the late 1960s. My brother, who shared my passion for the game, explained regretfully that he had taken his Soviet-born doctor to a Giants game but that he had failed in his efforts to explain the game to him. I turned to the doctor and said, "You must think we are obsessed with baseball." He responded in a clinical and matter-of-fact tone, "Yes, you are both obsessed with baseball."

It was a bit of a relief to have my baseball obsession confirmed by a mental health professional, but, of course, I had been aware of it for many years. This book is an attempt to draw on not only that obsession and the knowledge, experience, and questions that have grown out of it but also my experience as a political scientist working in and writing about international affairs, primarily in the former Soviet Union.

Anybody who has lived, worked, or studied in the countries that once made up the Soviet Union, particularly in the years closer to the collapse of the USSR in 1991, knows that institutions can seem permanent one day but disappear the next. Baseball is not the Soviet Union, and the analogy is fairly limited. But the transition from the unimaginable to the inevitable in a few short years is hard to miss in that part of the world, and it can be a useful approach to other institutions.

Assumptions about MLB abound, including that it has always played such a dominant role in organized baseball, that it has always been such a successful and lucrative business, and that television contracts will just keep getting bigger. This book seeks to identify, explore, and question such assumptions.

ACKNOWLEDGMENTS

ill Big League Baseball Survive? is a book about how institutions survive and evolve in changing environments; it is also the product of forty years of following, playing, coaching, talking, reading, and thinking about baseball. During these four decades, countless people have influenced my thinking about the game. The kids from the sandlots of San Francisco in the 1970s; the friends with whom I continue to while away more hours than I can ever count talking baseball, tossing a ball around, or watching a game; my former coaches and teammates; and the children I coached as an adult are just some of the people who have accompanied me during my lifetime of loving baseball. However, I want to mention a handful of individuals specifically. Micah Kleit and his colleagues at Temple University Press made this project much easier and more pleasant than I expected. Frank Cassinelli, Gia Kemoklidze, Deborah Kling, Greg Proops, and Joe Sheehan were very generous with their time while I was writing this book.

Several old friends, including Christian Ettinger, with whom I attended my first baseball game; Charles A. Fracchia Jr., who remains the biggest Giants fan I know and whose father still has not forgiven me for introducing him to baseball; John Maschino, with whom I have spent thousands of hours over the past thirty-five years discussing baseball, playing catch, and watching baseball on both sides of the continent; Charles Karren, who was the only Astro fan I knew as a child; and Mark Klitgaard, who remains loyal to the A's, are all part of my West Coast baseball support network. Tova Wang, Joseph D'Anna, Alan Metrick, Geoff Silver, and Nicole Gueron (my cousin who shares the family baseball gene) have played a similar role in New York. The members of the Baseball Freaks Facebook group have been a valuable source of friendship, encouragement, and humor throughout the time I spent writing this book. I am also grateful for the support of my writing companion, Isis the Dog, and the encouragement of my wife, Marta Sanders, who for many years told me I should write a book about baseball.

Three people in my baseball life deserve special mention. I have been very fortunate to have two sons, Asher and Reuben, who have inherited my love for baseball, and they are fortunate to be better players than their father ever was. Much of the initial curiosity that drove me to write this book came from looking at their experience as young baseball fans and players compared to mine. My forty years of being a baseball fan are unimaginable to me without my brother, Jonathan Mitchell. The hours we spent waiting for the ballpark express on the corner of Clay and Van Ness, shivering together at night at Candlestick Park, playing catch in the Presidio and the streets of San Francisco, poring over the box scores on weekend mornings, discussing the Giants and the Yankees, watching my sons play Little League, and taking my sons to ballgames at AT&T Park are memories I cherish. While this book reflects my uncertainty about the future of big league baseball, for most of my life I knew that I would share that future with my brother. This book is dedicated to him.

WILL

....

BIG LEAGUE BASEBALL

....

SURVIVE?

1

THE SELIG YEARS

In January 2015, Bud Selig stepped down as commissioner of baseball. He had served in that position since September 1992, although for the first six of those years, he had been acting commissioner. Selig's tenure of slightly more than twenty-two years was the second longest in baseball history. Only Major League Baseball's (MLB's) first commissioner, Judge Kenesaw Mountain Landis, served longer.

When Selig took over as commissioner, there were twenty-six Major League teams. To make the play-offs, teams had to win one of the four divisions, as there were no wild cards. There was no interleague play during the regular season, and steroid use was extremely rare and almost never discussed. Selig left the sport with thirty teams, fully one-third of which go the play-offs every year. Interleague play is now taken for granted, and the game is still recovering from a performance-enhancing drugs (PEDs) scandal that occurred on Selig's watch.

The year 1991 was the last full season before Selig took over as commissioner; and it ended with a dramatic seven-game World Series as the Minnesota Twins defeated the Atlanta Braves. Games Six and Seven of that World Series are considered among the most exciting postseason games ever. Game Six was won on an eleventh-inning walk-off home run by Kirby Puckett. That home run, due in part to the famous television announcer Jack Buck's saying, "And we'll see you tomorrow night" as Puckett's shot left the field, has become one of the most celebrated home runs in baseball history. The next night, Game Seven also went into extra innings and was also won by a walk-off hit, a pinch-hit single by Gene Larkin that gave the Twins a 1–0 win. The Twins pitcher in that game, Jack Morris, threw ten innings of shutout baseball, an outing that has become a central component of Morris's Hall of Fame candidacy that thus far has not ended with enshrinement in Cooperstown.

The 1991 World Series was viewed by an average of thirty-six million people per game. It was one of four World Series between 1986 and 1991 to average more than thirty million viewers per game. Since Selig took over, no World Series has been seen by that many viewers. The closest was the 1995 World Series between the Cleveland Indians and the Atlanta Braves that went seven games and had just under thirty million viewers per game. The 2014 World Series, which also went seven games, averaged fourteen million viewers per game.

Attendance was strong in 1991, as 56,783,759 people paid to see an MLB game, for an average of about 2.18 million per team. In 2014, 73,739,622 fans bought tickets to big league games, for an average of 2.45 million per game, an increase of 12 percent.

In 1991, Roger Clemens, the star pitcher for the Boston Red Sox who later became one of the highest-profile players associated with PED use, was the best-paid player in the Major League, making $5.3 million that year. In 2014, Zack Greinke of the Los Angeles Dodgers was the highest-paid player in baseball, beginning a multi-year contract at $28 million per year. The average Major Leaguer made $851,492 in 1991, or $1.48 million in 2014 dollars.[1] In 2014, the average big league salary was an estimated $4 million.[2]

In 1991, 1,034 players appeared in at least one big league game; 878, or 84.9 percent, were born in the United States, not including Puerto Rico. The remaining 15.1 percent of players came from the Dominican Republic (57), Puerto Rico (40), Venezuela (19), Mexico (12), Canada (10), Cuba (4), Germany (3), Jamaica (2), Panama (2), Australia (1), Belize (1), Curaçao (1), Honduras (1), Japan (1), Nicaragua (1), the United Kingdom (1), and the U.S. Virgin Islands (1).[3] Significantly, all three of the German-born players (Mike Blowers, Craig Lefferts, and Dave Pavlas) and the one Japanese-born player (Steve Chitren) were raised in the United States. Danny Cox, born in the United Kingdom, went to college in the United States. Thus, when Selig became commissioner, with the exception of the Australian Craig Shipley, big league baseball was played by men who had all grown up in the United States, Canada, the Caribbean, or Central and South America, in countries where (other than in Curaçao) either English or Spanish was the primary language. There was not a single Japanese, Korean, or Taiwanese player in the big leagues in 1991.

Of the 1,187 men who played in the big leagues in 2014, 852 or 71.7 percent, a significant drop from 1991, were American-born. In 2014, the 28.3 percent of players who were not American born came from the Dominican Republic (130), Venezuela (89), Cuba (21), Puerto Rico (21), Canada (18), Japan (12), Mexico (10), Colombia (5), Curaçao (5), Panama (4), Germany (3), Nicaragua (3), Taiwan (3), Australia (2) Brazil (2), South Korea (2), Aruba (1), the Bahamas (1), Jamaica (1), the Netherlands (1), and Saudi Arabia (1).[4] All of the Australians, Brazilians, Japanese, and Taiwanese who played in 2014 grew up in those countries, but all the players born in Germany, the Bahamas, and Saudi Arabia grew up in the United States. Didi Gregorius, the one Dutch-born player, grew up in Curaçao. By the time Selig's tenure as commissioner ended, baseball was still dominated by players from the United States, Central America, and the Caribbean, but more countries in the Caribbean; countries where baseball was relatively new, such as Australia and Brazil; and older baseball powers, such as Japan and Taiwan, were also sending players to the big leagues. By any measure, MLB became significantly more international during Selig's time as commissioner.

The internationalization of the game has been an unequivocally good development for baseball, raising the profile of MLB in many countries, introducing great players and highly marketable stars such as Ichiro Suzuki into the big leagues, and strengthening MLB's ability to draw the best players in the world. This globalization has been Selig's most unambiguously positive accomplishment, leading to a better, more fun, and more marketable product.

Selig's years as commissioner were also marked by tremendous changes in how big league baseball was structured. For decades, any attempts to change baseball had been met by resistance from traditionalists or purists. The introduction of two divisions in each league and one round of play-offs beginning in 1969 and of the designated hitter (DH) in 1973 was greeted with outrage by many baseball fans at the time. Hall of Fame baseball writer Roger Angell, who has spent decades beautifully and compellingly chronicling baseball, wrote of the DH in 1973:

> It is probably useless to complain at length about the league's shiny new thingummy . . . but one cannot forget that the game—the game itself, as played out there between the foul lines—has been wrenched out of shape. Gone now . . . is that ancient and unique concept of a player's total individual accountability. . . . Vanished, too, is the strategic fulcrum of baseball—the painful decision about pinch-hitting for your pitcher when you are behind in the late innings. . . . Now the game is farther away from us all, less human and less fun, and suddenly made easy.[5]

It is still not that unusual to find older fans who would prefer to get rid of the DH. Complaints about escalating salaries have been a constant for at least forty years. And any statistical tool more sophisticated than wins and runs batted in (RBIs) is criticized by some segment of baseball fans and kibitzers for taking the soul out of the game.

Even in this context, Selig's introduction of interleague play and two expansions of the play-offs were controversial. Both of these changes struck at traits that made baseball unique among American sports. For decades, the American League (AL) and the National League (NL) had been distinct organizations with different approaches on and off the field. In the 1950s, the NL was much faster to integrate, leading to NL's dominance in the All-Star Games in the 1960s, 1970s, and early 1980s. The AL adapted earlier to the live ball era, so in the 1920s, 1930s, and 1940s, it had a reputation for being more offense-oriented, with such sluggers as Babe Ruth,

Lou Gehrig, Jimmie Foxx, and Hank Greenberg making the home run king. The NL, on the other hand, developed a reputation for a more pitching- and defense-oriented game during those years.

These distinctions, real or imagined, were exacerbated because teams and players from the AL and the NL rarely played against each other aside from the World Series and the All-Star Game. This rarity meant that those games had an added level of excitement, but it also meant that some of the baseball's potentially best individual matchups and natural rivalries were not given an opportunity to flourish.

For example, the AL's Ted Williams was one of the greatest hitters in baseball history, but other than in All-Star Games, he never batted in an official game against Warren Spahn, Robin Roberts, Don Newcombe, or many of the other great pitchers of his time who played in the NL. Similarly, Mel Ott batted against Lefty Grove only in an All-Star Game despite their being among the best players in the game in the 1930s. Even in the modern era, potential rivalries between teams that shared a region or city were never given a chance to flourish. For example, the Chicago Cubs and the White Sox did not play a meaningful game against each other after the 1906 World Series until the advent of interleague play in 1997. Similarly, the Oakland A's and the San Francisco Giants played only five games that counted between 1968, when the A's moved to Oakland from Kansas City, and 1997. Those five games were, of course, the 1989 World Series, remembered by most baseball fans not for anything that happened on the field but rather for a major earthquake that struck the Bay Area shortly before Game Three was about to begin. Interleague play changed all that. To this day, many older fans dislike interleague play, viewing it as contrived, responsible for unbalanced schedules, and counter to the gestalt of the game, but many younger fans enjoy it and the new rivalries it has facilitated.

The expanded play-off system was also initially controversial but is now widely accepted and liked. In 1994, MLB switched from two to three divisions in each league and introduced a wild card position for the best second-place finisher. In 2012, a second wild card was added. Consequently, ten teams, or one-third of the total in MLB, make the postseason every year. The idea behind this change was to give teams that historically had little chance of winning a division a chance to make it into the play-offs. This goal was achieved as in the first four years following the implementation of this system, with twenty-one of the thirty teams having made at least one post-season appearance. This change was also meant to increase play-off revenue. Many fans like this system, but many others believe it renders the regular-season pennant race, long the most exciting part of baseball, less meaningful and makes it possible for lesser teams to find a back door route to a World Series victory. For example, between 2012 and 2015, three of the eight teams to play in the World Series won fewer than 90 games during the 162-game regular season, while the 2015 Mets won exactly 90 games.

Selig's tenure as commissioner was marred by two unambiguous blemishes. The first was the labor strike that led to the cancellation of the last third of the 1994 season and that year's postseason; the World Series was not played for the first time since 1904. When he left office in 2015, Selig identified the cancellation of the World Series that year as the "saddest" episode of his time as commissioner.[6]

The 1994 strike was a genuine crisis for baseball. At the time, many fans vowed never to return to the game. According to ESPN, "Attendance plunged 20 percent the following year [after the strike], from a record average of 31,612 in 1994 to 25,260."[7] Many worried about the future of MLB and talk of contracting franchises increased, but baseball recovered. That recovery was, in some respects, Selig's greatest accomplishment, but it also bore the seeds of what became the other most notable negative of Selig's time as commissioner.

It is not possible to know with certainty when the modern steroid era began, but it is quite likely that it began before the 1994 strike. During or immediately after the All-Star Game that year, one of my New York baseball friends looked beyond his East Coast myopia to ask me (the biggest Giants fan he knew), "Who's that bald white dude with the Giants with all those home runs?" He was referring to Matt Williams, who had thirty-three home runs at the time of the All-Star Game and ended up leading all of baseball with forty-three home runs in that strike-shortened year. Williams was linked to steroid use in 2002, but some suspect that he was using as early as 1994.

Regardless of when the steroid era began, it was in full swing by the late 1990s. The seminal event of baseball's poststrike recovery was the battle between Mark McGwire and Sammy Sosa to break Roger Maris's single-season home run record in 1998. At the time, the race was covered as a good-natured, all-American story, complete with racial diversity and two different but equally well liked protagonists. The best example of this spin was the December 21, 1998, issue of *Sports Illustrated* honoring Sosa and McGwire as "Sportsmen of the Year." The photo on the cover shows the heavily muscled men in Roman-style togas and gold-leaf crowns. The text of the accompanying article, which never mentioned PEDs or steroids, is unambiguously laudatory:

> McGwire and Sosa gave America a summer that won't be forgotten: a summer of stroke and counterstroke, of packed houses and curtain calls, of rivals embracing and gloves in the bleachers and adults turned into kids—the Summer of Long Balls and Love. It wasn't just the lengths they went to with bats in their hands. It was also that they went to such lengths to conduct the great home run race with dignity and sportsmanship, with a sense of joy and openness. Never have two men chased legends and each other that hard and that long or invited so much of America onto their backs for the ride.[8]

This feel-good story, along with many others like it, was written even after AP reporter Steve Wilstein spotted a bottle of androstenedione, a steroid, in McGwire's locker late in the 1998 season.[9]

Wilstein's discovery did little to diminish the excitement around Sosa and McGwire's home run chase in 1998. Over the next years, home run and other offensive records fell as baseball entered an era where bloated sluggers took the game to its highest scoring period since the early 1930s. From 1995 to 2000, the six years following the strike, runs per team per game ranged from 4.77 to 5.14

and thrice exceeded 5 runs per game. That benchmark had not been met since 1936, sixty years earlier. For most of these years, baseball officials did nothing to stop steroid use. Eventually, MLB conducted a few half-hearted investigations and ultimately handed out suspensions, but the steroid era lasted well over a decade, radically changed the feel and history of the game, and was never sufficiently addressed by Selig. For all the impressive advances and innovations Selig brought to the game, steroids will always be an undeniable, and unfortunate, part of his legacy as well.

The State of Baseball Today

Every year, baseball fans are told that the state of the game has never been stronger. Selig himself made this point in a 2013 interview toward the end of his long tenure as commissioner, saying, "Look at our attendance numbers. Look at our ratings. By any reasonable measurement, the grand old game has never been so popular."[10] Selig, who only stopped serving as baseball's commissioner and cheerleader in chief in 2015, said more or less the same thing at the end of every baseball season since the mid-1990s, after baseball had recovered from the damage from the strike of 1994.

According to some measures, Selig's optimism was accurate. Revenues remain strong at the big league level, and big television contracts continue to bring more money into the game than ever before. Additionally, as Selig also noted, and contrary to the occasional kvetch from retired players or curmudgeonly journalists, on-the-field play has never been stronger. The high salaries and growing international reach of American baseball has ensured that the best baseball players in the world are largely playing in the MLB and that the sport will continue to attract top athletes. The World Baseball Classic (WBC) has grown in popularity in recent years as well, further strengthening baseball's popularity outside the United States, particularly in such countries as the Netherlands, China, or Australia, which are not traditionally baseball powerhouses.

Baseball indeed has some impressive indicators of strong financial health. In 2014, more than 73 million tickets to big league baseball games were sold, meaning on average that each of the thirty big league teams sold more than 2.4 million tickets. That marked the twelfth consecutive year that overall ticket sales exceeded seventy million. By comparison, in the 1980s, the best year for attendance was 1989, when just over fifty-five million people bought tickets for an average of slightly more than 2.1 million tickets sold for each of the twenty-six teams, the first time that baseball ever averaged more than two million tickets sold per team. As late as 1975, the then twenty-four big league teams had never sold even a combined thirty million tickets.[11]

Attendance figures are not the only quantitative measures of baseball's wealth. Annual television revenue from ESPN, Fox, and TBS is currently $1.5 billion per year. MLB Advanced Media (MLBAM), the content provider in charge of baseball's official web presence, generates roughly $600 million per year. This income, shared between the teams, contributes substantially to the financial health of MLB, the high salaries for players, the profits made by individual teams, and the appreciation in value of most big league franchises.

According to an article in *Forbes*, when all sources of revenue, including local media deals, tickets, and other sales were taken into consideration, MLB's gross revenue in 2014 was $9 billion—an increase of 321 percent of the $2.14 billion in revenue (in 2014 dollars) that MLB generated in 1995.[12]

MLBAM has been an impressive source of supplementary revenue for MLB, but it has also offered fans exciting new ways to enjoy the game. Today, fans can watch any game outside their media markets on any day during the season on their phones, tablets, desktop computers, or televisions. While watching those games, they can review statistical data, pitch charts, scouting reports, and highlights. Much of baseball's success during the twenty-first century can be attributed to how well MLB has adapted to the new technological environment. Baseball did not shy away from the Internet but embraced it and crafted an excellent and technically sophisticated product for its consumers. Needless to say, this new technology has also provided fans the opportunity to talk about baseball online, buy and sell memorabilia, and otherwise more easily enjoy various aspects of the game.

Selig's annual statements about the health of the game were not pulled out of the air but reflected in the financial data and products being offered to fans. His successor, Rob Manfred, will almost certainly continue to report on the financial health of baseball. While these reports may be factual, they do not quite represent the entire truth.

The Other Side of Baseball's Success Story

On April 7, 2014, the Houston Astros hosted the awkwardly and redundantly named Los Angeles Angels of Anaheim. The Astros had begun the season by splitting their first six games, a decent start for a team that was not expected to go anywhere. The Angels had a slightly worse record of 2–4 going into the game, but behind C. J Wilson's eight strong innings in which he gave up only one run, they easily beat the Astros by a score of 9–1. Houston's lineup was young and not very well known, although their second baseman, Jose Altuve, would be recognized as a star before the season was over. The Angels' lineup was loaded and included future Hall of Famer Albert Pujols, a young center fielder named Mike Trout thought by many to be the best player in the game, and other well-known players, including Howie Kendrick and the controversial slugger Josh Hamilton.

Only 17,936 fans showed up to Houston's Minute Maid Park for this early-season Monday night game, but the attendance was not what made the game significant. It was the television audience—or, more accurately, the lack of one—that gave the game importance. The Nielsen rating for that game was 0.0, meaning that none of the TVs in the more-than-five-hundred Nielsen households in the greater Houston area were tuned to this game. The 0.0 rating does not mean that literally nobody in Houston watched the game, but it indicates that only a very small number of people did.[13] The Astros had also received a 0.0 Nielsen rating for a game late in the 2013 season, when they lost to the Cleveland Indians by a score of 9–2.

These two Astros' games are dramatic examples, but it remains true that watching baseball on television is not as exciting to viewers as MLB would like people to believe. In 2012, MLB added an additional wild card play-in game between the two wild card teams; those games are typically viewed by between three and five million people.[14] These are respectable numbers, particularly for a cable network, such as ESPN, but they hardly qualify as a ratings juggernaut. In 2015, because of the presence of the New York Yankees and the Chicago Cubs, both large-market teams with national followings, viewership for the AL and the NL play-in games approached eight million each.[15] Over the last decade, baseball's preeminent event, the World Series, still has usually drawn between fifteen and twenty million viewers per game, but this is a fraction of the twenty to forty million viewers who tuned in to watch World Series games in previous eras.

Game Seven of the 2014 World Series drew about 23.5 million viewers. This was not bad for the current era and a much higher number of viewers than any of the previous six games of the series had attracted. However, this was less than half the number of viewers who watched Game Seven of the 1991 World Series, another dramatic championship played between two small- to medium-market teams.[16] Significantly, Game Seven in 2014 drew about as many television viewers in the United States as the women's soccer World Cup final, which the United States won in the summer of 2015.[17]

Many factors are driving this downward trend, but primarily the different ways Americans consume entertainment and watch television in the second decade of the twenty-first century. Some might argue, yet again, that baseball has become boring, but even if that is not true, it is apparent that the declining number of television viewers is not good for an industry that still relies on television contracts to generate much of its revenue.

One cannot, of course, blame Selig or MLB for the changing ways Americans consume their media, but this evolution will have an impact on MLB. As more households eschew expensive cable-television packages, as television viewership continues to decline, and as younger Americans in particular no longer consume entertainment through traditional means, baseball could face even larger problems in this regard.

Currently, live sports is one of the main attractions of cable television, particularly for men. Therefore, as long as cable packages are still sold to customers, baseball fans will be forced to subscribe. This bundling will help ensure some revenue for MLB, but if fewer people are watching cable overall, the stations will not be able to charge as much for advertising and opportunities to push new sitcoms and the like during the play-offs. Thus, airing the World Series will not be as lucrative for stations, such as Fox, that currently have big contracts with MLB.

Disappointing television ratings are only one of the challenges facing MLB today and potentially threatening its future. Although game attendance figures remain strong, these figures are often based solely on ticket sales. The number of people actually attending the games is a different, and less encouraging, metric. Nowhere is this clearer than in Yankee Stadium, where the team consistently reports sellouts and impressive attendance figures,[18] but even a casual observer cannot help but notice the number of empty seats at many games. This disparity is not just a matter of people leaving early to beat the traffic or to catch an earlier subway home, but simply the result of people who have bought tickets—in many cases, season tickets—not attending the games.

If a team has trouble selling tickets, the causes could include an economic downturn, overpriced tickets, or the team's poor performance on the field dissuading fans from spending money to watch them lose. However, unused tickets may be symptomatic of a bigger problem: they indicate that ticket holders believe they have better things to do than to use the tickets for which they have paid good money, or that ticket holders could not resell tickets (or, in some cases, literally cannot give them away). This scenario represents a growing concern for a business that relies on the sales of expensive tickets as a significant revenue source.

Yankee Stadium is, of course, the game's most visible, and, other than Fenway Park, expensive, stadium, but the problem is not just limited to the new ballpark in the Bronx.[19] Empty seats can be seen throughout the regular season at most stadiums. In many cases, those seats represent unused rather than unsold tickets. In the short run, that situation may seem better for baseball, but those unused tickets are a measure of the fans' lack of enthusiasm about the game.

Baseball, like many forms of entertainment, is a product based on the idea of celebrities and a particular relationship that exists between celebrities and fans. The media's model of building baseball players into larger-than-life figures while covering up their faults has not been applicable for decades. We are far removed from the time when substance abuse by such stars as Mickey Mantle could be systematically ignored for more than a decade or when Babe Ruth's bouts of gonorrhea could be euphemistically, and almost universally, described as stomachaches.

A handful of current baseball stars are excellent at managing their images. Derek Jeter and Mariano Rivera, two recent Yankee greats and future Hall of Famers, are strong examples. However, many of the game's biggest stars in recent years, including Alex Rodriguez and Barry Bonds, were broadly disliked by baseball fans. An article in *The Onion*, a humor website, titled "Yankee Rookie Nervously Tells A-Rod How Much He Used to Hate Him as a Kid" summarizes this development very well.[20]

Some baseball stars have always been unpleasant to fans, rude to reporters, and had character flaws. Ty Cobb, Ted Williams, and, in some respects, Pete Rose are just some of the all-time greats who fit this description, but the relationship between celebrities and their fans has changed in the age of Twitter and a constant need for connections and information. In general, baseball has proved very adept at responding to technological changes, but this very adaptability may pose an unexpected, and more difficult to counter, set of threats to the game.

The evolving nature of baseball's broad role in society is further evidenced by the changes in youth sports. These changes have been occurring over the last several decades but have yielded an environment where almost no sandlot or other informal baseball play remains; instead, youth baseball is largely played in organized teams and leagues. While this evolution has led to some very strong youth baseball programs that are developing very good players, it has also relegated baseball to a niche sport that is no longer played by as large a proportion of American children, particularly boys, as it was in previous generations.

It is possible that this change will have no effect on the future of the game, but it is also very likely that children who seek out different activities and sports to play will continue to follow different sports and activities when they get older. The most obvious threat to baseball in this regard is soccer, but other sports and activities ranging from snowboarding to cycling could have a similar impact on baseball's popularity.

Baseball is not the only sport that faces a battery of challenges that threaten to disrupt its highest-level league. Basketball and football face similar challenges related to cable television, although football, largely because it is played only once a week, has a much more loyal television following. The Super Bowl remains the most broadly watched sports event in the United States, and every Sunday in the late fall and early winter, millions of Americans watch the teams in the National Football League (NFL) on television, despite the number of scandals and accusations of criminal behavior aimed at its players.

Youth football faces a different kind of a crisis, as more American families are reluctant to let their sons play organized football at all because of safety concerns. Clearly, the future of football is uncertain. It is possible that all professional sports now face a similar battery of challenges, but exploring those non-baseball issues is not the purpose of this work.

Big League Baseball's Current Position

To better probe or explore the possible future of big league baseball, it is necessary to have some sense of the development of the game at its highest level. The history of big league baseball is almost infinite, offering countless different angles from which to explore the game's evolution over the past century or more. It would be impossible, and not particularly useful, to probe all of those angles here. Nonetheless, of particular relevance is MLB's dominant role in organized baseball today. This reality informs a great deal about big league baseball, its economic strength, and its current good fortunes. Moreover, understanding how MLB reached its current status provides valuable insight, and an important foundation, for understanding what its future might look like.

MLB was not always such a hugely dominant force in baseball, even in the United States. For much of the twentieth century, and throughout all of baseball's nineteenth century, MLB competed with various minor leagues, the Negro Leagues, barnstormers, leagues outside the United States, and other forms of what, in 2014, Scott Simkus termed "Outsider Baseball" for status, the best players, and revenue.[21]

Today, barnstorming is almost nonexistent, and nearly all professional teams are affiliated with a big league club. A few independent leagues and teams exist, such as the St. Paul Saints and the Wichita Wingnuts, but these represent a very small proportion of the professional players in the United States. Additionally, even most international tournaments, most notably the WBC, are now, in one form or another, run by MLB. Leagues in countries outside the United States—for example, in Japan and Korea—are not part of MLB, but in many parts of the world where baseball is strong, such as the Dominican Republic or Venezuela, the best players are quickly funneled to MLB teams.

Thus, MLB is an increasingly dominant hegemon on the American and the global baseball scene. That hegemony affects almost every pitch that is thrown in the United States, from youth baseball all the way up to the World Series. It is a product of a confluence of events largely outside the realm of baseball, including such developments as the civil rights movement and population shifts following World War II. MLB's domination of the sport was not inevitable, but that is what has happened over the past fifty or sixty years. Just as it was not inevitable, it is also not irreversible. Other developments that extend beyond baseball, such as increased globalization, the rise of China as an economic power, and even the ubiquitous nature of social media, may begin to erode MLB's hegemony in the coming decades.

No league in any major sport enjoys a similar position to MLB either domestically or internationally. While the NFL and the National Basketball Association (NBA) are extremely popular multi-billion-dollar industries with lucrative contracts for players largely funded by cable providers and strong Internet strategies, they do not monopolize all of organized football and basketball in the United States the way MLB does for baseball. The National Collegiate Athletic Association (NCAA) enjoys a close relationship with the NFL and the NBA, but it is independent of those professional organizations. Although college basketball and football function essentially as minor leagues for the NBA and the NFL, respectively, they are not affiliated with those professional leagues. College baseball is becoming more popular in the United States, but it has not yet come close to the level of popularity enjoyed by college football or basketball. Moreover, college does not function as the minor or developmental league in baseball the way it does in other major sports, not least because of the extensive minor league system in baseball.

College teams, in any sport, have goals that are independent from those of professional sports. They need to generate revenue, keep their alumni donor bases happy, and win games in a way that does not apply to affiliated minor league teams. Similarly, college sports teams enjoy a loyal and constantly renewing fan base that is different from those of minor league teams. These different incentives ensure the independence of NCAA sports from the NFL or the NBA. Additionally, if the NCAA were ever to substantially change its football and basketball policies—for example, by offering fewer scholarships—it would create problems for the NFL and the NBA that these two leagues are currently unequipped to address.

MLB's role in global baseball is greater than that of any comparable institution in any other sport. The Fédération Internationale de Football Association (FIFA) is very important as a governing body in international soccer, but it does not play a leadership role in any individual countries. The NBA promotes its product overseas, but it does not organize international basketball. Football remains much more uniquely American than baseball and has a very small global footprint. Cricket has no global governing body that is largely the product of one country. Of course, individual baseball leagues exist in such places as Japan, the Dominican Republic, and Cuba, but (with the exception of Cuba) MLB has strong ties with these leagues. Additionally, not least because baseball has not been an Olympic sport for years, MLB organizes and sets the rules for the world's premiere international baseball tournament, the WBC.

This stronghold is particularly notable given that MLB itself is a relatively new entity. For most of the twentieth century, the

American and the National Leagues were separate organizations that made their own policies. For example, during the twentieth century, each league had its own umpires and even played under slightly different sets of rules. The most well-known rule difference was that the AL played with a designated hitter, while the NL did not.[22] A lesser-known rule difference was that if a league or a division ended in a tie, a one-game play-off was used in the AL, but a best-of-three format was used in the NL. There were other differences between the leagues as well. For example, the AL embraced the power game more quickly than the NL beginning in the 1920s. The NL, however, integrated more quickly than the AL.

For most of the twentieth century, player movement between the leagues was slightly less common as well. All of these variations contributed to a more competitive relationship between the two leagues. All-Star Games, for example, were taken much more seriously by everybody involved. For many years, the AL, because it was formed after the NL, was seen as something of an upstart league. Most glaringly, in 1904, the NL champion New York Giants refused to play the AL champion Boston Red Sox in what would have been the second World Series, because they viewed the AL as an inferior league. One of the legacies of this dynamic is that until the last few decades, writers and baseball people would, with decreasing frequency, refer to the NL as the "senior circuit" and the AL as the "junior circuit."

Until the two leagues merged in 2000, much of the governing power lay with the leagues themselves. The consolidation of power had been moving toward less separation between the two leagues, as such issues as negotiating collective-bargaining agreements between owners and players required collaboration between the two leagues, but this union was not finalized until 2000. Since 2000, MLB has become a much bigger brand, with the three initials being strongly identified with big league baseball. Even during the 1970s through the 1990s, although the initials were used as a kind of shorthand in writing, MLB was rarely pronounced as such. This prominence has changed over the course of the past fifteen years primarily because of MLB's efforts to brand big league baseball with those three letters and the success of MLBAM products.

Has Big League Baseball Survived?

Before asking the question of whether big league baseball *will* survive, it is worth probing the assumption that big league baseball has, in fact, survived *so far*. Regardless of the answer, baseball has unquestionably changed an enormous amount, not just in the years when Selig was commissioner but in the years before his tenure as well.

Over the past seventy-five years, big league baseball has evolved from a business located in only ten cities in the Northeast and the Midwest, played by white people, with only a few teams having anything approaching a farm system. Moreover, the big leagues competed with the Pacific Coast League (PCL), the Negro Leagues, and off-season barnstormers for attention, players, and revenue. The business was not particularly lucrative, as players often had to work in the off-season to make ends meet, thousands of tickets for almost every game went unsold, television contracts were still in the future, and owners often had to sell their best players after a few years.

The institution has transformed a great deal over the years, but some constants have emerged. Big league baseball still represents the best baseball around. It has always been dominated by the United States, American money, and American players. Since the late nineteenth century, it has consistently consolidated its hegemony to become a larger and wealthier business with each passing decade. The coming decades, however, could usher in changes for big league baseball.

2

LEFTY, JOSH, THE BARNSTORMERS, AND BRANCH

Today, only the most intense or nostalgic baseball fans remember Lefty O'Doul, but he was an interesting and important figure in baseball history. O'Doul is one of the people who is generally credited for helping popularize baseball in Japan.[1] He was also a fantastic hitter: his .349 batting lifetime average is fourth among players with 3,500 or more plate appearances. He led the National League (NL) twice in batting and once in on-base percentage. O'Doul's adjusted on-base plus slugging (OPS+), a statistic that measures a player's ability to get on base and hit for power, controlling for era and home ballpark, was 143. That is the same as such all-time great sluggers as Harmon Killebrew, Eddie Matthews, and, more recently, Mike Piazza.

Astute baseball fans will note that the parameter of 3,500 plate appearances is quite low. That is because O'Doul did not spend all of his playing days in the 1920s and 1930s in the American League (AL) or the NL, despite his ability to hit at any level. Instead, he spent two years in the heart of his career, at ages twenty-seven and twenty-eight, starring in the Pacific Coast League (PCL), where he hit .392 and .375 in successive seasons; he then chose to return to the PCL after reaching the decline phase of his career back east. O'Doul was a native San Franciscan who preferred to play nearer to his home. We now think of the PCL as a minor league, but it is not apparent that O'Doul or his fans thought of it that way in the 1920s and 1930s. O'Doul stayed involved with the PCL and baseball in San Francisco following his retirement as a player. He managed the San Francisco Seals of the PCL for more than a decade, beginning in 1935 when his best player was a young San Franciscan preparing to make the transition from the PCL to the American League. Unlike O'Doul, Joe DiMaggio, who went to the Yankees after the 1935 season, never played in the PCL again after succeeding in New York. O'Doul also ran one of San Francisco's better-known restaurants, Lefty O'Doul's. Nearly fifty years after O'Doul's death, his eponymous restaurant is still a destination for older Giants fans. By the mid-1940s, O'Doul's $39,000 annual salary with the Seals was "greater than [that of] most major league managers."[2]

Any discussion of the greatest players of all time, particularly of the first half of the twentieth century, is not complete without mentioning the great catcher and home run hitter Josh Gibson, a name better known than that of Lefty O'Doul to many baseball fans. Gibson, unlike O'Doul, never played a single game in the major leagues. Gibson was African American and was more or less finished as a player by the time Jackie Robinson made it to Brooklyn in 1947. Gibson played in the Negro Leagues, but based on the evidence, including assessments from white stars of the era, he was good enough to have played with anybody in the 1930s and early 1940s.

Gibson is only one of many great pre-1947 players who were excluded from Major League Baseball (MLB) because of their race. Other greats, including James "Cool Papa" Bell, Oscar Charleston, and Judy Johnson were as good as white stars of their era but never played in MLB. Baseball's brand of apartheid also extended to dark-skinned Latino players, such as Martin Dihigo. The quality of Negro League ball was inconsistent, the conditions were often quite tough for the players, and the teams and leagues changed frequently. Nonetheless, for half a century, the Negro Leagues formed an important part of the baseball landscape in the United States and often beyond, and they drew some of the best players in the world.

The consensus best Negro League pitcher of all time, and deserving of a mention in the discussion for the greatest pitcher to ever play the game, was Satchel Paige. Paige finally got his chance to play in MLB when he was already forty-two years old. All he did in his rookie year was go 6–1 with a 2.48 earned run average (ERA), two shutouts, and, for good measure, one save to help the Cleveland Indians win a very close pennant race in 1948. It is unfortunate that Paige never got a chance to pitch against the best white hitters of the 1930s and early 1940s when he was in his prime—except, of course, he did, just not in the context of an official big league game.

Paige was an inveterate barnstormer; and the leading white players of his day recognized the opportunity to make some extra money and to test their skills against the very best in the game by barnstorming with Paige—either on his team or on a team playing against him. Barnstorming was a product of the early days of baseball, when big league ball was played in only ten cities for half of the year. The absence of the Internet, television, and even radio in many cases meant that baseball fans from around the country were willing to pay to see the most famous players during the off-season. This void led to a culture of barnstorming, mostly informal games, played in rural America during the off-season. DiMaggio, Stan Musial, and Jimmie Foxx were among the all-time greats who batted against Paige in those games, with mixed success. Paige also found himself in barnstorming pitching duels against the best white pitchers of his era, including Dizzy Dean and Bob Feller.

In the first half of the twentieth century, barnstorming was not just for African American players; many white big leaguers did it to supplement their salaries as well. Barnstorming provided fans in the South, in the West, and outside the major metropolitan areas an opportunity to see good baseball and the biggest stars during the years before league expansion and television. Barnstorming also was supported by a large network of semipro teams that frequently provided opponents for the more famous barnstorming big leaguers as well as in-season baseball in places where the big leagues did not reach.

Branch Rickey may be the most famous baseball executive ever. He is widely credited with creating the modern minor league farm system that dramatically increased the scope of big league baseball's influence and for bringing Jackie Robinson to the Brooklyn Dodgers, thus breaking baseball's modern color line. Rickey was even portrayed by film legend Harrison Ford in the 2013 film *42*. Few people helped shape modern baseball as much as Rickey did.

After the Dodgers and the Giants left New York City for California in the late 1950s, Rickey sought to create a third major league called the Continental League. A 2009 book by Michael Shapiro states that "by the early months of 1959, Branch Rickey had so rigorously thought about the nature, structure and logic behind his new league that he was prepared to commit his plan to paper."[3] Rickey won some support for this proposal, but the project failed. It is nonetheless striking that the idea received a fair amount of discussion and debate. Ultimately, the New York Mets were created and awarded to New York, not least because the NL wanted to make sure the Continental League did not gain a foothold in the country's largest city. Thus, even more than a decade after the end of World War II and Robinson's integration of big league baseball, the assumption of the stability and the continued supremacy of the two major leagues was not close to the certainty it is today.

Today, it seems obvious that Rickey would never have succeeded in creating the Continental League. The American and National Leagues have maintained and even strengthened their dominance in the nearly sixty years since Rickey pursued his idea for a third league. However, at the time, MLB was fewer than twenty years removed from a period when it shared revenue and top ballplayers with the Negro Leagues and barnstormers of all kinds.

Additionally, fewer than fifty years before that era—a long time for big league baseball, but not so much for Rickey, who was almost eighty when he advocated for the Continental League—a third league *had* existed. The Federal League lasted from 1913 to 1915 before folding and is now forgotten by all but the most learned baseball historians. It was significant not because it was the product of baseball apartheid or international competition but because it drew on "the patterns of the past. They [the Federal League owners] offered the established stars more money than they were receiving."[4] Many very good players were happy to take the money and move to this new league, including future Hall of Famers Mordecai "Three Finger" Brown, Joe Tinker, Edd Roush, Charles "Chief" Bender, and Eddie Plank.

The Federal League lasted only two full seasons—it was a minor league in 1913 but competed directly with the AL and the NL in 1914 and 1915—but with teams in such cities as Chicago, St. Louis, and Pittsburgh, and with a generally high quality of play on the field, it was poised to challenge the two existing leagues. Part of the story of the decline of the Federal League helps explain some of the challenges Rickey faced in seeking to create the Continental League in 1960. The Baltimore Federal League franchise, one of the last holdouts in the failed league, sued the NL, each of its eight teams, and several others in 1917, accusing "defendants of conspiring to destroy its franchise by monopolizing the baseball business and restraining trade therein."[5] Baltimore lost its case, leading to the affirmation by Supreme Court Justice Oliver Wendell Holmes of baseball's exemption from antitrust and antimonopoly laws, known as the *reserve clause*. Justice Holmes argued that baseball did not count as interstate commerce, because "the fact that in order to give the exhibitions [baseball games] the Leagues must induce free persons to cross state lines and must arrange and pay for their doing so is not enough to change the character of the business [and qualify it as interstate commerce]."[6] This exemption, of course, despite its quirky understanding of interstate commerce, became central to MLB's rise and current status.

The stories of O'Doul, Gibson, Paige, Rickey, and many other top ballplayers and baseball figures who did not play in the big leagues but barnstormed and sought innovative ways to bring baseball to the public all reflect how big league baseball, until relatively recently, was only one aspect of a broader story of competitive baseball in the United States. Looking more closely at these institutions and how they withered, collapsed, or otherwise ended is critical to understanding MLB's current position.

The End of the Negro Leagues

When Jackie Robinson stepped onto the field as the first baseman for the Brooklyn Dodgers on April 15, 1947, baseball and America changed forever. Big league baseball did not become fully integrated immediately, as informal rules and policies limited the number of African American players to three on a team for at least another decade. Similarly, for the first years following Robinson's debut, most fringe players, utility infielders, and seldom-used relief pitchers were white, suggesting that the bar to make it to the big leagues was still set higher for African American players.

Despite these limitations, baseball rapidly evolved from reflecting a country where apartheid-like conditions dominated in roughly one third of the states toward representing a better and more just America toward which we can still aspire. In the almost seventy years since Robinson's debut, many African American players, including Willie Mays, Henry Aaron, Bob Gibson, Reggie Jackson, Rickey Henderson, Joe Morgan, Ken Griffey Jr., and Barry Bonds have been among the leading and best-known players in the game. Additionally, darker-skinned Latino players, beginning with Roberto Clemente and Minnie Minoso and continuing up to the current day with such stars as David Ortiz and Yasiel Puig, have followed Robinson and the first group of African American stars into MLB.

The integration of MLB accelerated the decline of the Negro Leagues. It is easy to interpret this relationship as direct—that is, once opportunities in MLB arose, the Negro Leagues rapidly collapsed because their best players were leaving—but this correlation is not exactly what happened. First, many of the top African American players following Robinson, including some who were a bit younger, such as Ernie Banks and Henry Aaron, played in the Negro Leagues as well. Banks played in the Negro Leagues as late as 1954, and Aaron in 1952, with the Indianapolis Clowns. Because MLB did not fully embrace integration in the years immediately following Robinson's debut, there was still room for the Negro Leagues, albeit in a limited and declining way.

The Negro Leagues, however, had been having financial problems since before 1947. The Negro Leagues are viewed by many as a parallel baseball universe to the segregated white American and National Leagues in the pre-Robinson era, but that was not quite the case. The Negro Leagues never enjoyed the stability and wealth of the American and National Leagues. In some years, the leagues stayed together and ended the season with a Negro League World Series, but in other years, the leagues did not last the season. Sometimes players left teams for more lucrative opportunities with other teams or to perform as barnstormers. On some occasions, teams ran out of money and folded midway through the season. The Negro Leagues are better understood as being one of the very highest rungs in the large and complex ladder of semipro baseball rather than as being a formal league comparable to the American and National Leagues.

Chuck Brodsky's moving and funny song "The Ballad of Eddie Klep" offers some insight into the decline of the Negro Leagues. Brodsky describes the moment Eddie Klep walked into the clubhouse of the Cleveland Buckeyes, a Negro League team, as being "just like when the sheriff walks into the saloon." He explains that Klep "in his Cleveland Buckeyes uniform . . . was a new twist on the law. / The marshalls kept their eyes on him and the hecklers ate him raw." Toward the end of the song, Brodsky makes it very clear that Klep was a white man playing for a Negro League team: "So, while Jackie played for Brooklyn and wore the Dodger blue. / Eddie crossed the other line, the one without a queue."[7]

The song nicely conjures images of the struggling Negro Leagues needing a stunt of some kind to put fans in the seats. It is significant that the Buckeyes relied on the stunt of bringing in a white player named Eddie Klep not in the post-1947 era of integrated big league baseball but in 1946, when Robinson was still playing in the Dodgers' minor league system in Montreal. The Buckeyes had been a long-standing member of the Negro American League and still had big stars on their roster, such as Chet Brewer, Sam Jethroe, and Quincy Trouppe, but in 1946, they, like many teams in the Negro Leagues, were in bad financial shape.

As MLB's integration became institutionalized and as informal, unwritten limits on African American players were lifted, the decline of the Negro Leagues accelerated. Robinson; Larry Doby, the first African American to play in the AL; and the generation that followed them led an exodus of talent from an already struggling institution. As these great players left the Negro Leagues, many African American fans followed. In a 2012 publication, Adrian Burgos asserts that "attendance at Negro League games dropped precipitously during the 1947 and following seasons."[8] In his 2004 book, Neil Lanctot makes a similar point, noting that "the overall attendance decline in black baseball during 1947 was startling."[9] The hollowed-out Negro Leagues simply could not compete with MLB by the mid-1950s, when it had become apparent to everybody that the best African American players were now in the NL rather than the Negro Leagues.

The Negro Leagues did not simply disappear in the mid-1950s but stumbled along in a sad imitation of what they had previously been. Barnstorming continued into the 1960s, particularly in the South and in rural areas, but eventually the combination of the end of segregation in the American South, the full integration of big league baseball, and the continued expansion of MLB led to the final decline of the Negro Leagues.

By 1970, the idea of an all–African American team, even if only barnstorming, would have offended the sensibilities of many Americans, regardless of race, and would not have been much of a draw. Like many African American institutions of the first half of the twentieth century, the Negro Leagues were, at least in part, a victim of integration and the civil rights movement.

The clear beneficiary of the end of the Negro Leagues was big league baseball. MLB ended up with a better product and with a broader audience to buy it. By the mid-1950s, it was apparent that African American fans wanting to see the best African American players were better off following the Brooklyn Dodgers, the Cleveland Indians, or the New York Giants than the Indianapolis Clowns or the Homestead Grays. Additionally, as the Negro Leagues disappeared, so did a competitor for MLB, making it easier for MLB to become the premium—and, in fact, only—elite professional baseball organization in the United States.

Third Major League or Top Minor League

In baseball today, the term "AAAA player" refers to a player who has nothing left to prove in AAA, the highest level of the minor leagues, but is not quite good enough to win a starting a job at the big league level. Juan Perez is an example of this kind of ballplayer: the backup outfielder for the San Francisco Giants bounced between AAA and the big club for most of 2014 but found himself in left field in Game Seven of the World Series, where he made an overlooked but nonetheless game-saving catch in the fifth inning.

The PCL was an entire league that could be described as AAAA. The caliber of play, the level of competition, and the fame of the players and teams were only slightly below those of the big leagues and stronger than in all the other minor leagues for white players. The contributions of PCL players and others to the big leagues from the turn of the century through the late 1950s is hard to overstate. Famous big leaguers such as Ted Williams; Joe, Dom, and Vince DiMaggio; Lefty O'Doul; Billy Martin; Lefty Gomez; Heinie Manush; Paul and Lloyd Waner; Mickey Cochrane; Earl Averill; and Ernie Lombardi are among the big league stars who spent part of their careers in the PCL. Additionally, many famous big league managers and coaches spent time in the PCL. Casey Stengel, for example, managed the Oakland Oaks in the PCL before returning to the big leagues to manage the New York Yankees in 1949.

In his 2012 book, Dennis Snelling states:

> The Pacific Coast League shattered all minor league attendance records. Its teams frequently outdrew major league franchises year after year. . . . Players repeatedly spurned offers to play in the major leagues because they wanted to remain in the PCL. For a time, it appeared the Pacific Coast League might become baseball's third major league.[10]

The PCL usually comprised eight teams in major West Coast cities, such as Portland, Seattle, Sacramento, Oakland, San Francisco, San Diego, and Los Angeles. The PCL was initially a league of independent teams, but beginning in the 1940s, some PCL teams had affiliations with MLB teams. By 1960, every PCL team had an affiliation of this kind, marking the consolidation of MLB influence over the once-independent PCL.

The PCL was a product of a time before television and jet airplanes. During the first half of the twentieth century, when the AL and NL teams were concentrated in the Midwest and the Northeast, the PCL filled a very important need on the West Coast. For baseball fans even in major West Coast cities, such as Los Angeles and San Francisco, it was not easy to see big league baseball; the PCL gave fans throughout the West a way to view high-quality games. Additionally, because MLB salaries for players were much more modest in the years before free agency, players in the PCL had mixed incentives to move over to the big leagues.

For such stars as Ted Williams or Joe DiMaggio, the choice was easy, as greater fame and wealth could be found in New York, Boston, or some other big league city, but that was not true for all players. For Californians who were good ballplayers but not Hall of Fame talents, abandoning the Oakland Oaks or the Los Angeles Stars for the St. Louis Browns or the Pittsburgh Pirates did not always make sense. Even if salaries were slightly higher in the American and National Leagues, the expense associated with moving east for the season and the time spent away from family were strong reasons for PCL players to remain where they were.

From the 1920s to the 1940s, big league salaries were still very good, but for a player from California, a decent salary could also be made playing closer to home in the PCL. Given that many players of that era held regular jobs during the off-season, the appeal of being close to home was even greater for West Coast players, who could more easily build their name recognition and explore postseason opportunities to make money by playing in the PCL.

Because the PCL was completely unaffiliated with MLB until the 1940s, it functioned and felt like a real league. The relationships between teams, fans, and players were defined by a continuity that, while far from complete, was much greater than what is found on affiliated minor league teams. Fans of the San Francisco Seals, the Los Angeles Stars, and the Oakland Oaks recognized that some of their best players would probably eventually make it east to the major leagues, but they also knew that many of the other players, such as PCL greats Ross "Brick" Eldred, Irvin "Fuzzy" Hufft, and Billy Raimondi, would spend their careers on the West Coast without ever playing in a single American or National League game. Similarly, because they were not dependent on major league teams for revenue or players, the owners and general managers of PCL teams had to build a fan base, ensure their teams were competitive, and generally provide a good product to their fans. Thus, for roughly the first half of the twentieth century, the PCL actually drew many players away from the big leagues, in some cases for their entire careers and in other cases for a few years at the beginning or end of their careers.

On balance, the PCL was not quite a third big league. Overall, the talent and quality of play was higher in the National and the American Leagues, but the best players in the PCL were usually good enough to play in the big leagues. Even some of the ordinary players were no worse than comparable players on weak big league teams. In his 2014 book, Scott Simkus, writing about the PCL of 1927, describes "the second-place San Francisco Seals" that "featured future Hall of Famer Earl Averill, a young slugger named Dolf Camilli and Lefty O'Doul . . . [and] had several other decent major leaguers in their lineup but lacked pitching," adding that "they would have gotten clobbered at the major league level over the course of a long schedule."[11]

Simkus bases this assessment on a quantitative approach that he calls the "STARS" system, designed to approximate the relative strength of leagues and teams across time. Simkus's methodology is strong, so his view of the PCL in 1927 should not be dismissed. However, while the Seals, for example, probably would not have finished in the first division in the AL or the NL in 1927, it should also be noted that for much of the first half of the twentieth century, some big league teams almost never finished in the first division either.[12]

The question of parity is always on the minds of the leadership of MLB and most other sports. The need for parity and the perception that the wealthier teams, such as the New York Yankees and the Boston Red Sox, have at times been too dominant have contributed to many reforms in baseball, including the more multitiered play-off system, compensation for teams that lose free agents, limits to how much can be paid to players in the amateur draft, and even the draft itself.

Baseball has reached a level of parity that is not at the extreme levels of the 1980s and early 1990s yet is still relatively high. Between 2006 and 2015, six different teams won the World Series, and eleven teams played in the Fall Classic. During those years, all but three teams—the Miami Marlins, the Chicago White Sox, and the Seattle Mariners—appeared in the play-offs at least once, while many teams made several play-off appearances. Obviously, if the play-offs are expanded so that one out of three teams makes it rather than one out of eight or ten, as was the case from 1903 to 1968, there will be the appearance of more parity, but the point is that MLB has worked hard to create that appearance in recent decades.

This effort was not always the case in baseball. Some, but not all, of this change can be attributed to the extent to which the Yankees dominated the AL from 1921 to 1964, a period of forty-four years in which they won twenty-nine pennants. This left little room for other AL teams to win, as until 1969 only the team that won the pennant made it to the postseason, which in those days was just the World Series. For example, between 1947 and 1964, only three teams represented the AL in the World Series. Other teams had runs of dominance as well; for instance, the New York Giants won eight out of fourteen NL pennants between 1911 and 1924.

It was not, however, dominance by such teams as the Yankees, the Giants, and the Dodgers from 1941 to 1956 or the Cardinals in the 1940s that made the lack of parity so pronounced—rather, it was the persistence of teams that were perennially *bad* for decades. The Philadelphia Phillies did not win a pennant between 1916 and 1949; the St. Louis Browns appeared in the World Series only once between 1903, when the first World Series was played, and 1966, by which time they had moved to Baltimore and become the Orioles. After getting swept out of the 1927 World Series, the Pittsburgh Pirates did not win a pennant until 1960. The Philadelphia Athletics had two mini-dynasties, one from around 1905 to 1914 and one from around 1929 to 1931, but bad financial times forced owner-manager Connie Mack to sell off his top stars after those good runs. By the time the Athletics made it back to the World Series, it was 1972, and they were two cities removed from Philadelphia. The Chicago White Sox won pennants in 1917 and 1919 but then had to wait forty years before winning another, and then more than forty to win the one after that.

Thus, during the years before the Dodgers and the Giants moved west, when the PCL was at its height, MLB had long periods of fielding essentially terrible teams. Between 1918 and 1948, the Philadelphia Phillies played better than .500 baseball only once. From 1930 to 1942, the St. Louis Browns never played .500 ball or finished better than twenty-three games out of first place. Similarly, the Philadelphia Athletics, after selling off future Hall of Famers Mickey Cochrane, Lefty Grove, and Al Simmons after winning pennants three years in a row from 1929 to 1931, began a thirteen-year period of finishing below .500 in 1934, never coming within fewer than seventeen games of first place during those years.

The best PCL teams, such as the Seals of the late 1920s, clearly could not have contended in the big leagues, but they were probably better than, for example the Phillies or the Boston Red Sox of that era. Similarly, the best PCL teams of the late 1930s were probably superior to the Athletics or the Browns of those years. A better team with, in some cases, comparable pay closer to home was a powerful incentive for many PCL players during the time before any AL or NL teams had moved to the West Coast. This disparity helped keep the PCL strong and contributed to preventing the big leagues from consolidating their grip on professional baseball.

The decline of the PCL as a high-quality independent league began in the late 1940s, when some PCL teams established affiliations with big league teams, but it can be more or less directly traced to the Brooklyn Dodgers' and the New York Giants' moving to Los Angeles and San Francisco, respectively, following the 1957 season. Until that time, big league baseball had never been played west of the Rockies, or even west of St. Louis. Within only twelve years, five big league teams would be settled in California, but by that time the PCL was a fully affiliated minor league, and it remains so today.

When the Giants and the Dodgers moved west before the 1958 season, MLB finally became truly national in its reach. Until that move, despite being widely recognized as the country's national pastime, at its highest level, baseball was still played in only a small geographical area of the United States. The westward migration by the Dodgers and the Giants to California had been preceded by other efforts to move MLB out of the Northeast, with the Athletics moving west from Philadelphia to Kansas City before the 1955 season and the Braves moving from Boston to Milwaukee two years before that.

The Giants and the Dodgers moved west before the expansion truly began, but they opened up the West to the expansion era. Of the fourteen teams MLB added beginning in 1962, six were in the West: the California Angels, the Seattle Mariners, the San Diego Padres, the Colorado Rockies, the Arizona Diamondbacks, and the Milwaukee Brewers. Milwaukee is, of course, not in the West, but for their first year, the Brewers were based in Seattle and known as the Pilots.

During these years, baseball also added teams or moved franchises to the South (for example, the Atlanta Braves and the Houston Astros) and to Canada (for example, the Toronto Blue Jays and, briefly, the Montreal Expos).

The PCL was the most cohesive and functional independent league that was damaged by these developments, but—at least as significant—expansion also effectively ended barnstorming, something that had been part of the fabric of baseball in the United States for decades.

Barnstorming and Semipro Ball

Today, in an era when MLB dominates all aspects of professional—and, to some extent, all organized—baseball, it is easy to see this system as natural. After all, MLB offers high-level competition in a clear structure with accurate record keeping. What more could a baseball fan want? Nonetheless, there is something much more organic about the less-structured, more-informal framework of barnstorming and semipro ball.

For a fan, the process of rooting for a big league baseball team requires accepting and getting excited about factors that are not exactly intuitive. Jerry Seinfeld described the phenomenon of rooting for a professional sports team as "standing and cheering and yelling for your clothes to beat the clothes from another city."[13] His point is not hard to understand: we root for teams because we like the cities they represent; because a loved one used to root for them; because a parent, grandparent, or sibling told us to; or because of some other quirk of fortune. These loyalties are often genuine, intense, and long lasting, but they are nonetheless arbitrary and often impersonal.

Additionally, the World Series winner is viewed as the best team in the big leagues that year, but it is not obvious why that status is important. The question of which team is the champion among thirty teams with which most fans have no strong direct connection is important only if fans believe it is important and create a storyline to explain that status. Moreover, the World Series does not even pit the best players against each other. From 1955 to 1965, for example, there were many World Series in which Willie Mays, the best player in the NL, did not participate. Similarly, Barry Bonds and Ken Griffey Jr., the greatest players of the 1990s, combined to play in only one World Series. These may seem like unsophisticated criticisms, but they underscore the contrast and appeal of semipro ball and barnstorming.

The connection between big league players and their fans is dependent on the media and the view of big league players as somehow larger than life. In semipro baseball, the connection is based on much more direct interaction between players and the community they represent and on the understanding that the teams include ordinary people who happen to be very good baseball players.

Semipro teams were an important part of baseball for much of the first half of the twentieth century. Semipro teams were organized around workplaces, towns, neighborhoods, counties, or some other connections. Because of this basis, rooting for a semipro team meant rooting for one's own town or county against a neighboring town or county, which offers a much more organic appeal. Determining whether the best players in our neighborhood are better than the guys one neighborhood over is much more natural than rooting for a bunch of guys from Japan, Venezuela, the Dominican Republic, and ten U.S. states as they take the field against a team whose players feature a similar range of backgrounds.

Semipro teams were not quite that simple or pure, as many companies hired people who were good players to do jobs that were not very demanding so they could play on their companies' team. Nonetheless, in general, the connection between semipro teams and the communities they represented was much stronger than what exists today in the MLB.

As might be expected, semipro baseball was never as well organized or clearly structured as big league ball. Teams formed, merged, dispersed, and reformed on a fairly regular basis. Leagues rarely lasted more than a few years, and many games were one-offs or challenges between teams rather than regularly scheduled matches within a league. Semipro ball was not a competitor to big league baseball or even to minor league baseball. Rather, it was an alternative based on a much more primal understanding of competition and athleticism. For many baseball fans, it was a very viable alternative, particularly as big league baseball for the first half of the twentieth century was for many Americans somewhat remote and inaccessible.

The relationship between the big leagues and the less formally structured world of semipro ball and barnstorming was synergistic and, taken together, provided fans throughout the country the best of both worlds. Because baseball is such an unusual combination of team and individual sport, matchups and personal accomplishments are extremely important. Any baseball fan—even one who, like me, is devoted to his or her teams and loves statistics—understands this.

Around 2010, I went to Yankee Stadium to see the Yankees play the A's. The Yankees took a lead into the ninth inning before giving the ball to pitcher Mariano Rivera. By that point in his career, Rivera was already a legend in MLB and broadly recognized as the greatest closer ever. He had also managed to remain well liked by baseball fans around the country despite being a career Yankee. I joined the other Yankee fans around me in cheering for Rivera as he began his warmups. The great closer did not disappoint, throwing about fifteen to twenty pitches—mostly cutters, but also a few fastballs. The pitches all registered between ninety and ninety-two miles per hour and quickly dispatched the A's hitters. As the game ended with Frank Sinatra's version of "New York, New York" playing over the public address system and the hometown fans cheering, I noticed two fans next to me decked out in green and gold who did not look quite as happy as the rest of the crowd. As they were leaving, one said to the other, "At least we got to see Rivera get a save." For those Athletics fans, seeing the greatest closer ever get a save was a memory they would cherish, even though it came at the expense of their team.

I have been to hundreds of big league games and have seen no-hitters, pennant-clinching games, and the final game of the World Series, but one of the most impressive events I have ever seen on a big league ball field—a memory that I still cherish more than thirty years later—occurred during batting practice before the 1984 All-Star Game at Candlestick Park. AL power hitters Reggie Jackson, Eddie Murray, Dave Winfield, and George Brett put on an impromptu home run derby that remains the most extraordinary exhibition of power hitting I have ever seen. This was before the days of official and highly publicized modern home run derbies or of steroid-fueled batting practices where thousands would flock to see Mark McGwire or Sammy Sosa. Instead, these four great sluggers and future Hall of Famers, who combined for more than 1,800 big league home runs over the course of their careers, simply took turns hitting home runs into the upper deck at Candlestick Park. The 'Stick was a classic postwar multiuse stadium that, because of its size and the wind, was not a good park for power hitters, but these players, seemingly at will, drove the ball into the upper deck, something very few players were able to do during games.

Individual accomplishments are part of the great appeal of baseball. Similarly, the matchup is also one of the most exciting and memorable aspects of the game. To see Lou Gehrig, Ted Williams, Willie Mays, or Barry Bonds hit was something special, but to see them take their cuts against Lefty Grove, Bob Feller, Sandy Koufax, or Randy Johnson was even more extraordinary. Some of these moments have become important, and well-known, slices of baseball history: the young Bob Welch striking out Reggie Jackson in Game Two of the 1978 World Series, the battles between Richard "Goose" Gossage and George Brett in the late 1970s and early 1980s when the Yankees and the Royals were the two best teams in the AL, or the many contests between Willie Mays and Sandy Koufax when the Giants-Dodgers rivalry was at its West Coast height in the mid-1960s are all prime examples.

These individual matchups were one of the principles on which barnstorming rested for many years. Barnstorming occurred mostly in the off-season, when teams of big league stars, lesser-known big leaguers, and others would travel throughout the country, playing at local fairgrounds, ballparks, and the like. Often they would play against local teams or against each other. Barnstorming baseball was part baseball and part spectacle. Teams would play actual games, but often they would be surrounded by non-baseball-related entertainment or such activities as foot races, which were only peripherally related to baseball.

Barnstorming was often very disorganized, with nothing approaching regular leagues. There were no real standings and the record keeping was generally shoddy, but fans around the country were given the opportunity to see the best players in the game and, moreover, to see the best possible matchups. This was particularly true given MLB's segregation until 1947. Between roughly 1925 and 1945, when Josh Gibson and Satchel Paige were among the very best players around, it was possible to see Gibson hitting against Lefty Grove, Bob Feller, and Dizzy Dean or to witness Paige pitching to Lou Gehrig or Ted Williams only through the context of barnstorming.

Because barnstorming was not subject to the same racial restrictions as MLB, there were mixed-race teams as well as teams with members of various different racial and ethnic groups. Interestingly, players on the House of David team, who were most famous for their long beards, were, despite their name, not Jewish. Rather, they were associated with a vaguely Christian sect. Women were also occasionally part of the barnstorming milieu, either as entire teams or as individual players.

Barnstorming emphasized baseball as spectacle. It did not seek to determine who was the champion or which records were broken; it simply offered fans the opportunity to see the kind of baseball they wanted. To some extent, good barnstorming was dependent on more organized leagues. The legends surrounding noted barnstormers Dizzy Dean or Babe Ruth, for example, were built through their exploits in the big leagues. Dean's pitching for the Cardinals and Ruth's play with the Yankees labeled them as superior players and thus made them more marketable as barnstormers.

Fans in the rural areas where barnstorming was most popular craved the opportunity to see big league stars who were hundreds or thousands of miles away during the regular season. Without the imprimatur of MLB, Ruth was just a plump guy who could hit the ball a long way, and Dean was just guy who threw hard and boasted a lot. The superior skills of these players, relative to other big leaguers, were not always evident to the casual observer of the game, but their legends and numbers were.

Barnstorming was an integral part of how ordinary Americans experienced baseball, and certainly of how they encountered baseball's biggest stars through the 1940s. For much of this time, barnstorming complemented big league baseball rather than competed with it. Big league baseball was not televised and was played only in a handful of cities in the first half of the twentieth century, so it was necessary to build big league baseball—and, in fact, baseball in general—into a national brand. Barnstorming was one of the ways this was done.

To get fans in small cities in the West, the South, or other parts of the country without big league baseball teams to care about, for example, who won the World Series or who were the best big league players, excitement around these topics had to be generated. Much of this was done by reporters who wrote extensively about big league baseball—which, despite everything, offered the highest quality baseball around—but barnstorming also played a key role. Barnstorming helped build the big league brand by bringing big league baseball—or, more accurately, big league *players*—to all corners of the country. A fan who saw Babe Ruth, Dizzy Dean, or Tris Speaker barnstorming in the winter would be more likely to pay attention to their exploits during the big league season the following summer. By bringing the best baseball to various parts of the country, big league baseball helped cement its position as the most elite form of the game, despite obvious problems of inclusion, most visibly, but not exclusively, around issues of race.

The Rise of Affiliated Minor Leagues

The PCL is generally recognized as having been the top minor league in the years before the Dodgers and the Giants moved west. It is significant that while the PCL of the 1930s and 1940s no longer exists—a place where teams enjoyed loyal fan bases, players often spent years, and the fans and media cared about pennant races and championships—but there is still a PCL that plays an important role in organized baseball. Today, the PCL has 16 teams, each of which is affiliated with a big league team. As a result of the consolidation of minor leagues in recent years, the PCL includes teams located as far east as New Orleans, Nashville, and Omaha. However, it still includes a number of teams in western cities, such as Sacramento, Tacoma, and Las Vegas.

The assertion of MLB's control over the PCL and the eventual elimination of nonaffiliated teams in that high-level minor league was one of the last steps in the creation of the official minor league systems. The process began in the 1930s and 1940s and is most identified with the St. Louis Cardinals and their general manager, Branch Rickey. By creating the modern minor league system, Rickey influenced baseball in a major way that would have guaranteed his legacy in baseball even if he had never moved to the Dodgers and brought up Jackie Robinson in 1947. Rickey was the general manager (GM) for the Cardinals from 1926 to 1942. During that period, the Cardinals, who had never before won a pennant, represented the NL in the World Series five times. Equally importantly, Rickey's farm system produced a number of stars, including Joe Medwick, Enos Slaughter, Dizzy Dean, Marty Marion, and Stan Musial. By the time Rickey left the Cardinals, most teams had begun to emulate his winning strategy, which reshaped organized baseball while strengthening MLB's position relative to all other leagues and teams—or at least the white ones—in the United States.

An extensive network of minor leagues, consisting almost entirely of teams that are affiliated with major league teams, is a structure that is much stronger in baseball than in any other sport. It has also contributed to MLB's hegemonic role in organized baseball. Today, minor league baseball is more popular than it was a generation or two ago. Most AAA teams, the highest level of minor league baseball, average between five and ten thousand fans a game.[14] These are not huge crowds, but for teams playing in secondary and tertiary media markets, they are impressive. These numbers are also frequently higher than the attendance for several big league teams in the 1970s. The appeal of minor league baseball usually rests on a combination of low ticket prices, fun and odd promotions, and the persistent, but false, belief that minor league baseball represents a purer form of the game, played for the love of the sport rather than for money.

In reality, minor league baseball is a reflection of the diversity and complexity, economic and otherwise, of baseball today. Many minor league rosters, particularly in the low minors, include highly compensated prospects who have received generous signing bonuses and low-paid players, frequently from the Dominican Republic, who earn very little. Players in the latter group are often following a dream of making it to the big leagues or of merely playing in the United States because it is better work than what can be found at home, but few of these minor leaguers ever make it to the majors or achieve stardom.

The lower pay for Dominican minor leaguers and the alleged poor conditions at training camps in the Dominican Republic run by big league teams have led some to assert that MLB is exploiting Dominican talent. A 2013 article in *Mother Jones* titled "Inside Major League Baseball's Dominican Sweatshop System" describes

> a recruiting system that treats young Dominicans as second-class prospects, paying them far less than young Americans and sometimes denying them benefits that are standard in the U.S. minor leagues, such as health insurance and profes-

sionally trained medical staff. MLB regulations allow teams to troll for talent on the cheap in the Dominican Republic.[15]

Additionally, several minor league players have sued MLB over their treatment. In early 2014, thirty-four minor leaguers filed a suit against MLB, essentially arguing that they were not compensated in accordance with U.S. law because, given the amount of work they were doing, they were not even making minimum wage.[16] This lawsuit had not been resolved as this book went to press, but if the economic structures of minor league baseball have to change, the repercussions will be felt throughout big league baseball, as teams will have to reallocate resources or perhaps find alternative ways of developing players other than an extensive minor league system. This lawsuit also demonstrates that despite the myth that minor league baseball is somehow more pure or genuine, an exploitative system exists that takes advantage of the dreams of young and sometimes desperate people.

Baseball outside the United States

Max Lanier, Sal Maglie, and Mickey Owen are not all-time greats, but they were all very good players in the 1940s and 1950s. Maglie, nicknamed "The Barber" because of his proclivity for throwing inside, is probably the best known of the three. During a ten-year career, he won 119 games and posted a 3.15 ERA. He was the ace of pennant-winning Giants teams in 1951 and 1954. After a short stint with the Indians, Maglie moved over to the Giants' archrivals, where he helped the Dodgers win the 1956 pennant by going 13 and 5 with a 2.87 ERA. He is also remembered by some fans as the pitching coach for the 1969 Seattle Pilots, one of the teams on which Jim Bouton pitched while writing the seminal book *Ball Four* (1970).

Lanier did his best work as a top left-handed pitcher for the Cardinals teams that dominated the NL in the early and mid-1940s. Over a fourteen-year career, he won 108 games and posted a 3.01 ERA. Owen is best remembered for not being able to hold onto a third-strike spitball from Hugh Casey, allowing Tommy Heinrich to reach first base in the ninth inning of Game Four of the 1941 World Series and leading to a comeback win for the Yankees in that game. Owen, however, was a fine catcher who played on three NL All-Star teams before his thirtieth birthday.

Lanier, Maglie, and Owen were among the best of the more than twenty major leaguers who left the big leagues in the 1940s to play in the Mexican League. Many Negro League players from the United States, including such superstars as Satchel Paige, Cool Papa Bell, and Josh Gibson, joined teams in the Mexican League as well. Thus, the Mexican League was the first organized league where white and black Americans played and competed against each other side by side.[17] Jorge Pasquel, the extremely wealthy Mexican who was the financial power behind the Mexican League, wanted to bring North America's biggest stars to Mexico but was unsuccessful. In his 2008 book, John Virtue reports, "Besides [Ted] Williams and [Joe] DiMaggio, Pasquel offered contracts to slugger Hank Greenberg and pitcher Hal Newhouser of the Detroit Tigers and to Cleveland Indians' pitcher Bob Feller. The offer to Greenberg was $360,000, to Newhouser $350,000 and to Feller $300,000, all for three years."[18]

The Mexican League fell apart after a few years, so many of these players, despite initially being banned from MLB for playing in the Mexican League, returned to the big leagues, where they continued to play through the 1950s. The Mexican League was a failure and ultimately could not compete with the U.S.-based major leagues. It is nonetheless notable that for a time in the 1940s, a foreign league was able to compete successfully with the major leagues for top, or near top, American talent. In this century, it is almost axiomatic that the best talent in the world is available to the thirty big league teams. The one exception involves players from Cuba, but even that may be changing given the thaw in U.S.-Cuban relations, a relatively new development.

Furthermore, the Mexican League at its height was a powerful threat to the growing hegemony of MLB. This threat was not lost on MLB owners and officials, who sought to challenge the Mexican League by, among other ploys, exploring the idea of creating a league in Mexico that would be owned and controlled by big league baseball and big league teams. In 1946, Larry MacPhail, the Yankees' GM, tried to get an injunction against the Mexican League to prevent it from trying to lure Yankee players to Mexico. Pasquel responded by seeking to challenge the reserve clause in court. Ultimately, Pasquel failed in that endeavor, but his actions led to significant reforms in big league baseball that helped the players. Baseball formed a commission, led by MacPhail, that issued the MacPhail Report that "established a minimum salary of $5,000 a season, a limit of 25 percent on salary *reductions*, which were then quite common, the first pension plan for players and $25 a week for training camp expenses."[19]

In the pre-1947 era, dark-skinned players from Latin America were excluded by the same racist agreements that kept African American players out of the big leagues. This meant that leagues and teams in such places as Mexico, Venezuela, the Dominican Republic, and Cuba featured some stars who were good enough to play in the big leagues but were excluded because of the color of their skin. Some of the best known of these players include Pedro Cepeda, the father of Hall of Famer Orlando Cepeda, and Luis Tiant Sr., whose son was a star in the 1960s and 1970s for several teams, most memorably the Boston Red Sox.

Baseball also thrived in Japan during the twentieth century, but no Japanese players were in the big leagues until the mid-1960s, and even then only one player for parts of two seasons. World War II made the idea of sending Japanese baseball players to the United States laughable for much of the 1930s and 1940s, but after the war, it took decades before Japanese players began to have an impact on baseball in the United States.

The superior quality of play in the United States was one of the reasons why foreign players had such a difficult time making it into the U.S. big leagues, but the best of those foreign players, such as Sadaharu Oh and Pedro Cepeda, almost certainly could have starred in the United States as well. Instead, such missed opportunities further ensured that big league baseball for many years did not centralize the best baseball talent in any way approaching how it does today.

Was MLB Dominance Inevitable?

From the vantage point of the second decade of the twenty-first century, it seems inevitable that big league baseball would consolidate, with MLB getting more dominant and ultimately dramatically limiting most other forms of professional and semiprofessional baseball. There are still a few independent leagues, but they are tiny and quirky and, other than having the occasional recognizable name on the field or in the dugout, have very limited visibility. In baseball, like politics, and probably life in general, everything seems inevitable once it has already happened. Additionally, the leap from unimaginable to inevitable often occurs very quickly. To some extent, this leap is what happened with big league baseball.

The consolidation of big league baseball was not inevitable. It occurred because of a combination of developments, some of which were directly related to baseball and some of which were not. It is certainly possible that if the postwar history of the United States, or of big league baseball, had gone differently, we would still have meaningful semipro teams, popular barnstorming, and even leagues that would compete for top baseball talent. None of those things exist now, but it is possible that they could return in the future. Just as MLB in its current form was not inevitable, it is similarly not guaranteed that its current form will last into the foreseeable future.

There are probably countless reasons why MLB was able to assume its unrivaled status in the organized baseball hierarchy, but several major reasons deserve some analysis. First, segregation in the United States ended. When Jackie Robinson joined the Dodgers in 1947, he made baseball one of the first major American institutions to be integrated, albeit partially.

On the one hand, this demonstrates that at least some people in baseball, such as Branch Rickey and Bill Veeck, the owner of the Cleveland Indians who integrated the AL in 1948, were progressive on civil rights issues; on the other hand, it also demonstrates that there were no guarantees that Robinson, Larry Doby, Roy Campanella, Willie Mays, and the other early African American players in the big leagues would be able to truly integrate the game. Had the larger civil rights movement not occurred, changing attitudes about race in America and making the most overt forms of racism broadly unacceptable, baseball would not have fully integrated. Racism in baseball continued to be a significant problem well into the 1960s and probably beyond, particularly for players who found themselves playing for teams in the Deep South, even superstars such as Henry Aaron. Aaron's Milwaukee Braves moved to Atlanta following the 1965 season. He encountered overt racism during those first few seasons with the Braves and was deluged with racist letters during 1973 and 1974 when he threatened and eventually broke Babe Ruth's career home run record. It was not until 1976 that Frank Robinson became the first African American to manage in the big leagues. African Americans and Latinos remain starkly underrepresented among managers and in front offices.

Although MLB, like the United States, has yet to fully overcome its racist past, it is sufficiently integrated, and was by 1960, so that no African American league or even barnstorming team could compete. This scenario seems natural now, but it occurred because of broader societal changes that had little to do with baseball itself. The civil rights movement in the United States also opened baseball up to many dark-skinned Latino players, who have helped make MLB the top global destination for baseball talent.

Today, MLB attracts top baseball talent from Japan, South Korea, Taiwan, the Dominican Republic, Panama, Venezuela, and numerous other countries. Again, this seems natural, but it was not always the case. The appeal of MLB for players from these countries is based on two ideas. First, MLB offers the best competition. For a Japanese star, such as Hideki Matsui, Ichiro Suzuki, or Yu Darvish, who has nothing left to prove in his own country, the prospect of testing his skills against the best players in the world is very appealing. Japan has the strongest baseball league outside the United States and is also a first-world country. Therefore, Japan has been able to exercise more leverage than other countries—again, with the glaring exception of Cuba—in keeping its top players from going to the United States.

Second, MLB offers extraordinary compensation. An agreement between MLB and the Japanese and Korean leagues known as the *posting system* lays out the ground rules for players from these two countries. A key component of this posting system is that the Japanese team has to agree to let the player go to the United States. This restriction obviously staunches the potential flow of all the top Japanese players to the United States, limiting the field to primarily those who have reached free agency. Nonetheless, such players as Masahiro Tanaka from Japan, David Ortiz from the Dominican Republic, and Mariano Rivera from Panama can earn much more money playing in the United States than they can anywhere else.

This pay gap is partially due to the economics of big league baseball, an institution that is well marketed and run with a constant eye toward increasing revenue, but it is also due to the size and wealth of the American economy. The growth of the American economy in the postwar era, particularly in comparison to the rest of the Western Hemisphere, was instrumental in making the United States the most desired destination for baseball players from Central and South America beginning in the 1950s, when they were first allowed to play in the big leagues. By the 1990s, when baseball began its most recent wave of globalization, the American economy was so much bigger than that of any other baseball-playing country that financial incentives for the best players in the world to come play for a U.S. team remained strong.

Within the United States, demographic changes and population shifts helped cement the supremacy of MLB. For example, people moving from the cities of the Northeast and the Midwest to the suburbs and the Sun Belt during the postwar period, but particularly beginning in the 1960s, brought their taste for big league baseball, and often their team loyalties, with them. In other words, people who left New York but grew up rooting for Willie, Mickey, or the Duke were unlikely to start rooting for a local semipro team in Texas, Arizona, or wherever else they moved.

MLB was not a passive bystander to this development. Rather, franchise moves and expansion followed population shifts. The establishment of expansion teams in Florida, Arizona, Texas, and southern California and the movement of existing teams, such as the Braves (from Boston to Atlanta by way of Milwaukee) and the Dodgers (to Los Angeles from Brooklyn), echoed these broader population shifts. Additionally, new teams in northern California, Washington State, Kansas City, and elsewhere meant that by the 1990s, very few Americans, except for those in Alaska and Hawaii, were more than a four-hour drive away from a big league team. This proximity was not an accident but a deliberate strategy by MLB. Franchise moves and expansion are taken very seriously by MLB and often decided with an eye to what is good for all of MLB rather than what favors the provincial interests of one or two teams.

The numerous technological innovations of the past seventy-five years or so have also had a dramatic effect on big league baseball and helped it build itself into a dominant national brand. Semipro ball and barnstorming, in particular, thrived in an environment without television or the Internet. When these forms of semiorganized baseball were at the height of their popularity, baseball games could be watched in person, read about in the newspapers, or listened to on the radio, but that was it.

These all were, and remain, great forms of media through which to experience baseball, but they are limited. Radio and newspapers are, other than a few photographs in the paper, devoid of images. A verbal or a written description of a great infielder from the first three decades of the past century, such as Frankie Frisch, making a fantastic stop or of a slugger, such as Jimmie Foxx or Babe Ruth, clouting a big home run is not the same as seeing it, and for many Americans, that was either impossible or extremely difficult until the television era.

Television changed all that and made it possible for fans throughout the country to easily see big league baseball. Notably, for the first decades, the availability of baseball on television varied substantially, with some media markets getting only a game or two each week while other teams televised many games. As late as the 1980s and early 1990s, fans in many parts of the country had access to only two games a week during the regular season as well as a handful of games, usually road games, played by their local teams—but this was still a lot better than having no baseball on television.

Once fans could see Willie Mays and Hank Aaron, and later Reggie Jackson and Tom Seaver, on television with some regularity, including during the All-Star Game and the postseason, the demand for barnstorming more or less disappeared. Similarly, semipro teams and unaffiliated minor leagues could not compete with big league baseball on television. As the reach of cable television expanded, this disparity became even more apparent.

In the last two decades, new technologies such as podcasts, MLB.TV, the Internet, and social media have helped bring MLB to an ever-growing audience, leaving even less room for other forms of professional or semiprofessional baseball. It is possible that the Internet could have had a different effect, creating more visibility for independent leagues or baseball outside the United States, but MLB was able to preclude this chance by staying ahead of the technological curve beginning in the mid-1990s.

MLB's position, success, affluence, and relationship to almost every other form of organized baseball in the United States, including youth baseball and college baseball, to some degree, is the result of a confluence of events, such as technological breakthroughs and demographic changes over the past seventy-five years, and of smart strategic thinking by the owners of baseball teams and their allies in the commissioner's office.

MLB has done an excellent job of promoting itself, adapting to the changing environment in which it is played, and pushing away all potential rivals. Nonetheless, a central question facing baseball's ability to maintain this status is how much more it will have to adapt to continually changing circumstances inside and outside the game. As baseball becomes more globalized, for example, MLB may have to meaningfully expand beyond North America. If that happens, MLB may have to change its season schedules and structures or risk the emergence of financially competitive rival leagues. Such shifts could change MLB in many respects and undermine the continuity that is central to appreciating baseball's history. Similarly, if baseball is unable to retain its appeal to younger fans and becomes more identified with an older and overwhelmingly male demographic, it will be hard for the game to continue to generate the kind of revenue on which it has grown to depend.

3

GIA, BERT, AND MASANORI

Gia Kemoklidze is a baseball man. He is the kind of guy who seems most comfortable wearing sweatpants, a team windbreaker, and a baseball cap. Kemoklidze enjoys talking baseball, and although English is not his first language, he is fluent in the idiom and slang of the sport. He is a stocky, middle-aged man who looks like he probably played a corner infield position and hit with some power as a younger man. Kemoklidze, however, never played an inning of professional, college, or even high school baseball, yet he has dedicated much of his career to it. As a coach of younger children, he has great patience for teaching the fundamentals of the game and an impressive capacity for hitting fungos to youths learning to play the infield or outfield and for pitching batting practice.

Kemoklidze also helps manage a men's baseball team and a women's softball squad. This task involves raising money for supplies, scheduling games, and working out the logistics around traveling to the games as well as being a presence on the field offering guidance and technical advice to his players.

Thousands of people like Kemoklidze live across the United States, men and women whose love for the game has kept them on the field, trying to teach the next generation of baseball and softball players, putting in long hours for modest compensation because of their love of the sport, doing whatever they can so that the kids in their area get a chance to play ball, and, yes, hoping to find the next Willie Mays or Derek Jeter.

Kemoklidze, however, is not American, nor does he spend his days in Latin America, the Caribbean, or East Asia. Kemoklidze is Georgian, hailing from the small country just south of Chechnya and east of Turkey that until 1991 was part of the Soviet Union. Georgians love sports, particularly team sports. It is not unusual for the Georgian soccer or rugby teams to defeat Russia, their giant (and not particularly friendly) neighbor. These events are usually cause for great celebration in Tbilisi, Georgia's capital.

Baseball, however, is largely unknown in Georgia. Accordingly, Kemoklidze spends a great deal of time securing fields where his teams can play and practice, generally having to do the grounds keeping himself. Equipment is also a problem. I have tried to help him over the years by shipping used, and sometimes new, equipment to him in Georgia, but he often is concerned about such matters as running out of baseballs if the national team hits too many batting practice home runs. When I met with him for an interview in a small cafe in Tbilisi, he was very pleased to see the dozen brand-new baseballs I had brought him from New York.

Georgia is a long way from having a strong baseball program, but Little League, with help from the U.S. embassy, is becoming more popular there, and Kemoklidze is constantly seeking more tournament opportunities for his national teams. It is not inconceivable that if the World Baseball Classic (WBC) were to expand, Georgia could win a seed there in the next decades. It is similarly possible that a talented young Georgian could find his way to the big leagues in a shorter time frame. If that were to happen, this country of fewer than five million people would suddenly become much more interested in America's national pastime.

Kemoklidze, who encountered and fell in love with baseball at the end of the Soviet period, first learned the game from Cubans, some Americans, and a small handful of Soviet citizens, most of whom were ethnic Georgians. He told me that baseball is a good fit for Georgians, as his countrymen like team games that require fast thinking and quick decision making. Kemoklidze tells me Georgians do not run marathons but are naturals at recognizing whether a pitch is a ball or a strike.[1] Bert Blyleven is also a baseball guy, but in a very different way than Kemoklidze is. When I first became a baseball fan in the 1970s, Blyleven was understood to be a pretty good pitcher, reliable, known for what many viewed as the best curveball in the game, but at least a cut below Steve Carlton, Tom Seaver, Jim Palmer, and the other superstar pitchers from the mid-1970s to the early 1980s. Blyleven gained additional name recognition in the early days of ESPN, because a young Chris Berman, fond of making up puns based on players' names, used to refer to Blyleven as Bert "Be Home" Blyleven.

Blyleven was much more than just a pretty good pitcher with a silly nickname that never really caught on. He also became an important symbol during the Sabermetrics revolution, particularly during the years from 1998 to 2011. Blyleven was the prototype of a pitcher whose greatness did not come through in conventional statistics. He did not reach the magic threshold of three hundred wins, won twenty games in a season only once, never won a Cy Young Award, finished in the top ten in Cy Young Award voting only three times, and made only two All-Star teams. He also never led the league in wins or earned run average (ERA) and led the league in strikeouts only once.

But a closer look at Blyleven's career tells a different story. Blyleven was an excellent postseason pitcher, going 5–1 with a 2.47 ERA in eight starts, including three in the World Series. Over a span of nineteen years, he finished in the top ten in ERA and strikeouts ten and fifteen times, respectively. At the time of his retirement, he was twenty-third in career wins and, amazingly, third in career strikeouts.

More advanced statistics made Blyleven seem even better. The Wins above Replacement (WAR) formula, an attempt to create a measure of overall contribution to winning baseball games, rated Blyleven the best pitcher in the American League (AL) in 1981, the best player in the AL in 1973, and one of the top ten pitchers in his league ten times. According to WAR, when he retired, Blyleven was the eighth-most-valuable pitcher *ever*. That measure was bolstered by numbers that were almost as impressive in such areas as Fielding Independent Pitching (FIP), strikeout-to-walk ratio, and adjusted ERA (ERA+).[2] Because of this discrepancy between conventional and more advanced statistics, for more than a decade, Blyleven was at the center of a heated debate concerning the Hall of Fame. In 1998, his first year of eligibility, Blyleven received support from a very modest 17.8 percent of the voters.[3] Over the next fourteen years, the controversy over Blyleven's Hall of Fame candidacy became an annual affair for baseball fans and writers, until he was finally elected in 2011. Blyleven is an important figure in baseball because the understanding of him as a Hall of Fame–caliber pitcher is evidence of a genuine and significant shift in how people have come to understand the game.

Blyleven is also the answer to a great trivia question: ask fans who won the most games of any foreign-born pitcher, and they will likely first think of great Dominican pitchers, such as Juan Marichal and Pedro Martínez—but the answer is Rik Aalbert Blijleven (as the name is spelled in Dutch), who was born in the Dutch city of Zeist. By the time he was five years old, Blyleven's family had settled in southern California, so the future Hall of Famer grew up playing baseball in the United States, the country where he has lived almost his entire life.[4]

But Blyleven's connection to his native Netherlands did not end when he was a child. More than a decade after he retired, Blyleven served as the pitching coach for the Dutch team in the WBC in 2009 and in 2013. The Dutch entry in the WBC became a favorite of baseball fans in both those tournaments. In 2009, they twice beat a Dominican team that had a lineup that would not have looked out of place at a major league All-Star Game. Jose Bautista, Robinson Cano, Nelson Cruz, and David Ortiz were among the Dominican sluggers the Dutch held to three runs in two games. In 2013, the *honkballers*, as they are called in Dutch, made it all the way to the semifinals before the Dominican players, on their way to the championship, had their revenge and defeated the Dutch 4–1. Both years, the Dutch team included players from Dutch Islands in the Caribbean, such as Curaçao, and from Holland.

More than four decades before the WBC was first played, the 1964 San Francisco Giants were one of the more interesting teams ever assembled. The team was very good, winning ninety games and finishing in fourth place in a very close race, only three games behind the National League's (NL's) pennant-winning St. Louis Cardinals. The team had six future Hall of Famers that year, including Orlando Cepeda, Willie McCovey, Willie Mays, Juan Marichal, Gaylord Perry, and an aging former Brooklyn Dodger center fielder named Duke Snider, who had once been part of the triumvirate of extraordinary center fielders playing in New York in the 1950s.

The best player on that team was, as might have been expected, Willie Mays. Mays was in his prime and still the best player in baseball in 1964. He finished sixth in Most Valuable Player (MVP) voting despite having the highest WAR in the league. In 1964, Mays hit .296, but his on-base percentage, as a result of his eighty-two walks, was .383. Mays also managed to lead the league with a slugging percentage of .607, due largely to the forty-seven home runs he hit despite playing his home games in the huge, windy, and cold Candlestick Park. Although he was already thirty-three years old, Mays managed to steal nineteen bases while only getting caught five times and for good measure, won his eighth of what would eventually be twelve straight Gold Gloves. In 1964, Mays was an all-time great player at the height of his game.

One of the least-valuable players on that team was a thirty-four-year-old reliever who pitched 10.1 mediocre innings over six games, giving up six walks and ten hits and chalking up an inflated ERA of 4.35 before being sold to the Houston Colt .45s on May 20. The change of scenery was apparently good for Don Larsen, as he salvaged a decent season with the not very good Colt .45s, going 4–8 with a 2.25 ERA for his new team. Larsen was eight years removed from the highest point in his career, when as a New York Yankee he threw the only perfect game in World Series history.

Larsen, Snider, Mays, Marichal, McCovey, and two of the Alou brothers (Jesus and Matty) made that Giants team very interesting, but one of the most intriguing Giants that year was a twenty-year-old rookie pitcher who was called up on September 1 and played in only nine games. That pitcher was a young Japanese man named

Masanori Murakami, the first player to make it to the big leagues from his country. Murakami was excellent out of the bullpen in the stretch drive in 1964, striking out fifteen and walking one, while going 1–0 with a save and a 1.80 ERA. The next year, Murakami was a very respectable 4–0 with a 3.75 ERA in forty-five games, all but one as a reliever for the Giants. Murakami then returned to Japan, where he pitched very well for another sixteen years before retiring after the 1982 season.

For the two seasons he played with the Giants, in 1964 and in 1965, Murakami was very popular. His presence on the team was broadly recognized and celebrated by the media. After he agreed to come back to the Giants for the 1965 season, following some contract-related controversy, Robert Fitts wrote in 2015, "San Francisco was once again caught up in Murakami mania. Mashi's return headlined the sports section of every Bay Area newspaper and was picked up by UPI and AP news."[5] However, after his return to Japan, Murakami was quickly forgotten, and almost three decades would pass before another Japanese player made it to the big leagues.

For Giants fans growing up in San Francisco in the 1970s and 1980s, Murakami was somebody from what seemed like the distant past. Intense fans knew his name and that he was the first Japanese player in the big leagues, but little was known about the Japanese leagues, although they were presumed to be inferior. Most fans viewed Murakami's presence on the Giants as a stunt, usually forgetting the value he brought to the team during the year and change he played in San Francisco.

Kemoklidze, Blyleven, and Murakami are very different figures in baseball history. One is an all-but-unknown man who has dedicated his life to baseball in a country where few people have ever thrown a baseball or swung a bat. Another was, depending on whom you ask, one of the twenty to seventy-five greatest pitchers ever. And the third was a good, but fringe, player from half a century ago who is well known in his own country but in the United States is known to only the most studious fans of the game. Yet they all reflect an important part of the story of baseball—its ongoing globalization. A century and a half ago, baseball was almost exclusively America's game. It is not quite the world's game yet and may never achieve that status, but the sport is a lot more global than ever before, and it becomes more global every year.

Baseball Leagues outside the United States

Every four summers when the World Cup takes place, much of the world turns its attention to soccer. During this quadrennial event, Americans, particularly in recent years, pay some attention to the World Cup, but most of us, at least those of us who are sports fans, keep focused on our own summer game. Any American who has traveled, particularly in Europe, during the World Cup has been asked, with varying degrees of politesse, to explain why the rest of the world loves soccer, but Americans like baseball. This is the kind of question that reveals far more about the person posing the question than most responses reveal about Americans.

It is not true that the whole world loves soccer except for us pesky, quirky Americans. Soccer is the world's most popular team sport, but it is not exactly popular throughout the whole globe. It is extremely popular in Europe, Central and South America, and Africa, but it is a peripheral sport in the United States, Canada, much of the Caribbean, and parts of East Asia, where baseball is more popular. Nor is soccer the most popular sport in China, where basketball is probably the most favored team sport. In India, Pakistan, Bangladesh, and a handful of smaller countries, cricket remains the national pastime, far outpacing soccer.

Thus, while soccer's position as a global sport is often overstated, the notion that baseball is uniquely American reveals a distinct strain of Eurocentrism. Baseball is now played in numerous countries, albeit perhaps a bit afield from Europe and the European view of the world. Many baseball fans are aware of baseball's popularity in the Caribbean, Central America, and East Asia; its increasing popularity in Australia; and its slow growth in Europe.

Casual fans might assume that baseball's popularity outside the United States is a relatively new phenomenon, particularly in Japan and other parts of Asia. It would be natural to think that the sport was introduced to Japan by U.S. soldiers after World War II, but that assumption would also be wrong. Baseball's roots in Japan, as well as in Korea and Taiwan, go back at least to the early part of the twentieth century.

As early as the 1920s, big league players barnstormed in Japan from time to time. The most notable of these barnstorming trips to Japan occurred in late 1934, with a group of U.S. ballplayers that included future Hall of Famers Earl Averill, Jimmie Foxx, Lou Gehrig, Charlie Gehringer, Lefty Gomez, and Babe Ruth, who was still the biggest name in baseball despite being at virtually the end of his big league career. The team was managed by Connie Mack, who would also later be inducted into the Hall of Fame.[6]

Two other intriguing members of that barnstorming group were Lefty O'Doul and Moe Berg. O'Doul is recognized as being one of the Americans most responsible for popularizing baseball in Japan. O'Doul had first visited Japan in 1931 and then returned in 1932 and 1933. In 1932, O'Doul spent much of his time in Japan working with players and coaches to improve their skills. After World War II, O'Doul went back to Japan to help repair the baseball relations between the United States and Japan.[7] O'Doul's work to support baseball in Japan was recognized in 2002, when he was posthumously elected to the Japanese Baseball Hall of Fame.

One of O'Doul's interesting legacies in Japan involves the Yomiuri Giants. As the best and the most visible Japanese team, they are the Japanese equivalent to the New York Yankees, yet their name and their colors, orange and black, were chosen because they were modeled on the New York Giants, O'Doul's team, which was still the marquee baseball team in the United States in the early 1930s.

Berg was never the hitter that O'Doul was. Berg was a longtime backup catcher of the good field no hit variety. He played for the Dodgers, the White Sox, the Indians, the Senators, and the Red Sox over the course of a fifteen-year career. Berg's legacy is not so much based on his generally limited on-the-field contributions; instead, he is remembered for being one of the first reasonably prominent Jewish big leaguers. Additionally, Berg was an unusually well-educated and cerebral man, particularly when compared to other ballplayers of his era. He had a degree from Princeton, was a polyglot, and had a deep knowledge of physics. As a ballplayer, Berg spent his free time on the road reading newspapers, going to libraries, and visiting museums, not activities generally associated with ballplayers in the 1920s and 1930s—or, for that matter, any time before or since.

During World War II, Berg served his country with distinction in a number of capacities. He is perhaps most famous for his 1944 assignment with the Office of Strategic Services (OSS), the precursor of the Central Intelligence Agency (CIA), when he was asked to go to a lecture by German physicist Werner Heisenberg in Zurich. The OSS asked Berg to decide, based on Heisenberg's comments, whether he thought Germany was ahead of the United States in the race to create an atomic bomb; if so, he was to shoot the German scientist.[8]

During that 1934 barnstorming trip, Berg took many photographs, often breaking away from the team to take pictures. In his 2012 book, Robert Fitts describes how Berg defied Japanese law to take photographs of various strategic sites, including several straits, harbors, and coastal areas used by the Japanese navy. In Hokkaido, according to Fitts, "neither the proscription nor the officials stopped Moe Berg. Defying the warning, Berg whipped out the camera and filmed the area."[9] Berg later gave those photographs to the U.S. military to help them target and otherwise strategize about the war with Japan.

Professional baseball in Japan began in earnest in 1935 with the founding of the Japanese Occupational League (JOL). The JOL is the antecedent of today's Nippon Professional Baseball (NPB) organization. Because of the physical distance between the United States and Japan and then the difficult relations of World War II, baseball in the two countries, while still largely the same game, evolved on different but asymmetrical tracks. While Japanese fans have always known a fair amount about professional baseball in the United States, the reverse has never been true. Before 1990 or so, few American baseball fans would have been able to name one professional Japanese player other than the great Sadaharu Oh, who had retired in 1980.

During the last few decades of the twentieth century, the NPB was known to American fans as a place where American ballplayers went when they were at the tail end of their careers or when they could not make it in the big leagues. Some of these players included relatively big names, such as Warren Cromartie, Willie Davis, Don Money, and Cecil Fielder. Fielder had a very unusual stint in Japan, because he went there as a twenty-five-year-old and batted .302 with thirty-eight home runs in 1989, his one season with the Hanshin Tigers, before returning to the United States and establishing himself as one of baseball's premier sluggers in the 1990s.

Despite the presence of American and other Western players, the NPB has never been a truly global league. There have always been limits on the number of non-Japanese players on each team. Moreover, few American or other foreign players have enjoyed long careers in Japan. Instead, they have usually played only a short time, often at the end of their careers.

The NPB is the oldest, most established, and best professional baseball league in Asia, but it is not the only one. Baseball has also been played for more than a century in Taiwan and in Korea. In his 2004 book, Joseph Reaves asserts, "Baseball was introduced to Korea in 1905 by a U.S. missionary named Philip L. Gillet."[10] However, adds Reaves, "Baseball may have been brought to Korea by a U.S missionary, but it would be the passion and policies of Japanese soldiers, administrators and educators that enabled the game to survive and prosper."[11] The Korean Baseball Organization's first season was in 1982, and the Chinese Professional Baseball League, the league in Taiwan, first began to play in 1990. Neither of these leagues is as strong as the NPB, but top players from Korea and Taiwan have excelled in the United States over the past twenty years.

Baseball has been played in many parts of Latin America for more than a century, but for that region, the gravitational pull of big league baseball in the United States has always been stronger than it has been in Asia. Because of their proximity to the United States, many countries in this region had less-formal baseball leagues, although some of these leagues, such as the league in the Dominican Republic, date back to the early part of the twentieth century. Additionally, barnstorming trips to the Caribbean by big league players occurred with some frequency during the first half of the twentieth century. Beginning around the 1950s, the Dominican Republic, Puerto Rico, Venezuela, and other countries in that region began to send their best players to the United States. Winter baseball leagues in such places as Puerto Rico and the Dominican Republic have long been popular destinations for big league players trying to work on some part of their game, stay in shape, or recover from an injury during the off-season.

Following Fidel Castro's ascent to power in 1959, Cuba had a different path than the rest of the region. Baseball in Cuba has continued to thrive during the decades since Castro came to power, but Cuban baseball was cut off from the United States. Teams from Cuba played in Caribbean tournaments and other international settings but otherwise rarely faced American teams or played in the United States. Similarly, Cuban players during these years were unable to come to the United States as freely as players from elsewhere in the region. Those who did—for example, Livan and Orlando Hernandez, Rey Ordonez, and Yasiel Puig—had to flee Cuba and establish residency in a third country before committing to sell their services to the highest American bidder.

For the first half of the twentieth century, Latin American baseball had strong ties to the North American Negro Leagues. African Americans in the United States were excluded from the big leagues because of their skin color, but they could play in Latin America, where the leagues did not discriminate on the basis of skin color or ancestry. Thus, Negro League stars frequently barnstormed in the Caribbean, played on Caribbean teams, and otherwise contributed to baseball in that region. None of these leagues and very few of these teams offered the consistent quality of big league baseball, but they included some of the best players in the game.

Who Played in the Big Leagues?

Today, the people playing big league baseball come from many different countries and at least four different continents. American-born players still represent a plurality of all big leaguers, and they are also an ethnically diverse bunch, with substantial numbers of Irish American, Italian American, and Jewish American players as well as white Protestant Americans, African Americans, Latinos, and players who trace their roots to many other European countries that have sent immigrants to the United States. This diversity, of course, was not always the case.

The racial segregation of Major League Baseball (MLB) from the late nineteenth century until 1947 is very well known, but the exclusion of Latino players during most of those years is less well known. Many Latinos were excluded because of their dark skin, while those who played were generally described as "Spanish"; their roots in Latin America were rarely mentioned. Nonetheless, the history of Latinos in baseball is extremely complicated, particularly during the period when African Americans were excluded from the big leagues.

In his 2007 book, Adrian Burgos notes that

> thirteen of the sixteen major league teams that existed prior to 1947 had at least one Latino player perform in uniform before Jackie Robinson's 1947 debut. That these players, most of whom were racialized as nonwhite Others or of "Spanish" ancestry, secured access illuminates how team and league officials manipulated the league's racial policy to sign players who occupied locations along the color line other than that of blacks.[12]

Pre–Jackie Robinson Latino stars included Dolf Luque, an excellent pitcher for the Cincinnati Reds in the 1920s, and Al Lopez, an American-born player whose parents were Spanish immigrants to the United States by way of Cuba. Lopez had a nineteen-year career as a catcher and was elected to the Hall of Fame in 1977 primarily for his work as a manager. Another great Latino of the pre-1947 period whose career overlapped with Robinson's was Ted Williams. Williams, generally viewed as one of the greatest hitters ever, was born in San Diego to a Mexican mother; Williams was his father's surname. The question of how Lopez, Williams, or Luque fits into the racial and ethnic history of baseball is subjective but speaks to the nuanced stories of Latinos in the big leagues.

Native Americans also occupied a complicated place in the racial politics of baseball. They were not excluded, but very few made it to the big leagues. Those who did, such as Hall of Fame pitcher Charles Bender and catcher John Meyers, were often known as "Chief." For Americans of European descent, baseball rarely had any formal barriers, although prejudice against Italian, Jewish, and other players was not uncommon during much of the twentieth century. However, the demographics of the big leagues loosely followed immigration patterns. Early twentieth-century players were frequently of English, German, or Irish ancestry, as demonstrated by such names as Keeler, McGraw, Wagner, Mathewson, Ruth, and Gehrig. However, by the middle of the century, that had changed somewhat as, for example, Italian Americans began to make their mark on the game.

The first Italian American baseball superstar was Joe DiMaggio. One of three brothers who played center field in the big leagues, the DiMaggio brothers grew up in an Italian American neighborhood in San Francisco called North Beach. Joe also spent his entire career playing in New York, which had a huge Italian American population. Among the Italian American stars who played alongside DiMaggio on the Yankees were shortstops Frank Crosetti and Phil Rizzuto, catcher Yogi Berra, and infielder Billy Martin, whose Anglicized last name belied his Italian roots.

Despite being one of the best players in the game, playing on a team in New York alongside other Hall of Fame Italian Americans such as Rizzuto and Berra, throughout his career DiMaggio was called "Dago," or "The Big Dago." DiMaggio was more of a trailblazer for Italian Americans than many remember or than younger fans may be able to imagine. The idea of a graceful, dignified, and superbly talented Italian American such as DiMaggio was new to many white Protestant fans in the 1930s, a time when Italians were often portrayed as dirty, mobbed up, or otherwise not quite American. A 1939 *Life* magazine profile of DiMaggio, then in his fourth season, notes that "although he learned Italian first, Joe, now twenty-four, speaks English without an accent and is otherwise well adapted to most U.S. mores. Instead of olive oil or smelly bear grease he keeps his hair slick with water. He never reeks of garlic and prefers chicken chow mein to spaghetti."[13]

By mid-century, Jewish players, although in much smaller numbers, had begun to make their mark on the game. Hank Greenberg and Al Rosen were the first major Jewish stars, followed by Sandy Koufax a few years later.

By the 1960s, baseball was almost fully integrated, with players representing an increasing diversity of backgrounds. Americans of almost all backgrounds, although notably few of Arab or South Asian descent, could be found in the big leagues beginning around that time. However, baseball still drew players almost entirely from the United States and Latin America. Even the occasional European-born players in the 1970s, such as Bruce Bochy and Bert Blyleven, had all grown up in the United States.

Today, big league baseball is played by people from Venezuela, Panama, Japan, Korea, many islands in the Caribbean, Australia, and an occasional European country. In 2010, fully one-quarter of big league players were foreign-born, up from 12 percent twenty-five years earlier. The 88 percent of big league ballplayers who were American-born in 1985 represented only a slight decrease from the 90 percent who were American-born in 1960. Thus, the modern age of globalization in baseball is only, at most, thirty years old. By contrast, in 1935, all but 6 of the 484 men who played in the big leagues had been born in the United States.[14]

The dramatic increase in the number of countries that send players to the big leagues began with Latinos, who began to make their mark on the game in the 1950s and 1960s. Initially, this change was uneven, as some teams—notably, the Pittsburgh Pirates and the Los Angeles Dodgers—aggressively scouted in Latin America. Few teams in the late 1950s and early 1960s were more active in that part of the world than Murakami's Giants. The Giants found Orlando Cepeda in Puerto Rico, who became the second Puerto Rican to be elected to the Hall of Fame after the Pirates' Roberto Clemente.

The Giants also found some of the first great big leaguers from the Dominican Republic, including, most prominently, Hall of Fame pitcher Juan Marichal. Felipe, Matty, and Jesus Alou, a trio of brothers who had grown up with Marichal, were also among the early Dominican players on the Giants. Slowly, the trickle of players from Latin America increased as Venezuelans, Panamanians, Mexicans, and even Nicaraguans also began to gain visibility on big league rosters.

The next very significant step toward the globalization of big league baseball was the substantial increase in the number of Asian players to make it to MLB, primarily from Japan, but also from Korea and Taiwan. These players came to the big leagues through a very different path than Latin American players did. In such places as the Dominican Republic and Venezuela, big league teams were, and continue to be, free to scout and sign players more or less as they want. Players from these countries are not eligible for the amateur draft, and only some limits are placed on how teams can spend their money there. Cuba is, of course, a long-standing exception to this policy.

Japanese players are treated differently in this regard. Because the NPB is recognized as an organized league with some legal rights, Japanese players cannot simply sign with big league teams at will. Instead, since the late 1990s, they must be *posted*, which means that big league teams bid for the right to negotiate with Japanese players who are seeking to come to the United States. Because of this system, Japanese teams are compensated when their players go to the United States. This policy also drives down the salaries of the Japanese players, as posting fees can be quite high.

After Murakami's brief trial with the Giants in the mid-1960s, it was almost thirty years until the next Japanese player appeared in a big league game. Hideo Nomo's excellent season with the Los Angeles Dodgers in 1995, during which he was voted Rookie of the Year and finished fourth in Cy Young voting, seems more significant as more time has passed.

Unlike Murakami, Nomo was almost instantly a star. As a twenty-six-year-old rookie in 1995, he went 13–6 with a 2.54 ERA, while averaging a league-leading 11.1 strikeouts per nine innings. In his first start, against the Dodgers' archrival San Francisco Giants, Nomo threw five innings, giving up only one hit while walking four and striking out seven. Despite Nomo's impressive debut, the Dodgers lost that game 4–3 in fifteen innings. Only 16,099 fans attended that game, and probably very few stayed until the end. Nomo's second start, in Colorado against the Rockies, did not go well, as he gave up seven earned runs in five and two-thirds innings. His third start against the Cardinals was also rough.

The phenomenon that came to be known as Nomomania—whereby Nomo briefly became one of the biggest names in baseball, often pitching to sold-out crowds, particularly when the Dodgers were at home—really began when he made his second home start and struck out fourteen Pirates in seven shutout innings. In 1995, baseball was recovering from the strike of 1994 that had led to the cancellation of the World Series and a great deal of fan anger toward players and owners. Those fans who had stuck around in 1995 were looking for something about which to get excited. Before the steroid-driven home run record race of 1998 between Sammy Sosa and Mark McGwire caught the attention of fans, there was the story of the hard-throwing lefty from Japan with the catchy name and the extraordinary strikeout rate. In many ways, Nomo was *the* baseball story of 1995.

Nomomania was such a major phenomenon partially because Nomo pitched for the Los Angeles Dodgers, a West Coast team that played in a city with a large and historic Japanese American community. It is likely that if Nomo had pitched as well with the Milwaukee Brewers or the Baltimore Orioles, Nomomania would not have been as big a deal.

Nomo's Dodgers were also the same team that fourteen years earlier, in another strike-shortened season, had been the home of a rookie lefty from another country who had captured the imaginations of baseball fans. Fernandomania was an important chapter in the growing role of Latinos in the big leagues as Fernando Valenzuela became a star pitcher and media figure as the most famous Mexican ever to make it to the big leagues. Again, the huge Mexican American community in Los Angeles buoyed Valenzuela's fame and visibility. In 2015, Jeff Katz noted that, as a result of controversy surrounding the displacement of Mexican American families in the area where Dodger Stadium was built, tensions between the team and the Mexican Americans in Los Angeles had helped keep support for the Dodgers unnaturally low among that key demographic group. Accordingly, "the Los Angeles Dodgers had been on the prowl for a Mexican star to heal the rift between the team and the Latino community."[15] Fernando was that star.

The excitement around Nomo meant that poststrike baseball was back and that it was going to be different and more global. After

Nomo's great 1995 season, baseball was never again a game played by men from only the Americas. Within a few years, other Japanese stars, including pitcher Hideki Irabu, slugger Hideki Matsui, and the incomparable Ichiro Suzuki, made it clear that Japanese players had become a permanent part of North American baseball.

This round of globalization was not limited to players from Japan, nor was it limited to only a few high-profile stars. In addition to such stars as Nomo, Matsui, and Suzuki, more ordinary Japanese players, including Mac Suzuki, So Taguchi, and Kei Igawa, also played in the big leagues. By 2005 or so, only a decade after Nomomania, the presence of Japanese players was no longer news on most big league teams. Occasionally, the news that major Japanese stars, such as pitchers Masahiro Tanaka and Yu Darvish, were preparing to be posted would become a big story. These events, however, were covered much more like the bidding war for a star free agent than from the Japanese angle specifically.

The immediate impact Nomo had on the Dodgers and on all of baseball, in addition to the number of not just players but stars from Japan in the few years following Nomo's debut, suggests that Japan had produced top baseball players for many years. Such players as Ichiro Suzuki and Hideki Matsui came to the United States within a few years of Nomo and found themselves making All-Star teams and playing big roles on winning teams. Thus, it is reasonably apparent that during the thirty years from 1965 to 1995 when there were no big league players from Japan or elsewhere in Asia, big league baseball was missing out on some of the world's top talent. At the time, few fans or people in baseball lamented this situation, but it is now evident that the competition in MLB during these years was not as good as it might have been.

The greatest player in Japanese baseball history is still Sadaharu Oh. Oh, who starred on the Yomiuri Giants from 1959 to 1980, played most of his career between the time Murakami left the Giants and Nomo joined the Dodgers. He never played in the United States, as that option did not exist during his career, so it cannot be known whether the man who hit more big league home runs in the NPB than Barry Bonds did in the NL would have made it in the United States. However, many big leaguers saw Oh play, and while few believed he would have hit eight hundred home runs in the United States, many thought he would have been a good player nonetheless. Hall of Fame manager Joe Torre said of Oh, "He was pretty good size. He coulda competed over here." Tom Seaver, a star big league pitcher during much of Oh's career, commented, "He sure hit me. He was a superb hitter. . . . If he played in the United States he would have hit twenty to twenty-five home runs a year. . . . He'd be a lifetime .300 hitter." Brooks Robinson was succinct in his description of Oh: "He could have played right here in the big leagues with the best players in the world."[16] These statements are impossible to prove but are further evidence that at least some Japanese players in the 1970s and 1980s could have contributed in the United States.

As early as 1955, several years before Oh started his career, the New York Yankees made a post–World Series trip to Japan to play against Japanese teams and All-Stars. During that trip, Yankees' manager Casey Stengel said:

It may be four or five years, but I think the next great innovation in American baseball will be a Japanese star. . . . I saw about five fellows over here who could hit our boys' pitching, and when I say hit, I mean they whanged that ball 395 to 410 feet. And remember, we had the lowest ERA in the American League.[17]

In 1998, only three years after Nomo's debut, the New York Yankees won the World Series. That team won 114 regular season games and is considered one of the greatest teams ever. One of their many strengths was a bullpen led by closer Mariano Rivera. Rivera was in only his third full season in 1998, but today he is widely viewed as the greatest closer ever, he has the most saves of any reliever in history, and he is all but certain to be a first-ballot Hall of Famer. The Yankee bullpen, however, was deeper than Rivera. Another key member of that bullpen was Graeme Lloyd, an Australian in his seventh major league season who was excellent that year at limiting opposing batters to under one hit or walk per inning while being used mostly against left-handed batters. Lloyd's ten-year career ended by 2003, but baseball in Australia has continued to develop since then.

In addition to players from Australia and Japan, by the first decades of the twenty-first century, it was not uncommon to see Korean players in the big leagues, including Chan Ho Park, Hee-Seop Choi, and Shin-Soo Choo. A smaller number of players came to the big leagues from Taiwan, the third major baseball-playing country in East Asia. The most famous of these has been Chien-Ming Wang, who was the ace of the Yankee pitching rotation in the mid-2000s before succumbing to injury and age.

The increasing internationalization of baseball, particularly with regard to Asian players, is no accident. MLB understood the value of raising the game's profile overseas, particularly in Asia, and crafted a strategy to do so. Popular players, such as Nomo and Ichiro Suzuki, have been aggressively promoted by MLB. Additionally, seven times since 1999, two teams have opened their seasons with a series outside the United States. Four of those series have been in Japan, and one was in Australia. The other two were in Mexico and in Puerto Rico.[18]

Foreign media from Asia and Latin America have been encouraged to cover baseball, and MLB has been helpful in facilitating this. Such stars as Ichiro, Wang, and Choo enjoy extensive coverage of their MLB exploits in their home countries. One very visible example of this occurred after the sixth and final game of the 2009 World Series. The game itself was the kind of game that only a Yankee fan could truly enjoy, as the Yankees cruised to a 7–3 victory. However, on that evening in the Bronx, Hideki Matsui, once Japan's greatest slugger but also a longtime member of the Yankees, went three for four with a single, a double, and a massive fourth-inning three-run home run off future Hall of Famer Pedro Martínez. Matsui ended up driving in six of the seven Yankee runs that game.

Matsui's night helped him earn the MVP for that World Series. At the presentation of the award, a few minutes after the final out of the game, dozens of Japanese reporters, photographers, and other members of the media converged on the field to record the moment. It was a much larger celebration than usual for World Series MVP honors, and the extensive coverage in Japan only helped MLB solidify its popularity there. It was also evidence of how global MLB had become. The Japanese reporters clearly saw Matsui's accomplishment as further evidence, as if any were needed by 2009, of the ability of Japan's players to excel at the highest level. The Japanese reporters chanted for Matsui and cheered him on in their language, making the somewhat misnamed World Series more true to its grandiose title than ever.

Where Baseball Is Played Now

Today baseball remains a sport that is primarily played in North America, the Caribbean, and East Asia, but it is beginning to make inroads elsewhere, including in Australia and in the Netherlands. There is no obvious reason why Australia has become a growth country for baseball, other than the passion Australians hold for many team sports and the strong relationship that exists on many levels between Australia and the United States. The Netherlands' baseball connection is due mostly to the Dutch presence in the Caribbean islands, such as Curaçao and Aruba.

Baseball has roots in Australia going back to the mid–nineteenth century, but it has never been that country's primary sport; soccer, rugby, Australian rules football, and other sports have generally eclipsed baseball. Nonetheless, baseball leagues and organizations have sporadically existed there for decades. The current incarnation is the Australian Baseball League (ABL), a six-team organization that began playing in 2010. The ABL is not an informal league with no connection to MLB; one of its initial founders was MLB. While baseball is still not a top-tier sport in Australia, the ABL is evidence that the sport is growing and that MLB is committed to its success in that country.

Despite baseball's deep history and growing popularity in Australia, no great players have yet come out of Australia. Such players as Dave Nilsson, Grant Balfour, and Graeme Lloyd, who rank among the best Australians to play in the big leagues, have been valuable role players but not big stars.

The Netherlands is different in this regard. The Dutch-born Bert Blyleven, although raised as an American, became a Hall of

Fame pitcher. Additionally, at least two players from Curaçao have become big league stars. Interestingly, both Andrelton Simmons and Andruw Jones were, or are, known primarily for their defense. Simmons is a two-time Gold Glove winner and an extraordinary defensive shortstop viewed by some as the best defender at his position in the game today. Over the course of his seventeen-year career, five-time All-Star Jones won ten Gold Gloves while slugging 434 home runs. Another player from Curaçao, Hensley Meulens, has become one of the game's most respected batting coaches and has helped his San Francisco Giants win three World Series.

The Netherlands is one of several European countries where baseball has long been a minor or fringe sport. It is easy to imagine baseball fans in the Netherlands, Germany, or Italy feeling a bit like soccer fans did until recently in the United States. They were fans of a sport that almost nobody knew anything about and that to outsiders looked slow and complicated. Despite that perception, teams and leagues in the Netherlands have played since the early twentieth century.

Other than Blyleven, who cannot really be considered a product of the Dutch system, the first Dutch player to make it to the big leagues was Win Remmerswaal, who appeared in twenty-two games for the Boston Red Sox in 1979 and 1980. As a boy, I remember being puzzled by Remmerswaal's strange and difficult-to-spell name, but other than making that impression on many fans, he did not particularly stand out during his brief and mediocre career, in which he was 3–1 with a 5.50 ERA. It was only with the debuts in 1996 of Ralph Milliard and Andruw Jones that Dutch ballplayers, even by way of the Caribbean, began to make an impact on big league baseball.

In addition to Australia and the Netherlands, other European countries have been playing baseball for years—most notably Italy and Germany. These and other European strongholds of soccer do not, however, represent baseball's biggest growth opportunities. MLB is also seeking to expand to such countries as South Africa, a major regional power, and China, which have scant experience with baseball but are potentially enormous markets. Baseball has long been popular in Taiwan but until recently had almost no presence or impact in China. That has changed in the last decade or so, as MLB International has sought to raise baseball's profile in the next global superpower.

Jim Lefebvre, a former Los Angeles Dodger infielder and a hitting coach for a few different teams, has spent several years in China trying to strengthen baseball's popularity there and even coaching China in international tournaments. Similar efforts have been made to promote baseball in South Africa.

Central to understanding the development of baseball in such countries as China, South Africa, Australia, and other places where it has until very recently been on the fringes is the role that MLB has played in promoting the sport. MLB has helped found foreign baseball leagues, organize clinics and other efforts to teach the game to aspiring players in these countries, and—most visibly— promote international tournaments.

Thus, in recent years, MLB has sought to promote baseball internationally and to channel baseball's growth into existing MLB structures. By doing this, MLB is trying to draw top athletes globally to baseball and to strengthen the organization's brand around the world. A decade or two ago, there was very little chance that the top athletes in China or Australia would give baseball a second thought, but that is changing. It is still going to be many years before the best young arms in Australia are used to pitch in baseball rather than bowl in cricket, but it is not completely unthinkable in the coming decades.

In smaller countries, the equation is different. In Gia Kemoklidze's Georgia, a country of about four million people among whom soccer and rugby are the most popular team sports, all it will take will be a player from Georgia's national team to make the big leagues, or to even come close, for MLB to win the allegiance of a few hundred thousand new fans. Kemoklidze dreams of a Georgian who is now a boy making it to the big leagues. He asks PE teachers all over the country to let him know if they see a boy who is good at throwing rocks, for he has informal ties with scouts and recruiters in the United States. When I asked Kemoklidze what would happen if a Georgian ended up in the pitching rotation or starting lineup for a big league team, he smiled and told me that player would be a "national hero" who would finally make baseball popular in Georgia.[19]

The most visible structure through which MLB has sought to bring more countries into baseball has been the WBC. Three of these multinational tournaments have taken place thus far, and all have been won by longtime baseball powerhouses: Japan in 2006 and 2009 and the Dominican Republic in 2013. The players on the Japanese champion teams were not as well known in the United States because they drew heavily from the Japanese leagues, but a few of their players, including Daisuke Matsuzaka, the star of the 2006 tournament, went on to successful big league careers. The 2013 Dominican team's roster, however, featured other well-known and highly accomplished big leaguers, including Santiago Casilla, Fernando Rodney, Octavio Dotel, Carlos Santana, Robinson Cano, Jose Reyes, Hanley Ramirez, Miguel Tejada, and Nelson Cruz.

The WBC includes traditional baseball powers, such as the Dominican Republic, Cuba, Taiwan, Korea, Venezuela, the United States, Japan, and Puerto Rico, which, despite being legally part of the United States, fields its own team. It also includes second-tier baseball countries where the sport is already quite popular, such as Canada, Mexico, Australia, the Netherlands, and Panama.

More significantly, the WBC also is open to countries where baseball is relatively new. Among those countries that have appeared in the WBC are China, South Africa, Italy, Brazil, and Spain. The competition for these spots has been frequently determined through tournaments in the fall before the spring WBC. For a team such as China's, a spot in the WBC is considered an accomplishment and recognition that its baseball program is progressing. For a country such as Georgia, a spot in the WBC is a long-term goal that is a challenge, but not out of the question.

The WBC is not the first international baseball tournament. Baseball was an Olympic event from 1992 to 2008, with Cuba winning the Gold Medal three times and the United States and Korea once each. Other international baseball tournaments have taken place at such events as the Pan American Games as well as semipro tournaments that included teams from the United States, Canada, and the Caribbean.

The WBC is different from these other tournaments because it is not the product of an international organization, such as the International Olympic Committee (IOC) or soccer's Fédération Internationale de Football Association (FIFA). While the WBC has been supported by the International Baseball Federation (IBAF), it is very closely tied to MLB and its American leaders.

The WBC would not be nearly as exciting or interesting if it did not enjoy the support of MLB. Because of this support, top MLB players are encouraged to participate in the WBC. Over the years, such players as Roger Clemens, Barry Bonds, the aforementioned Dominican stars, Adrian Gonzalez, Justin Morneau, Angel Pagan, Miguel Cabrera, Andruw Jones, Pablo Sandoval, and Ichiro Suzuki have appeared in the WBC. Because of the demands on pitchers preparing for a long season and the corresponding concerns about arm injuries, the WBC has generally drawn higher-profile big league hitters than pitchers. The WBC also has a unique set of eligibility rules that have been created in an effort to dilute American talent and to give smaller countries more opportunity. The eligibility rules for 2013 were as follows:

- The player is a citizen of the Federation Team's country or territory, as evidenced by a valid passport the player holds as of January 1, 2013; or
- The player is currently a permanent legal resident of the Federation Team's country or territory, as evidenced by documentation satisfactory to WBCI and the International Baseball Federation ("IBAF"); or
- The player was born in the Federation Team's country or territory, as evidenced by a birth certificate or its equivalent; or
- The player has one parent who is, or if deceased was, a citizen of the Federation Team's country or territory, as evidenced by a passport or other documentation satisfactory to WBCI and the IBAF; or
- The player has one parent who was born in the Federation

Team's country or territory, as evidenced by a birth certificate or its equivalent; or

- The player presents documentary evidence satisfactory to WBCI that, even if he has not been granted citizenship or been issued a passport, the player would be granted citizenship or a passport in due course under the laws of the Federation Team's country or territory had the player applied for such citizenship or passport.[20]

Two things are immediately apparent about these rules. First, they employ a very lax definition of eligibility, making it very easy for Americans to play for the country from which their parents immigrated to the New World. Accordingly, the 2006 Italian team featured Italian American big leaguers Nick Punto, Jason Grilli, and Chris Denorfia. The presence of these players made Italy stronger and helped generate more excitement around the Italian team. The second thing that stands out is the last stipulation, which defines a player as eligible if he "would be granted citizenship or a passport in due course under the laws of the Federation Team's country or territory had the player applied for such citizenship or passport." This means that if a player is eligible for citizenship in a given country, that player can play for that country. This is substantially a clause that would allow American Jews to play for Israel. While Israel does not have a strong baseball program, in recent years, American Jews including Kevin Youkilis, Ryan Braun, and Sam Fuld have played, and in some cases starred, in the big leagues. Israel has not qualified for the WBC, because the timing of the qualifying round precludes big leaguers' participation, but if the country ever made it, it could bolster its team roster with big league stars and show respectably.

It is also striking, from a political perspective, that the WBC has a policy that recognizes the connection that Jews have with Israel. It is very hard to imagine FIFA, the IOC, or any other international organizations taking a similar implicitly pro-Israel position. However, MLB is an American organization, and American Jews, like other people in their country, love baseball and are involved in it at all levels.

MLB and the Future of International Baseball

The WBC and other efforts to support baseball around the globe are part of a long-term strategy for MLB to increase its fan base and revenue over the coming decades. Thus far it has been well executed and enjoyed some success, but a potential paradox is also built in to this approach: MLB's strategy seems to embrace the idea that the highest level of baseball will continue to be played in the United States under more or less the same structures that have been in place for a very long time. According to this view, such countries as Australia, the Netherlands, and China may have their own leagues, but they will continue to feed their best players to the United States, thus operating as something of an alternative, more international minor league system.

For MLB to maintain its current structure while simultaneously becoming more global, it needs to strike a precarious balance that requires encouraging the development of baseball in many different countries and continuing to build ties with different leagues in those countries while ensuring that the best players in the world remain in MLB. Until now, the flow of the most elite players has been essentially unidirectional, with strong players from Japan, Taiwan, Venezuela, the Dominican Republic, and elsewhere coming to the United States, while weaker and older American players have occasionally gone to play for Asian teams. Obviously, Cuban baseball has largely existed outside this structure, but some great Cuban players have made it to the big leagues.

Not all the best players in Japan, Taiwan, Korea, or certainly Cuba end up in the big leagues, but those who do come to the United States are among the very best in those countries. Outside Cuba, for the past fifty years or so, it has been true that the best players in Latin America end up pretty quickly in the big leagues. The result is that MLB can now claim to draw the best players in the world, more than at any other time in history.

This seems like the natural state of affairs for MLB, and for its position in global baseball, but it is also a result of American economic power, the relative poverty of much of Latin America, and economic disparities between Asia and North America. These economic differences, however, are not as dramatic as they once were and will continue to shrink as time passes.

MLB has never entertained the idea of expanding to major cities in the Dominican Republic, Mexico, Japan, Korea, or Taiwan, despite the popularity of baseball in those countries. Instead, the system of independent leagues that increasingly send their best players to MLB has worked out very well with regard to the bottom line and to the quality of play on the field for MLB.

But if baseball continues to grow in popularity, fans in Japan and Korea, for example, could begin to question why their best players leave the country for the United States and only return to represent the national team in such tournaments as the WBC. This current structure is based on an implicit notion of the United States as an economic and, indeed, political hegemon, at least in the baseball world, that is less relevant as time passes.

4

THE ETERNAL AND
EVER-CHANGING GAME

Part of the existential appeal of baseball is that it is both timeless and ever changing. While it is true that Ty Cobb, Johnny Evers, or Wee Willie Keeler, if they were alive today, would recognize much of the game as it is played on the field, there is also a great deal that would be unfamiliar to them. The notion of the platoon advantage or a LOOGY[1] would be completely foreign to Keeler, whose famous contribution to baseball strategy was "Hit 'em where they ain't." Evers probably never gave much thought to walk-up music and would be surprised to see a new ball used every time the previous one touches the ground. It would not take long to explain the designated hitter (DH) rule to Cobb, known as the Georgia Peach, but the technology of the twenty-first century would be almost impossible to explain easily to anybody from that era. MLB.TV, pitch charts, pitch framing data, and the like have changed how baseball is played and watched, with more changes to come in the future.

The changes in baseball over the last few decades have affected the game at all levels from the big leagues to youth baseball. Four general areas that deserve special attention are the economics of the game, the technologies of baseball, youth baseball, and globalization. Since globalization is discussed extensively in a previous chapter, it needs less attention here.

The Economics of Baseball Today

To the contemporary fan, it is axiomatic that baseball is a massive multi-billion-dollar industry where players make huge salaries, owners turn tremendous profits, tickets are expensive, television contracts are enormous, and souvenir T-shirts, caps, and the like are a lucrative retail business.

This was not always the case. For much of its history, despite its unique position in the culture and national gestalt, baseball was not such a big business. Well into the 1980s, for example, most games were played in stadiums that were frequently less than one-third full. Although high-profile stars, such as Babe Ruth, always made good money, ordinary players, and even some very good players, were not extremely well paid. Even in the 1970s, many players still had winter jobs, such as coaching, substitute teaching, or working for local businesses. Richie Hebner, a slugging corner infielder with the Pirates, the Phillies, the Tigers, and the Cubs spent the off-seasons during much of his career digging graves, a factoid that baseball-card collectors learned from Topps during the 1970s.

Baseball's rapid growth over the past thirty years has been dramatic and significant. Younger fans and those without great memories may not remember that from the 1960s through the early 1990s, the financial struggles of individual teams and of the game itself was a persistent baseball storyline. Moreover, the pace of baseball's economic growth, estimated today to be a $9-billion industry, has been startling.[2] Jon Pessah's 2015 book's description of the state of the game in late 1992 captures the feeling in Major League Baseball (MLB) as the industry was beginning to shift away from this decades-long slump: "The amount of money pouring into the game has never been greater. A decade ago baseball was a $300 million business. This season it will bring in $1.6 billion and the projection for next season is $1.75 billion."[3] Compared to today, those numbers that were so pleasing to ownership in the early 1990s are downright paltry.

I became a fan of the San Francisco Giants in the mid-1970s, a few years after the great Willie Mays had been traded and later retired. They were not a good team at that time, but I remained a loyal fan. In the 2010–2014 period, they emerged as the best organization in baseball, winning three World Series in a five-year span, selling out every home game, and building a strong fan base throughout, and beyond, northern California. While not yet on the same level as the Yankees or the Red Sox, the Giants have begun to build a national following, making them among the most popular teams in many media markets outside the Bay Area.

When discussing this phenomenon, I am frequently asked whether I used to get strange looks wearing my Giants hat in New York when I first moved here. The answer, of course, is yes, but the full answer is that for much of the 1970s and 1980s, I got weird looks walking around *San Francisco* in my Giants hat. During those years, big league baseball and the Giants were seen as some quirky event that took place in a mostly empty and often freezing cavernous ballpark in the southeastern corner of the city, not as a pastime central to the city's identity and a source of entertainment for families, tourists, and young people, as it is today.

It is true that the Giants were a moribund franchise when I was growing up, but they were not the only one: the San Diego Padres, the Oakland A's, the Cleveland Indians, and later the Seattle Mariners were not generating a lot of enthusiasm in those years either. Even the good teams did not sell out their ballparks the way they do now.

By the 1970s, baseball had more or less taken its current form. African Americans and Latinos, such as Joe Morgan, Reggie Jackson, Luis Tiant, and Cesar Cedeno, were among the leading and best-known players of the decade. The DH rule was introduced into the American League (AL) in 1973. The 1970s were the first full decade with a postseason that consisted of more than just a World Series. Although the modern bullpen had not yet fully evolved, relievers, sometimes known as firemen, were part of the game. Hall of Fame relievers Goose Gossage and Rollie Fingers starred throughout the decade. Sparky Lyle, Pedro Borbon, and Mike Marshall were big names as well. Marshall was the first reliever in either league to win the Cy Young Award, when he was voted the best pitcher in the National League (NL) in 1974. Marshall pitched in an extraordinary 106 games for the pennant-winning Dodgers that year. Lyle won the award for the AL three years later while helping pitch the Yankees to the pennant.

Attendance figures from the 1970s, however, demonstrate that baseball had a different economic profile then and was essentially smaller. Games were frequently played in front of mostly empty stadiums. Salaries were growing, but they were not close to what they are today. There was simply less money around baseball forty or even thirty years ago.

Three teams in the 1970s were very strong for the entire decade. The Pirates won the NL East in 1970, 1971, 1972, 1974, 1975, and 1979. The Reds captured the NL West title in 1970, 1972, 1973, 1975, 1976, and 1979. The Orioles won the AL East in 1970, 1971, 1973, 1974, and 1979. Two other teams excelled in part of the decade. The Oakland A's won five consecutive AL West titles from 1971 to 1975, while the Yankees won the AL East from 1976 to 1978 and again in 1980. The A's and the Yankees also won their divisions in 1981, but because of the strike that year, the data are a bit skewed.

The attendance figures for these teams in all or part of the 1970s are quite striking (see Table 4.1). Despite fielding very good teams throughout the decade, the Reds averaged just slightly more than 2 million fans a year, and the Pirates and the Orioles just slightly more than 1.5 million fans a year. The Yankees did significantly better in their big years but still drew poorly compared to contemporary standards. The team that drew the best in the 1970s was the Dodgers, averaging almost 2.5 million fans a year. By contrast, from 2000 to 2009, the Angels, the Dodgers, the Giants, the Red Sox, the Astros, the Mariners, the Cubs, and the Yankees all averaged more than three million in attendance per year.

The story of attendance in Oakland during the 1970s is long, fascinating, and not very upbeat, but it is worth knowing. The 845,693 figure that was the lowest of their good years occurred in 1974. The A's won the World Series in 1972 and in 1973 and were on their way to winning again in 1974, fielding a team that included perennial All-Stars Sal Bando, Bert Campaneris, and Vida Blue and future Hall of Famers Reggie Jackson, Jim "Catfish" Hunter, and Rollie Fingers—yet they could barely draw an average of ten thousand fans for each of their seventy-six home dates.[4] To put that

TABLE 4.1. ATTENDANCE FROM 1970 TO 1979			
Team	Worst	Best	Average
Reds	901,784	2,629,708	2,055,068
Pirates	670,974	1,501,132	1,196,290
Orioles	899,950	1,681,009	1,085,456
Yankees (76–80)	2,012,434	2,627,417	2,323,316
A's (71–75)	845,693	1,075,518	951,658

number in perspective, the only other recent team to win three World Series in a row was the 1998–2000 Yankees. In the third year of that run, the Yankees drew more than 3.2 million people. Attendance in Oakland reached a nadir when the team drew a total of 306,763 for the entire 1979 home season. The team was bad, and the ballpark was falling apart, but that is still an appalling figure for a big league team.

A game in Oakland between the A's and the Mariners on April 17, 1979, demonstrated the challenges facing the game in general and the A's in particular during this period. The Mariners were only beginning their third year of existence, while the A's were still recovering from losing virtually an entire championship team to free agency between 1975 and 1977. The two teams had fought for sixth place in a seven-team division in 1977 and 1978 and would do the same that year, with the Mariners finishing just above the A's.

The game was the second of a three-game set that the A's swept from Seattle. It was a reasonably exciting game won on a walk-off single with two outs in the bottom of the ninth by a now-forgotten backup catcher named Jim Essian. Both lineups were filled with similarly unremembered players, such as Jeff Newman, Wayne Gross, and Dave Heaverlo of the A's and Julio Cruz, Larry Cox, and Odell Jones of the Mariners. Perhaps the two most famous players to appear that day were Willie Horton, Seattle's slugging thirty-six-year-old DH who had been a fixture for more than a decade with the Detroit Tigers, and the Mariners' shortstop, Mario Mendoza. Mendoza was a shortstop who hit .215 over a nine-year career but is most famous for lending his name to the "Mendoza line." The

Mendoza line is the point below which big league hitters cannot fall and still manage to hold a job in the big leagues, regardless of how good they are in the field.

The significance of that game was that only 653 people were in attendance, the lowest number for a big league game in years and one that has not been approached since that time. That game was no fluke; fewer than five thousand people in total turned up to watch all three games in that series between two weak and not very interesting AL West teams. The pitiful A's attendance throughout much of the late 1970s was influenced by the poor quality of the team, the lousy ballpark, and rancor toward A's owner Charlie O. Finley for dismantling the fantastic A's teams of the 1971–1975 era, but that tells only part of the story.

In the 1970s, as the attendance figures above show, baseball was in a bit of a crisis. It was very far from apparent that the sport would come into the twenty-first century in such strong shape; in fact, it was not clear whether it would survive at all. The A's were not the only team in the Bay Area that struggled badly in the 1970s, which was viewed as proof that the Bay Area was not big enough for two teams. The San Francisco Giants, for their part, averaged fewer than 592,000 fans per year from 1974 to 1977. The combined attendance of under 2.4 million for those four years would now be considered a bad one-year figure for most teams, including the Giants. In 1976, the Giants were almost sold and moved to Toronto, but that city was awarded an expansion franchise instead. As late as 1992, the Giants, today one of baseball's most successful franchises on and off the field, were rumored to be leaving San Francisco for Florida.

During the 1970s, the stars who played for Bay Area teams included Willie Mays, Willie McCovey, Juan Marichal, Bobby Bonds, Rickey Henderson, Reggie Jackson, Catfish Hunter, Vida Blue, and Rollie Fingers, but neither team, even when it was winning, could draw good crowds. Interestingly, the Bay Area team that drew the most in the 1970s was not one of the five A's or the one Giants division winner, but the 1978 Giants, a team that grabbed the attention of a generation of post–Willie Mays fans despite ending up in third place.

The 1970s were an interesting time in the Bay Area. There was a lot going on there, from Patty Hearst and the Symbionese Liberation Army (SLA) to the first real stirrings of the gay rights movement, the consolidation of the social upheaval of the 1960s, the Black Panther movement, the assassinations of Harvey Milk and George Moscone, the Zebra killings, Jonestown, and more. Perhaps the problem was not with baseball but with the Bay Area itself.

The Dallas–Fort Worth market was probably less like the Bay Area than any other in baseball in the 1970s, but Bill Pennington's 2015 book describes the popularity of the Texas Rangers in the early 1970s by saying, "The average high school football game outdrew the average Rangers game often by thousands of fans. . . . In 1974, it is likely the average Texan could name more Dallas Cowboys cheerleaders than Texas Rangers baseball players."[5] The numbers support Pennington's assertion, as between 1971 and 1973, the Rangers never drew even seven hundred thousand fans in a season.

Something in the culture was changing in the 1970s, and baseball could not quite keep up. The national pastime appeared to be trapped between the ascendant popularity of football on the right and the counterculture on the left. According to Pennington:

> Economically, the game was suffering as attendance had dropped significantly. Crowds of seven thousand or five thousand were not uncommon at many ballparks. At first it appeared to be a backlash against the players for their April [1972] strike, but there seemed to be more at play than that. In the early 1970s, baseball was paying for a policy shift in America. . . . [B]aseball was an established institution and anything linked to "the establishment" was unpopular in many quarters of America at the time.[6]

Notably, while attendance was consistently lower, some television ratings were much higher. In the 1970s, for example, the World Series was a national event, not the niche event it has become today. In the 1970s, the ratings for the World Series ranged from a low of 19.4 when the Reds played the Orioles in 1970 to a high of 32.8

when the Yankees played the Dodgers in 1978.[7] The last time a World Series drew a rating of better than 19.4, the lowest of the 1970s, was in 1995, when it got a 19.5 rating.

The rise in attendance since the 1970s, particularly when linked to the increasing cost of attending games, has brought more revenue into the game than ever before. Although World Series ratings are down, the size of cable contracts are not. This is the financial equation that is at the heart of today's baseball economy, but declining television viewership and the number of empty seats at many games—a data point not picked up by attendance figures, which are based on ticket sales—could be among the early warning signs that the foundation of baseball's economy is not as strong as it looks.

Baseball after the Sandlot

When I was growing up, two of my closest friends were twin brothers named Peter and William. They transferred to my school in third grade and remained classmates until we graduated from high school. William and I even went to our first year of college together. I have remained friends with both of them. In school, Peter was a star athlete. He was a good outfielder, was fast on the bases, and had a good arm. His best sport, however, was basketball. He was an aggressive defender, good shooter, and extraordinary rebounder. Peter worked hard to become a great basketball player, and it showed when he was on the court.

At the time, William was viewed as unathletic. At our somewhat-sports-crazy all-boys Catholic school, Will was one of the few kids who showed little interest in basketball, baseball, or even soccer. William shared his twin brother's strength and coordination, but his tastes ran more toward drumming and punk rock and less toward organized sports. He was always able to join in and hold his own in a pickup basketball game, but he was never as good as his brother.

William, however, was in reality anything but unathletic. He just expressed his athleticism in different ways. In San Francisco, a city where, for obvious reasons of topography, skateboarding is taken very seriously, he was a very accomplished skater. He could fearlessly and gracefully speed down our city's hills, always power sliding to safety to avoid being hit by an oncoming car or simply falling off his board. During the last few years of high school, Peter focused almost exclusively on basketball, starring on the school team. William continued to eschew team sports but began to spend more of his free time out at Ocean Beach, braving the cold and the waves to surf. Anybody who can swim through the rough waves and undertow at Ocean Beach and surf those waves is axiomatically athletic, but in the framework of that time, we did not see it that way.

Almost all of my classmates from high school would have described Peter as the more athletic of the two twins back in 1985—the year we graduated—but if they were growing up today, it would be different. Now William's athletic skills would be much more broadly recognized. Moreover, they would be actively encouraged by the adults in the life of a young person such as William. In the late 1970s and 1980s, skateboarding was associated with punk rock, disrespect for elders, and radical politics and was seen as vaguely threatening. Surfing was largely viewed as a uniquely Californian way to waste time. There were no lessons for these activities, no structures created by adults to facilitate surfing or skating, and virtually no recognition that these were even legitimate athletic events. My point here is not simply to reflect on how much young people's lives, for better or for worse, have changed, but to examine the impact of this shifting attitude on baseball and the future of MLB.

I was reminded of this change a few years ago when my own son was in eighth grade and playing on his school basketball team. As in many urban schools today, basketball was the sport that drew the most attention and was the most competitive at his school. My son did not have a lot of experience playing basketball, but because he was tall and reasonably athletic, he made the team and played mostly as a sixth man, backing up the center and the forwards. In the finals, his team's star center fouled out, and my son had to play the final six minutes. He played ably, providing good defense while getting a few rebounds as his team held on to win.

A month or so later, I attended my son's first school baseball game of the year. My son had not played on his school baseball team much in the past, opting for more competitive youth baseball programs. However, in his last year of middle school, he decided to play on the school team. Watching his school team play, it was striking how the same boys who were so athletic and skilled on the basketball court were more or less lost on the baseball diamond. One boy, who had been the star power forward, went up to the plate holding the bat as if it were some native curiosity whose purpose he was trying to determine.

Together, the stories of William and Peter and my observations almost thirty years later while watching my son's school teams reveal much about youth sports today, and what that might mean for baseball. There are several different elements to consider, but together they reflect the evolving context in which young Americans are being exposed to baseball and other sports. This change raises several important questions for an institution whose success still relies on the intergenerational transfer of loyalty and on the fandom of grown-up Americans, particularly, but not only, men, who played the game as children.

Finding reliable data on youth baseball activities is difficult, because little data is available regarding, for example, sandlot baseball, playing running bases, and throwing a ball against a wall, all forms of the game that were central to many American childhoods until relatively late in the twentieth century. The data that are accessible tell a complex and nuanced story.

The Aspen Play Project summarizes two of the key points about youth sports generally and youth baseball in particular. The 2014 report first notes that

> fading is the era of sandlot or pickup ball, a form of play that organically promoted innovation and fitness among generations of Americans. A leading annual survey of participation trends notes that "casual play continues to decline dramatically" (SGMA, 2010). . . . There's a lack of mainstream options for the moderately interested athlete. As soon as travel teams are formed, in-town rec leagues often begin to fade.

The report also finds that

> most of our largest sports are seeing major drop-offs in par-
> ticipation, as organized opportunities consolidate around
> the most talented, committed or well-resourced players.
> Among children ages 6–12, participation rates have de-
> clined in basketball (down 3.9 percent since 2008), base-
> ball (14.4 percent), soccer (10.7 percent), softball (31.3 per-
> cent), and football (29 percent).[8]

The point about the "fading . . . era of sandlot or pickup ball"
resonates with anybody who is able to remember what life was
like in the United States before about 1990. This evolution is not a
reflection of something intrinsic to baseball but rather the result of
factors that, in most cases, have little to do with the game. A combination of changing parenting styles; an increase in the number
of athletic options; a significant rise in the popularity of indoor
activities, such as video games and other screen-based recreation;
and various other factors have conspired to make pickup baseball
much less common than it used to be.

Many children today lack the amount of unstructured free time
that lent itself to pickup sports. Others prefer to spend their time
indoors with a range of entertainment options that did not exist
even a generation ago. Sandlot baseball was never perfect; fields
and equipment were often inadequate. Anybody who ever played
pickup baseball knows how rare it was to get eighteen kids to play,
so such permutations as having one-half of the outfield being out of
play, making the pitcher's mound as good as first, or using invisible
pinch runners were common. Similarly, because of the lack of catching gear, pitching was often more of the "let the batter hit it" variety rather than the "try to get the batter out" kind. Despite these
shortcomings, sandlot ball engendered a great love of the game and
gave generations of young players, including, perhaps particularly,
those who were not the best players, the opportunity to play a lot.
The sandlot ensured that everybody played, and it was therefore
easy for the next generation of baseball fans to develop.

The decline of the sandlot is only part of the changing environment. Another key piece is that, according to the report, "organized opportunities consolidate around the most talented, committed or well-resourced players." This development has several impacts. First, it means that the better and more serious players receive more and better coaching from a younger age. This situation is to some extent complicated by economic issues; for instance, travel, good equipment, and private lessons with a good pitching coach are expensive. This problem is particularly acute among players who are just starting to play, a period when individual coaching can make a real difference in how players present themselves and impress coaches. Younger players who do not have these opportunities often find it difficult to keep pace with these highly coached players and lose interest in the game. Interestingly, by the time players are eleven or twelve, talent wins out, and no amount of private lessons or fancy gear can obscure the inability of an untalented child to hit or throw a fastball.

Additionally, today the stronger youth baseball players, as well as athletes in other sports, are encouraged to focus on only one sport from a younger age than ever before. Until relatively recently, athletic boys tended to follow the calendar in organized youth sports and in the sandlot, playing baseball in the spring and summer and switching to football and basketball in the fall and winter, but that has changed. There are several reasons why this evolution in youth sports has occurred. First, it seems intuitively obvious that by playing only one sport, practicing it intensely year-round, and not wasting time and effort learning other sports, a player will become better at his or her chosen sport. However, the data indicate that this is not true.

It is not altogether surprising that playing only one sport can lead to injury because of overuse of muscles and actions relevant to that sport. According to an article in *Orthopedics Today*, "Specialization in youth sports has led to an increased number of overuse injuries in young athletes, often amounting to acute injuries or withdrawal from play." This has specific relevance for pitchers:

"Parents think the more you pitch [for example], the better you are going to be in terms of playing further into college or into the professional level, but we believe, as physicians, the more you throw at that level, the less chance you have of a long career playing baseball or moving on to the next level because of the overuse injuries we see limiting these players long term," Grant L. Jones, MD, an orthopedic surgeon and professor at Ohio State University, said.[9]

The American Academy of Pediatrics has also found that "children who participate in multiple sports have a lower risk of overtraining syndrome compared with single-sport athletes."[10]

In addition to the increased chance of injuries, it is far from clear that focusing on only one sport, particularly beginning at a young age, is the best way to excel even at that one sport. David Epstein, who has studied how people excel at sports, observes:

When you look at studies of adult elite versus sub-elite athletes, the elites have accumulated more practice hours in their sport. No big surprise. But I really wanted to see if that pattern held over the entire lives of athletes, and it turns out that it absolutely doesn't. . . . Once I saw that pattern coming up again and again, I started talking to researchers who study skill acquisitions, from soccer to chess, and they talked to me about evidence suggesting that, early on, athletes should sample a variety of sports, gain a range of physical skills during that period of brain flexibility—age 12 is also the general cutoff for changing your native language—and only focus in and specialize later.[11]

For young baseball players, the best way to become a better pitcher might be to spend the fall playing soccer, building up lower-body strength and coordination rather than throwing another one thousand or so pitches on an arm that is already tired from the spring and summer. Similarly, taking a mental break from the study and practice of hitting may allow a player to tackle those tasks with renewed vigor, and perhaps better perspective, once that season rolls around again.

The access to such good coaching at a young age, and the focus on only one sport, may or may not have a long-term effect on player development. Epstein summarizes the most recent findings on year-round sports: "Children are playing sports in too structured a manner too early in life on adult-size fields—i.e., too large for optimal skill development—and spending too much time in one sport. It can lead to serious injuries and, a growing body of sports science shows, a lesser ultimate level of athletic success."[12] Ironic, but not quite counterintuitive, findings such as these notwithstanding, the growing trend of young people focusing on one sport, whether baseball or any other, has an effect on young people and on baseball more generally.

A corollary of the movement toward year-round participation in one sport is providing youths, often at considerable expense, with highly specific training or coaching. Youths as young as eight years old can find coaches to work with them not just on baseball generally but on hitting, pitching, catching, or other position-specific skills.

This niche is driven more by supply than by demand. For players with college or some professional experience who may coach in the spring and summer and need to make money in the off-season, offering private, often highly specialized lessons becomes a very reasonable option. These coaches, either consciously or not, play on a class of parents who, caught in the maw of the parenting industrial complex, are desperate to give their kids an advantage to increase their chances of a college scholarship. It is not hard to persuade these parents that their child's success relies on access to private lessons.

Many of the people who offer these lessons believe in what they do, love baseball, want to teach it to children, and are genuinely interested in helping their clients succeed. They are not, however, offering a product that is essential for success. Anybody who has been around baseball at any level knows that position switches occur all the time and that any player with a very strong arm can be converted to a pitcher as late as the high minors and certainly in high school. Every time I see a young person paying for private catching lessons, for example, I am reminded that Buster Posey, the best all-around catcher of his generation, became a catcher not even in high school but toward the end of his college career. Posey is not the only example. Kenley Jansen, the star closer for the Los Angeles Dodgers, started out as a catcher and did not start pitching until his fifth year as a professional. Within a year of making that transition, he was in the Dodgers' bullpen to stay. Star Kansas City Royals outfielder Lorenzo Cain did not play baseball at all until he was in the tenth grade.

The rise in the tendency for athletes to begin specializing in one sport year-round has had impacts on youth sports generally, and youth baseball particularly. The players who receive year-round training and a great deal of game experience are excellent. The best nine- to fifteen-year-old players today have benefited from more and better coaching than previous generations and, if they have managed to avoid injury, are probably as good as any in history. However, they also have a different approach to playing baseball. From a young age, something that for most kids a generation or more ago was a game that was played for fun is, for the better players and those with more ambitious parents, now seen as an opportunity for a scholarship or even a professional contract, and therefore something to be taken seriously; the weaker players, in many cases, have simply stopped playing. Thus, the number of children having fun playing baseball may be fewer than ever. As Fred Engh argues in his 2002 book, "Parents with the best of intentions are turning their children into miniature workaholics. . . . Children can't even take a couple of months' hiatus from a sport for fear of falling behind peers."[13]

Because the top players in all sports now specialize from a younger age than in previous generations, the best basketball, soccer, or football players, for example, no longer play baseball or do not have the opportunity to play it enough. This is particularly significant given that baseball is built around two skills—throwing and hitting—that have little relevance for other sports. Thus, the best athletes, unless they have specialized in baseball, increasingly lack the skills to play it properly. The result is that in many youth baseball settings, the middle of the skills bell curve has been removed, leaving only those who are either very good or those whose parents are desperate to see their children have some form of physical exercise or outdoor activity. This is probably true of all sports but is felt more acutely in baseball, again because of the difficulty and nontransferable nature of the game's building-block skills.

Accordingly, the better players opt out of recreational leagues and switch to travel or other more competitive programs, effectively making recreational baseball leagues for children over the age of ten increasingly difficult to maintain. Therefore, in many communities, baseball has become a niche sport, played extremely well by a small number of youths but not played at all by many others. What is happening to youth sports and youth baseball is a reflection of a changing culture, not a pathology specific to baseball. However, it is not good for the long-term health of the game. Rejuvenating the fan base was easy when all boys played baseball when they were younger, regardless of whether they were good, and when baseball became serious only for talented American boys late in high school. With fewer young people playing and enjoying the game, baseball will have to work harder to gain the next generation of fans.

Significantly, we are now in the second generation of declining numbers of young Americans who play baseball. Debbie Kling, the longtime president of Manhattan's West Side Little League, one of the largest Little League organizations in the country, notes that "it used to be that every American boy played baseball. You can no longer assume that because of the competition from other sports— most particularly soccer, but also lacrosse [and] basketball." Kling, whose involvement in youth baseball began as a team parent in 1991, adds that when the league asks parents how they want to volunteer, "there are fewer people who put down coach, particularly head coach, when they register. Often you get people whose experience is less than I would prefer. I end up having to settle." Kling makes these comments in reference to men who are mostly now in their late thirties and early forties and did not play baseball growing up. Additionally, when asked about the quality of play she sees today compared to a generation ago, Kling says it is "clearly weaker," adding that even the umpires tell her this.[14]

Frank Cassinelli, a long-time San Francisco baseball figure who has coached high school baseball in private, Catholic, and public schools there almost every year since 1978, offers a similar assessment of youth baseball today: "At the high school level, the quality [of play] has gone down in the city. We're getting kids at the high school level who have played in middle school who do not have the skills that they should have developed at the middle school level." Cassinelli attributes this issue to "the lack of kids playing youth baseball at the park-rec level or the Little League level."[15]

It may be that big league baseball can survive more or less unchanged in an environment where fewer Americans in each generation are deeply familiar with the game in the way that can come only from spending many hours playing baseball in the sandlot or in a more organized structure. However, there is substantial reason to think this is not the case.

One of the reasons why baseball fans love baseball, and why nonfans find it boring and incomprehensible, is that to fully appreciate the game, one must understand much more than what is happening on the field. This is probably true of all sports, but more so in baseball, where what occurs on the field is slower and less action- or motion-packed than is the case with most other sports. Part of this understanding can come from reading about, watching, or discussing baseball with more knowledgeable fans, but part can really come only from getting experience on the field.

There are, of course, many paths other than playing to becoming a baseball fan. Some immigrants from non-baseball-playing countries embrace the game as a symbol of their love for their new home. Some fans discover baseball through friends or serendipitously. Fans can be initially attracted to baseball because of its grace and beauty, one memorable year for their hometown team, a love of statistics, or many other great attributes of baseball. Being a baseball fan is nonetheless a trait that is often passed down from one generation to another. That is certainly how many intense fans I know, including my own children, came to their love of the game.

Many people become fans who never played baseball as kids, but playing as a young person clearly helps facilitate the process. Interestingly, this connection is also something that MLB appears to believe:

"The biggest predictor of fan avidity as an adult is whether you played the game," MLB commissioner Rob Manfred said. An MLB spokesman cited fan polling conducted by the league last year as proof. When asked to assess the factors that drove their interest in sports, fans between the ages of 12 and 17 cited participation as a major factor more often than watching or attending the sport. That was particularly true among male fans in that age group, 70% of [whom] cited "playing the sport" as a big factor in building their interest.[16]

The methodology reported in the *Wall Street Journal* piece quoted above is somewhat flawed, because youths between the ages of twelve and seventeen can report on only what makes them baseball fans in the present. This anecdotal evidence does not help determine why baseball-loving adults of any age became fans. Nonetheless, it is a piece of evidence that suggests some, possibly strong, connection between playing baseball as a youth and being a fan as an adult.

What about the Girls?

The gendered language in the previous section was deliberate. Baseball differs from such sports as soccer and basketball, as well as less-popular sports, such as lacrosse and various track and field events, because it remains segregated by gender. While boys and girls play soccer and basketball from a young age all the way through college, and at the professional level as well, baseball begins to phase out those girls who play at all by around age ten or eleven. At that age, the girls who have shown a talent for baseball are encouraged to move to softball, because that is the game competitively played by women in high school and for which college scholarships are available.

Because girls, even those who are excellent baseball players, do not have opportunities to play, very few girls have the experience of playing baseball at a genuinely competitive level and are therefore less inclined to become fans when they grow up. Comedian, social critic, and astute observer of baseball Greg Proops spoke to this issue more bluntly in an e-mail interview with me: "Why would you care if you played hoop and soccer all year? What is in it [baseball] for women?"

Proops's assertion about baseball's not appealing enough to women is supported by data, but with some nuance. For example, in her 2012 dissertation, Kelly Balfour notes that "where many believe sport to be a male domain and thus much marketing is focused toward men, women are found to make up nearly 44 percent of the fan base." She adds:

> It was found that females were motivated to be sports fans based on social motives such as utilizing fandom as a way to spend time with their families and for the cheering aspect of the game. . . . While females were found to be fans due to social aspects and the entertainment value of the game, male fans were found to be fans based on their love for the game and enjoyment they gain from learning about the game itself.[17]

Balfour's research suggests that women fans are more common than many might think, but they are not fully integrated into the fan experience, perhaps because they are drawn to the game for different reasons than the men and boys who are the targets of most of baseball's marketing efforts. It is also worth noting that Balfour focuses on whether people are fans at all, not the intensity of their fandom, an aspect that would likely skew more heavily male.

Not all the data tell a story of women as fans of baseball that is as positive as Balfour suggests. In a 2014 article, using data from Nielsen ratings, Derek Thompson asserts that "Major League Baseball shares the most male-heavy audience, at 70 percent, with the NBA."[18] In either case, it is apparent that by either increasing the number of women baseball fans or strengthening the passion of existing women baseball fans, baseball could increase its revenue.

Some women continue to play baseball in high school and beyond, but they represent a small minority. There is a national women's baseball team in the United States, but few Americans are aware of its existence. Several attempts at creating women's baseball leagues over the years, most notably the All-American Girls Professional Baseball League during World War II that is best known for inspiring the 1992 movie *A League of Their Own*, have ultimately failed.

Jennifer Ring's description of how her daughter, who later went on to play on the U.S. women's national team, was consistently pushed away from baseball by parents, coaches, and others provides a good picture of the barriers facing girls who want to play baseball at a competitive level after the age of nine or so:

> When my daughter was twelve years old, the age limit for Little League, she was expected to give up the sport she loved and switch to softball. She was pressured to change games "for her own good," with the counterintuitive argument that she was so good at baseball, she shouldn't squander her talent on a sport in which she had no future. . . . This rationale occasionally took the form of astonishing responses to her finest moments on baseball diamonds: the better she played baseball, the more forcefully she was urged to play softball.[19]

Malaika Underwood, the star power hitter on that Team USA squad, describes her frustration with how boys and girls are treated differently on America's ball fields and proposes a solution:

> I've actually thought that ideally we should have Little League Baseball, where boys and girls could play together until a certain age and then, instead of having high school baseball and high school softball, have high school boys' baseball and high school girls' baseball, just like we have boys' basketball and girls' basketball. It's the same sport. Soccer is the same way. Tennis is the same way. So why not baseball? I mean, ask anybody. . . . [B]aseball is America's pastime, right? So why can't girls play it?[20]

Ring describes a dinner with her daughter and two other members of the national women's team during a tryout:

[I] was regaled by their war stories as "the only girl" on their baseball teams until they discovered Team USA. Both girls had proved themselves as athletes and good teammates. . . . Still, both had vivid memories of what they referred to as "The Silence": the first moment with a new team when the boys suddenly noticed a girl in their midst.[21]

That dinner, which occurred in 2010, demonstrates how for many players, not to mention parents and fans, the idea of women and girls playing baseball is still viewed as strange or even wrong.

Girls play softball largely because they always have, or at least because they have been encouraged to play softball rather than baseball for more than a century. Dorothy and Harold Seymour describe softball's ascendancy circa 1909: "At the outset female physical training instructors approved of the new game. . . . [T]hey expressed the view that although regulation baseball contained the greatest educational possibilities, it presented problems for women: the hard ball, the heavy bat, the long throws and the complex rules."[22] This is sexist reasoning that, for some reason, still helps deny girls and women the enjoyment of playing baseball. It also contributes to preventing millions of Americans from becoming bigger baseball fans.

The roots of the sexist exclusion of women and girls from baseball run deep: "But neither our wives, our sisters, our daughters, nor our sweethearts may play Base Ball on the field. They may play Cricket, but seldom do; they may play Lawn Tennis, and win championships; they may play Basket Ball, and achieve laurels; they may play Golf, and receive trophies; but Base Ball is too strenuous for womankind, except as she may take part in grandstand."[23] The condescending and discriminating nature of comments such as these is not a big surprise, given that Albert Spalding wrote those words in 1911. It is, however, surprising and significant that the basic position reflected in those comments still limits baseball to boys and men more than a century later.

There are few things MLB could do that would have a bigger impact on its popularity and future success in the coming five- to ten-year window than encouraging girls to play baseball and supporting efforts by school districts, colleges, and youth sports programs to make this transition. This shift could very quickly and dramatically expand the potential fan base for big league baseball, as within a few years there would be a generation of women who were more familiar with the game. This opportunity is particularly significant, because basketball and soccer are games that girls play a lot. If soccer's mass popularity breaks through in the United States, it will be in no small part due to women fans who played it as girls. By continuing to simply cede this enormous part of the American population to other sports, MLB is making a big mistake and letting sexism and outmoded thinking triumph over fairness and good business sense.

Moreover, by continuing to exclude girls and women from playing baseball in high school, college, and most youth baseball programs, baseball damages its own image and places itself on the side of gender discrimination rather than alignment with equality and forward thinking. Politics aside, there is little doubt that many institutions, from basketball to the Supreme Court, that were once thought of as being for boys and men only are now open to girls and women. Baseball continues to lag on issues of gender equality, damaging itself financially and otherwise.

The Grandpa Demographic

Baseball is already a sport that has an aging fan base. This is clear from watching the ads during most baseball games, which sell Viagra, heart medicine, and the like to the grandfather demographic. During episodes of his popular podcast, *The Smartest Man in the World*, Proops frequently refers to baseball as an "old white guy sport." He fleshes out this view via e-mail by arguing that "baseball has high ticket prices, white guy stars, and a lack of sex appeal like the NBA has. MLB's idea of improving baseball is crap instant replay and clocks for the batters. Yawn." It should be kept in mind that these comments are coming from a middle-aged man who is an intense baseball fan with a deep knowledge of the game. But despite his affection for the game, Proops has correctly, if informally, identified some the flaws of baseball today.

In a 2014 article, Ira Boudway describes baseball as having "the oldest fans of the four major U.S. professional sports. During the World Series last fall, according to data gathered by *Sports Media Watch*, roughly half of TV viewers were 55 or older—and only 6 percent were under the age of 18." He adds, "Every year, the median viewing age gets one year older. It's a trend line that ends in a graveyard." The difficulty big league baseball has confronted in its efforts to draw younger fans has many contributing factors, including the length and price of games, the additional distractions and forms of entertainment available to young people today, and the late starting time of most postseason, and all World Series, games. Additionally, the changing nature of how, and of how many, young people play the game is a major contributing factor.[24]

How We Consume Baseball Now

Forty years ago, when an annual attendance of two million was considered pretty good for a big league team and when most of the best young male athletes in America changed sports with the seasons, people consumed all forms of entertainment very differently. Movies could be seen only in theaters or when they happened to be broadcast on television; eight-track and cassette tapes were considered technologically sophisticated ways to listen to music; newspapers and magazines existed only in hard-copy form; and baseball could be heard on the radio, seen live at the ballpark, or, in most media markets, viewed a few times a week on television during the regular season. In addition, all postseason games, as well as the All-Star Game, were broadcast on national network television.

Not only were baseball games only available in a few forms, and infrequently seen on television; most data about the game were also relatively scarce. During the season, many newspapers printed incomplete statistics about the home team or teams, plus top ten listings for batting average, home runs, runs batted in (RBIs), wins and occasionally other measures. The weekly publication of the *Sporting News* was the moment when fans could get more complete data on all the major and most minor leagues, but this information was always at least a few days behind events. Fans on the East Coast usually had to wait until two days after the completion of night games on the West Coast to see those box scores. Video highlights were shown on weekly baseball shows, such as *This Week in Baseball*, and occasionally on the nightly news.

In the pre-Internet age, baseball was consumed in other ways as well. Baseball books were, and remain, central to the baseball experience. Forty years ago, the baseball section was the biggest of any sport in the bookstore. That remains true today. Baseball has not relinquished its position as the most literary of all American sports. Various magazines and books were published at the end of every season and at the beginning of the new seasons, aggregating statistical and other relevant information. The *National League Green Books, American League Red Books*, individual team media guides, annual *Who's Who*, and other similar works were very useful for fans at that time. *The Baseball Encyclopedia* was published every few years beginning in 1969. This resource was invaluable to serious fans and scholars of the game and could be found behind more than a few bars, where patrons could use it to settle arguments about the game's history.

Today, reflecting the radical changes in media and technology over the past thirty years, baseball is consumed very differently. Most of these changes stem from the rapid growth of Internet-related technology, but cable television first began to change how people watched baseball in the 1980s by making televised baseball more available to fans. This transition began with the Braves and later the Cubs televising all their games nationally, but it quickly transformed to a point where almost all teams had cable contracts to broadcast their games. In addition to making baseball more accessible to people, this development reinvigorated the television market for baseball and began to bring more cable money into the game.

In general, the impact of Internet-related technology has been in two primary areas. First, these technological changes have made more of everything related to baseball, including statistics, videos, and archival material, available to fans. Second, the technological developments over the past decades have made baseball information more directly available to fans than in the past.

In general, the way Americans consume news and entertainment has changed so dramatically in the past quarter century that it is almost unrecognizable from previous forms. Various derivations of the Internet, including social media; handheld technology; blogs; new media companies, such as MLB Advanced Media (MLBAM); archived video of the kind found on YouTube; podcasts; and websites that provide data and information, are now among the resources baseball fans rely on to follow and enjoy the game. Of course, this shift is true of all forms of entertainment and news, including other sports, film, comedy, politics, weather, music, science, and the like.

The age of broadcasting, for baseball and everything else, has gradually given way to narrowcasting and, ultimately, egocasting. J. C. R. Licklider first used the term *narrowcasting* in 1967 to mean "the rejection or dissolution of the constraints imposed by a commitment to a monolithic mass-appeal, broadcast approach."[25] In 2012, Rob Peters defined narrowcasting as having "traditionally been understood as the dissemination of information (usually by radio or television) to a narrow audience, not the general public. Narrowcasting involves aiming media messages at specific segments of the public defined by values, preferences or demographic attributes."[26]

In a 2004–2005 issue of *New Atlantis*, Christine Rosen defines *egocasting* as "the thoroughly personalized and extremely narrow pursuit of one's personal taste." Egocasting arises from "technologies [that] are increasingly capable of filtering culture so that it suits our personal preferences."[27] For baseball fans, egocasting means that a fan of, for example, the Boston Red Sox can stream all the Red Sox games during the regular season, begin the day by listening to a few Red Sox podcasts on the way to work, check in on favorite Red Sox blogs every day, and study the Red Sox box score after every game. However, that fan can do all that while barely paying attention to the other teams. As a result, that fan could be more familiar with the Red Sox twentieth-ranked prospect than with the starting lineup of the Chicago White Sox or the Atlanta Braves.

In the age of egocasting, fans are able to follow only the parts of the game that they care about. One fan might be interested in pitching prospects, another in photos of old ballparks, another in Sabermetrics, and yet another in the history of a favorite team. Many different passions motivate different baseball fans. The challenge for MLB is to either rebuild a mass audience or find a way to turn a profit on all of these different kinds of baseball fans.

The Internet has lowered the bar for publishing on any topic. Just as anybody can create a political blog with his or her views, no matter how wacky, or post regular entries about fashion or music, the same is true for baseball. There is now more writing about baseball than has been broadly available than at any time in history. Some of this may be terrible, but much of it is very good. The breadth of writing available to the baseball fan today is extraordinary. There are traditional news sites, Sabermetric-oriented sites and bloggers, countless blogs analyzing and discussing every team, writings specifically on prospects, and more. No fan can possibly keep up with more than a tiny proportion of the baseball analysis that is now available online.

There is also what sometimes feels like an infinite amount of baseball-related video available online. During the season, highlights are available through such sites as MLB.com and ESPN.com not just for the previous night's games but for all games from recent seasons. MLB.com also has an enormous archive of historic video and games. YouTube has thousands of hours of baseball video available, ranging from funny interviews with ballplayers from thirty years ago, to fans' reactions to their teams' winning, to homemade highlight films, clips from games over the course of the past half century, and even a few hundred complete games from much of that period.

The second decade of the twenty-first century has seen the beginning of the data revolution that will probably continue for many years and has begun to reform how people consume entertainment, participate in politics, do business, advertise, and communicate. It has also already begun to change how baseball fans experience the game they love. More than almost any other sport, baseball has always been steeped in data. The game lends itself to a statistical accountability, because what happens to every pitched ball can be documented. It also lends itself to innovation, as new statistics are frequently created to try to explain the game better, and to the magic of numbers more generally. Round numbers, such as three hundred wins, a .300 batting average, or thirty home runs, evoke images and meaning for fans. Specific numbers, such as a fifty-six-game hitting streak, sixty-one home runs in 1961, 755 home runs, or a .406 batting average, are inextricably linked to baseball history.

A fan today not only can access Baseball-Reference.com—a free baseball encyclopedia, which, for a nominal annual fee, also allows members to do searches and manipulate the data in several useful and endlessly entertaining ways—but also, through such sites as Retrosheet.org, can find the box score or similar arcana for almost every game of at least the past seventy years. Minor league and other historical data are also available at numerous sites. Equally significantly, sites that provide pitch count and pitch tracking information, such as BrooksBaseball.net, share information that in the past was largely proprietary, if it existed at all.

Additionally, watching a game, particularly on a handheld device, is now an experience that fully integrates statistical data. By touching the screen, a fan can pull up statistical information on any player involved in the game. Increasingly, it is possible to examine specific plays through quantitative angles. For example, through MLB's *Statcast*, it is now possible to see how fast a runner was running or a catcher was throwing on a stolen-base attempt.

These developments have had two distinct impacts on the ways in which baseball is experienced. First, because egocasting is increasingly widespread, there is much less consensus around baseball than there used to be. Many fans know a great deal about the teams and players for whom they root, but they are less involved with the sport more broadly. This individualization has contributed to the generally declining ratings for the World Series and play-offs, as many fans lose interest if their team is not playing. In previous generations, there was agreement that the World Series was an important event for all fans, and even for many nonfans, but that attitude has changed.

This disappearing consensus has also contributed to the decline in players who are famous beyond the world of baseball and baseball fans. From roughly 1920 to 1980, baseball was always characterized by a small handful of players who transitioned from baseball stars to national figures, even national heroes. Babe Ruth, particularly in the 1920s, is the most obvious example of this, but others include Joe DiMaggio in the 1930s and 1940s; Jackie Robinson, Willie Mays, and Mickey Mantle through much of the 1950s and 1960s; and Reggie Jackson and Pete Rose in the 1970s. Derek Jeter may have played a similar role for most of his career, but nobody else has approached that stature in at least a decade.

The Internet has also weakened the credibility and relevance of the baseball expert and has had similar effects in many other fields, such as politics and music. The relatively few obstacles to anybody who wants to create a baseball blog or podcast and the increased availability of statistical information and video have made it much easier for people without direct access, status, or titles to write or talk about baseball and to build an audience.

For decades, experts, usually in the form of sportswriters or broadcasters, played a key role in mediating how baseball was received and understood by the broader fan base. Experts helped determine who the best players were or why teams won. It was difficult to challenge their expertise, because they had access to the players and information to help support these ideas, while the rest of us got the *Sporting News* once a week.

Sometimes these experts were great writers, making World Series games come to life for readers around the country, but at other times they were the protectors of conventional wisdom, spreading tropes about some teams' and players' having more desire than others or about the personalities of specific players. Not surprisingly, most of these experts were conservative, viewing scornfully high-priced salaries for players and being skeptical of most innovations and new methodologies for understanding the game. The ongoing clash between younger, more Sabermetrically oriented writers and fans and older, more conservative writers and fans maintaining the value of traditional statistics and intangibles is illustrative of the declining role of experts in baseball. This debate frequently presents itself in arguments such as the one regarding the 2012 AL MVP race, in which the Sabermetrically inclined supported Mike Trout, largely because of his league-leading 10.8 Wins above Replacement (WAR), while more traditional analysts supported Miguel Cabrera, who was the first player to win the triple crown since 1967, leading the league in home runs, RBIs, and batting average, but who largely because of his poor defense and twenty-eight GIDPs,[28] generated only a 7.2 WAR.

The rise of narrowcasting and egocasting, exacerbated by the declining impact of experts, is not good for a form of entertainment that relies on a mass audience, and particularly a mass audience watching the same set of events at the same time. It is apparent that the days of NBC's *Game of the Week*, *Monday Night Baseball*, or enormous ratings for postseason baseball are in the past. Even current programs, such as ESPN's *Sunday Night Baseball*, may not survive or draw decent ratings much longer.

MLB has not simply experienced the Internet revolution; it has played an active role in staying abreast or ahead of technological changes. Accordingly, MLB has managed to offer baseball fans an extremely good product that has become more diversified and innovative as technology has changed. Although many of the blogs, websites, and podcasts about baseball have developed independently of MLB, MLB has also led the way in making older baseball video available, created MLB.TV to sell access to televised baseball games to fans through a subscription program, and consistently used technology to make more information available to fans.

The new media context for baseball has also meant that baseball is increasingly played in a more global media environment. Baseball is becoming more global not just because players from all over the world come to the United States, and one Canadian city, to play in the big leagues but also because the game is played in many countries and is beginning to change as a result. The most glaring example of this change is in Japan, where baseball fan culture is already different from that in the United States. Writing in 2009, Ingrid Williams describes going to a game in Japan where

as soon as the game began, so did the coordinated cheering. Led by cheer captains in the outfield bleachers, the batting team's fans chanted, sang and rhythmically banged plastic

bats for every pitch to every batter. Their deafening, syn-
chronized roar dominated the dome. Each hit ignited a burst
of still louder cheers and frantic towel waving.

Yet the fans of the team in the field maintained a re-
spectful hush, interrupted only by an exuberant wave of
applause after each out. Questionable calls were never
booed. No jeers rang out when an error was made. These
fans radiated only love for their teams.[29]

In his 2002 book, Joseph Reaves also notes that

in Japan—in Asia—the game is different. . . . The style of
play is different. The style of managing is different. The
style of umpiring is different. And the styles of watching,
wishing, hoping and cheering are different. . . . The way the
game is played is, indeed, important. It is incredibly reveal-
ing on any number of levels—cultural, political, economic,
psychological.[30]

As the game gets more global, additional demands will be made
on MLB, because as markets in foreign countries grow and fans in
those countries want a product more tailored to their needs and
understanding of baseball, MLB will need to adapt as well. This
evolution will include economic and structural decisions, such as
whether to have more teams play games in Asia or to eventually
expand beyond North America, as well as questions regarding how
the game itself is played. For example, MLB is played according to a
set of unwritten rules that primarily focus on conduct but include
tactics and strategy as well. The unwritten rules about strategy
include prohibitions against teams with big leads stealing bases or
bunting, and players bunting to break up a no-hitter late in a game.
The rules about conduct primarily focus on players' not seeking to
show each other up and treating the game itself in a solemn way.
These rules, however, are culturally bound and do not reflect how
the game is played around the world. Comedian and Mets fan Chris
Rock has observed of baseball, "It's the only game where there's a
right way to play the game—the white way. The way it was played

100 years ago, when only whites were allowed to play. This code doesn't exist in other places where they play baseball, like Korea[,] where bat-flipping is an art form, or the Caribbean[,] where the games are a carnival."[31]

The issue of unwritten rules' bearing a uniquely American— and, as Rock argues, white American—imprimatur is not in itself a major concern. It is, however, illustrative of the way big league baseball, despite its increased international flavor, remains tailored for American audiences. Bat flips, for example, are a fun part of the game for Korean audience and fans. Unwritten rules against them in the big leagues limits the game's appeal in South Korea. Perhaps for the game to become more genuinely international, American hegemony in MLB's structure, governance, rules for field play, and other areas may be challenged.

Conclusion

Changes related to the globalization of baseball, how young people play sports in the United States, and how forms of media are created and consumed will challenge MLB. The constant stream of new fans and the consistent intergenerational transfer of passion for the game that has sustained baseball and, indeed, made it an American institution for more than a century can no longer be guaranteed. The breadth of athletic activities pursued by young people today affects the game similarly. If my childhood friend Will's young son develops his father's passion and skill for skateboarding, he will not have to pursue his athletic passion as a punk-rock rebel earning dirty looks from adults as he speeds down the hills of San Francisco as his father did. However, given who his father is, that possibility cannot be ruled out entirely. Instead, Will's son can find skateboarding teams for young people, receive lessons from skilled skateboarders other than his father, and, if he is good enough, enter tournaments or get a sponsor. Those options were not available to my good friend in the 1970s and 1980s. Will's son and thousands, perhaps millions, of other kids in this generation can pursue athletic activities, such as skateboarding and surfing, that were barely recognized as sports a generation ago. Millions of others will grow up playing soccer, basketball, and lacrosse and rarely, if ever, even swing a baseball bat. If MLB is still a major American sport with a mass following in 2030 or 2040, it will not be because of a generation of middle-aged men who grew up playing the game.

MLB has worked to stay ahead of the technological changes that have sped through American culture over the past twenty-five years or so. The result, for the most part, is a better product. Fans today now have access to more information, a greater diversity of writing, high-level statistical analysis, and a seemingly infinite archive of video information. Much, but not all, of this material has been directly provided by MLB.

Although MLB has succeeded in integrating its product into the newest technological developments, two major challenges raised by these developments remain unanswered by baseball. First, the new age of egocasting makes it difficult to develop mass audiences of the kind necessary to sustain baseball as an enormous, and enormously wealthy, industry. While there is now something for every kind of fan available on the Internet, the game is lacking events or even players about whom all fans can get excited.

Fans who care only about prospects, follow only the Seattle Mariners, love the statistical side of baseball, want to look at photos of old stadiums, like to listen to snarky young analysts, prefer curmudgeonly older former ballplayers, want to watch World Series or All-Star Games from their youth, or enjoy the game in almost any form can now choose from the panoply of options available on their computers and telephones. MLB, however, cannot guarantee good ratings for the World Series, has fewer household names playing than at any time in recent memory, and rarely sees on-the-field events break out of the sports pages. Solving that paradox will be essential to MLB's survival in its current form.

The second challenge facing MLB is also facing many different types of organizations, institutions, companies, and individuals in the new Internet economy—how to monetize the products they are creating and making available to the public. Many of the new resources available to fans cost nothing to consume other than the price of an Internet connection or a phone plan and a computer, a tablet, or a phone. Some of the available products are not cheap to create, yet they bring no revenue to MLB. Podcasts on baseball are almost all free, as are most blogs, all of YouTube, and access to statistical data. Some of these sites or podcasts make money through advertising revenue, but that money does not go to MLB in most cases; rather, it goes to the individual owner and creator of the content.

One of the major exceptions to this dilemma is MLB.TV. This is an extraordinary product that for the cost of approximately $150 a year offers fans access to every ballgame every night during the regular season. If, for example, the Brewers are playing the Cubs, fans can choose between the Brewers' or the Cubs' radio feed or television broadcast, thus having four different ways to follow that game. Teams that have Spanish-language broadcasts offer additional options. This is a fantastic arrangement for many fans.

Some fans, however, benefit more from this than others. Fans living far from their favorite teams can watch all their teams' games. Similarly, fans who simply love baseball can watch several games a day or skip around from game to game. This product is less useful to ordinary fans, because currently all games broadcast within the media market where the fans are located are blocked. Postseason games are not always available either. Thus, for the casual fan who wants to watch his or her hometown team and a bit of the play-offs, this product is all but useless.

MLB.TV is the best effort MLB has made to monetize its impressive array of Internet products, but thus far it has met with mixed success. In 2015, for example, approximately 3.5 million people subscribed, in one form or another, to MLB.TV.[32] At $150 per subscription, that constituted roughly $525 million in revenue for MLB. That is a substantial amount of money, but it is not comparable to the roughly $1.5 billion in revenue MLB still gets from its cable contracts. Moreover, MLB.TV's blackout policy is increasingly frustrating for fans, but if that policy changes, local cable contracts for individual teams will also decline.

Until around 1990, baseball was defined by a fan base that, at least for men, had come to its passion for the game in no small part through playing it. Similarly, until that decade, baseball was largely consumed either on the radio, on television, through the newspapers, or in person. Those pillars of popularity have radically changed in the past twenty-five years, even as, ironically, those years coincided with baseball's reaching new heights of wealth and, by some measures, popularity.

Baseball's success during this period has obscured a demographic reality that will, at some point, threaten the game. Making fans out of people who did not grow up playing the game raises difficult challenges for MLB, particularly given the diversification of athletic options for young participants and for adult fans. Similarly, baseball's embrace of new technologies has been impressive, admirable, and a boon for most fans, but revenue provided by cable television is still central to baseball's wealth and hard to imagine continuing at today's levels after the current contracts have expired.

5

JOHN ROCKER AND
RUSS HODGES

n 1999, John Rocker of the Atlanta Braves gave an interview to Jeff Pearlman, who was writing a profile of Rocker for *Sports Illustrated*. At the time, Rocker was a twenty-four-year-old relief pitcher who had just finished a very successful season, saving thirty-eight games for the pennant-winning Atlanta Braves. Rocker was a hard-throwing lefty who had shone even more in the postseason that year, allowing no earned runs in thirteen innings of work. However, when Pearlman asked Rocker his views about New York, a city Rocker had visited when his Braves had gone there to play the Mets and the Yankees, the native Georgian responded by echoing the bizarre, paranoid rhetoric that New Yorkers frequently encounter from people who do not like the big city—thus immediately making himself a controversial and, particularly in New York, not very popular figure:

> I would retire first. It's the most hectic, nerve-racking city. Imagine having to take the 7 train to the ballpark, looking like you're [riding through] Beirut next to some kid with purple hair next to some queer with AIDS right next to some dude who just got out of jail for the fourth time right next to some 20-year-old mom with four kids. It's depressing.

Rocker also added his thoughts on the Big Apple and geopolitics:

The biggest thing I don't like about New York are the foreigners. I'm not a very big fan of foreigners. You can walk an entire block in Times Square and not hear anybody speaking English. Asians and Koreans and Vietnamese and Indians and Russians and Spanish people and everything up there. How the hell did they get in this country?[1]

Rocker's bigoted views accelerated the collapse of his career. He found himself the target of angry fans and confrontational questions from the media in many cities, not just in New York. Rocker was an effective pitcher for only two more years and was out of baseball following the 2003 season.

Rocker's postbaseball life has been that of a minor media personality, appearing on reality television shows and the like. His desire for the media spotlight has probably increased since his playing days, while his gift for inflammatory words has not gone away.

Almost half a century before Rocker's controversial comments, perhaps the single-most famous play in baseball history occurred as Bobby Thomson hit a three-run home run in the bottom of the ninth inning of the third and final game of the play-off between the Brooklyn Dodgers and the New York Giants, two teams from Rocker's favorite city. The Dodgers and the Giants had ended the 1951 regular season tied for first place in the National League (NL). Thomson's home run gave the Giants a 5–4 win in that game and put them in the World Series against the Yankees.

Any avid baseball fan is familiar with Thomson's home run and the accompanying words of Giants announcer Russ Hodges: "The Giants win the pennant! The Giants win the pennant!" The video of that hit can be seen frequently when ESPN or some other network or website counts down the greatest moments in baseball history. It is also easily seen on YouTube. Hodges, however, did not call that game on television; he was a radio announcer on WMCA, a New York station. The radio broadcast was linked to the video after Hodges's home run call became famous.

Thomson's home run was known as the "Shot Heard 'Round the World," echoing the 1837 poem by Ralph Waldo Emerson. It was called that because the play-off between the Dodgers and the Giants was broadcast to U.S. military personnel in most of the far-flung places where the United States had a military presence in 1951, most notably Korea, as this was during the height of the Korean War. In 1951, naturally, American military personnel heard the dramatic game on the radio but could not watch it on television. Hodges's call of Thomson's home run is the most enduring legacy of a period in baseball when radio was more important than television, but it also encapsulates how central radio was to the game and to making big league baseball a national—and, by 1951, a nascent international—institution.

A Changing Society and the Consolidation of Big League Baseball

The consolidation of big league baseball was due to some factors that went well beyond the control of any team or league officials. For example, the rise of the United States as a global power in the early twentieth century, but particularly after World War II, ensured that the ability to pay high salaries was significantly greater in the United States than elsewhere, thus limiting the possibility that baseball leagues outside the United States could compete for the best players.

Similarly, the industrialization and immigration in the United States of the late nineteenth and early twentieth centuries also contributed substantially to the popularity of baseball. Although in the lore, baseball is often viewed and described as a rural and pastoral sport, it also thrived in immigrant communities in big cities during these years. The rapid urbanization of this period meant that potential audiences and fan bases could be found in enough cities to sustain big league baseball.

Baseball's rise, and the consolidation of Major League Baseball (MLB) within that, was also bolstered by the technology of much of the twentieth century. Baseball's relatively slow pace, particularly when compared to other sports, such as football or basketball, made it a natural for radio, where, absent any visual, announcers need time to explain what is occurring on the field and have extra time to build a relationship with the audience. Anybody who has listened to a basketball or a football game on the radio knows it is simply a poor substitute for television. Baseball, on the other hand, is frequently at least as enjoyable on the radio as on television.

Radio played a critical role in making MLB the national brand for baseball and in expanding audiences and fan bases in areas of the country where there were no big league teams. The synergy between baseball and radio has never existed for most other sports, but the conditions for its development were perfect during the middle of the twentieth century.

In a 1978 biography of Hall of Fame pitcher and announcer Dizzy Dean, Curt Smith describes how

> during the 1930s and the next decade beyond, with television an incipient vision, radio thrust baseball into the nation's living rooms, creating millions of new-found fans. . . . Radio alone did not lift baseball from its medieval station to a more enlightened level, but it assuredly led the way. . . . Even in its formative stages, radio endowed each season's climax—the World Series—with a stunning and unprecedented appeal. . . . [T]he Series lured a national cult which quickly developed and never ebbed.[2]

Smith's argument that big league baseball was able to expand as a national institution because of radio is reasonably straightforward, although the reality is somewhat more complex, but baseball's relationship with television has never been quite that simple. In fact, the nadir of baseball's popularity, the period from roughly 1968 to 1976, dovetailed with the rise of football on television.

In 2008, James Walker and Robert Bellamy described this period as one in which "the relative failure of baseball's *Monday Night Baseball* compared to the overwhelming success of *Monday Night Football* marked the diverging fortunes of the two sports."[3]

Whereas baseball seems to be made for radio and, at least at first glance, less so for television, the reverse is true for football. As television expanded into almost every American household during the 1950s and 1960s, football began to make inroads into baseball's fan base. During this period, attendance plummeted in baseball, as television ratings for the Super Bowl, an event that began in the late 1960s, exceeded those of the World Series, causing many in the leadership of MLB to begin worrying about the sport's losing its preeminence.

In 2008, Walker and Bellamy attributed football's enduring popularity on television to the game's having

> certain structural features that make it a near perfect match for the type of television coverage ABC lavished on it. The rectangular playing field is technically easier to cover. The limited number of games makes every contest seem important. Football is played in the fall and early winter when worsening weather in much of the U.S. increases television viewing levels.[4]

The Future of Baseball and Television

Baseball and television have always had a complex relationship. If television had never been invented, it is likely that football and basketball would still be considerably less popular than baseball. However, in the last decade or two, MLB has figured out how to make television, particularly cable television, extremely lucrative. Ironically, the organization figured that out just as the media environment was shifting once again.

Baseball's current challenge is sustaining interest and revenue, both of which have been substantially dependent on cable television over the past twenty years or so, in a time when television viewing is changing and declining. The media today is full of stories about how fewer people, particularly young people, are watching television.

In 2014, a *Time Magazine* headline blared, "Fewer People than Ever Are Watching TV."[5] *Marketing Charts* asked rhetorically, "Are Younger People Watching Less TV?"[6] *Business Insider* announced, "BRUTAL: 50% Decline in TV Viewership Shows Why Your Cable

Bill Is So High."[7] In 2014, Bloomberg noted, "US Pay TV Subscriptions Fall for First Time as Viewers Cut the Cord."[8] These are just a few of the countless articles that have addressed this issue in recent years. The data on television viewership only reinforce these headlines. The *Time* article notes that by late 2014, fully 2.8 percent of American households did not own a television, an increase of more than 100 percent from the previous year. The article points out that, according to Nielsen, in 2014, the average American adult watched 141 hours of television a month. That may sound like a lot, but it was down from 147 to 148 hours in each of the previous three years and represented a "more precipitous decline in TV viewing than any previous year."[9]

In early 2015, *TechHive* warned, "If 2013 and 2014 were disappointing, 2015 could turn out to be an annus horribilis for traditional television in the United States. Especially if the remainder of the year is anywhere near as bad as research firm Nomura says January was for live television."[10] Citing the 12.7 percent decline in television ratings in January 2015 compared to 2014, *TechHive* argued, "The writing is on the wall for traditional television as more and more people are cutting the cord and moving to streaming services such as Netflix, Amazon Instant Video, and Hulu—not to mention the growing population of so-called 'cord-neverism' people so strongly opposed to the idea of cable-TV subscriptions as to never bother with them."[11]

These data confirm the anecdotal experience of any American who has spoken with young people, walked around a college dorm, visited American homes, or, in many cases, even examined their own behavior—the age of television as the primary medium for entertainment, news, and sports is clearly in transition, although it is not over yet.

The decline in television ratings is not due to increased numbers of people reading books or taking long walks in the evening but instead a result of the rise of, as *TechHive* mentions, streaming video providers and new hardware, such as smartphones, tablets, and, for example, Apple TV. In its various forms, MLB.TV itself is one of these streaming options.

MLB.TV is an excellent product. In many ways, it is better than the product MLB has generally offered on cable television. This will be truer when MLB.TV works out its blackout-related problems, but even now it offers more baseball and more perspectives on baseball than traditional television ever has. Fans can usually choose between at least two broadcast teams when watching a game on MLB.TV. It also offers a much more in-depth look at the game through extensive video replay, a wealth of data for every game, and programs, such as *Statcast*, that make a deeper dive into the science of the game.

But although the product may be better, the business model is not. Over the past ten to fifteen years, cable has been an excellent source of revenue for MLB, allowing the organization to sign lucrative contracts and spread that money around to all thirty teams. In turn, MLB simply had to facilitate and give access to its partner cable networks. Fox, ESPN, and other networks were responsible for putting the broadcasts together, selling advertising, and selling cable subscriptions to customers. All of these things were related. The better the product MLB could provide, the higher the ratings and the more subscribers the networks would get, allowing them to generate more revenue from subscriptions and to charge more for advertising. These results then made it possible for MLB to demand more from competing networks when it was time to renegotiate a new contract. That system worked well for a while, but it is becoming increasingly difficult to maintain.

The Demographics of Television's Decline

Declining television ratings are bad for MLB's future cable contracts, but these slides are not evenly spread throughout the population; they are more acute among younger people. In a 2014 *Washington Post* article, Cecilia Kang notes:

> TV is increasingly for the old, and the Internet is for the young. . . . The median age of a broadcast or cable television viewer during the 2013–2014 TV season was 44.4 years old, a 6 percent increase in age from four years earlier. Audiences

for the major broadcast network shows are much older and aging even faster, with a median age of 53.9 years old, up 7 percent from four years ago. These television viewers are aging faster than the U.S. population. . . . The median age in the U.S. was 37.2, according to the U.S. Census, a figure that increased 1.9 percent over a decade. So to put that in context of television viewing . . . TV audiences aged 5 percent faster than the average American.[12]

This finding is also intuitive. Young people watch videos, news, and sports through Netflix, iTunes, or similar platforms. Young couples or roommates moving in together no longer subscribe to cable—they simply continue whatever contracts they have with streaming services.

The entertainment market has moved unequivocally away from mass and uniform consumption. Although movies, pop singers, and television shows are marketed to large audiences, they are no longer always consumed that way. Music can now be purchased in digital form, one song at a time. Television programs can be purchased one season or even one episode at a time and then watched whenever the viewer wants. These new systems work for platforms that are based on either a direct subscription or an item-by-item model, as they receive money directly from the viewer either every month or every time he or she decides to buy something. But for advertisers, the calculations are trickier.

For baseball, this new framework will be difficult as well. The success of cable television is that many networks are packaged together and sold to a broad public. A sports fan may never watch E! or the Discovery Channel but still has to pay for it in most cable packages. Similarly, somebody who loves movies might watch only IFC, Showtime, and the like but still end up paying for ESPN and Fox Sports. This packaging of stations allows cable providers to make money and extend the reach of all stations, including sports stations, into more homes. However, pressure from viewers and the availability of alternatives to cable will make it difficult for cable providers to continue this practice.

Currently, baseball sells its flagship online product through

MLB.TV at approximately $150 for a one-year subscription. The question of how many people will want that product at that price in ten years is one that should weigh heavily on MLB. Right now, MLB.TV generates a not-insignificant amount of revenue, roughly $600 million a year. This is a nice sum of money if it supplements cable revenue, which totals roughly $1.5 billion a year, but it is not close to being enough to replace cable revenue or to compensate for the shortfall if the next cable contract is not as big. MLB's current TV contract expires following the 2021 season. If trends in television viewership continue, the context in which that contract will be negotiated will be even worse for baseball than the current one.

Baseball needs to keep this subscription-based system in place, because the market for individual games during the regular season would be very small. Few regular season games today command widespread attention. Even pitching duels between division rivals, such as Clayton Kershaw of the Dodgers and Madison Bumgarner of the Giants or Matt Harvey of the Mets and Stephen Strasburg of the Nationals, are only local events during the regular season. It would, therefore, be very difficult for big league baseball to sell access to games on a game-by-game basis in a sufficiently profitable manner, particularly if the product remained available for free on the radio—a medium that many older fans still prefer.

Babe Ruth and the Emergence of the Baseball Celebrity

Baseball's popularity is deeply tied to the culture of celebrity around its best players and occasionally others involved in the game. In its early decades, John McGraw, who was renowned as a player and as a manager, Christy Mathewson, Ty Cobb, Adrian "Cap" Anson, Frank Chance, and other famous people drew fans to the park and were emulated by the young.

But none of those players were ever as famous as baseball's first true superstar, Babe Ruth. Ruth, still widely considered the greatest ballplayer ever, was more than a celebrity—he was a sui generis American folk hero. Today, he is a mythic figure for baseball fans and, perhaps, for a larger swath of the American people. A powerful man on legs that always seemed too skinny and whose statistics still do not seem quite believable, Ruth was one of the best pitchers in baseball before shattering all power-hitting records after becoming a full-time outfielder. In his 1975 biography, Marshall Smelser argues that Ruth's fame reached its height when technology was just beginning to bring the game to new levels of popularity. Smelser states that Ruth became a national figure at a time when "baseball, in particular, was a running adventure story with new climaxes almost every day." According to Smelser, Ruth benefited because "he was a cartoonist's dream subject. Even his name helped. It is easy to say Babe Ruth, and the word Babe is just unlikely enough to be unforgettable. Ruth was the people's ballplayer. When he hit a home run the Yankee fans were pleased with themselves and for the moment at least, found peace of mind."[13] That last sentence is a very good expression of what it means to be a fan rooting for a favorite ballplayer.

Don Mattingly, who was briefly one of the best hitters in baseball as a member of the New York Yankees in the mid- and late 1980s before becoming one of the worst managers in baseball with the Los Angeles Dodgers, once said of Ruth, "Honestly, at one time I thought Babe Ruth was a cartoon character. I really did, I mean I wasn't born until 1961 and I grew up in Indiana."[14] Another Ruth biographer describes the Babe as "the patron saint of American possibility," adding that "his success will be a lottery ticket in every empty pocket. . . . His fame will be manufactured in part, packaged, kept alive by a host of inventions, but its core will be performance."[15]

Ruth's obituary in the *New York Times*, penned by Murray Schumach, eloquently expresses the breadth of his celebrity:

> Probably nowhere in all the imaginative field of fiction could one find a career more dramatic and bizarre than that portrayed in real life by George Herman Ruth. Known the world over, even in foreign lands where baseball is never played, as the Babe, he was the boy who rose from the obscurity of a charitable institution in Baltimore to a position as the

leading figure in professional baseball. He was also its greatest drawing-card, its highest salaried performer—at least
of his day—and the idol of millions of youngsters throughout the land. A creation of the times, he seemed to embody
all the qualities that a sport-loving nation demanded of its
outstanding.[16]

Ruth's celebrity in the 1920s is understandable. He was not only
the greatest player the game had ever seen; he also changed the
entire way the game was played by making the home run a genuine
offensive weapon and generally shifting offense away from speed
and toward power. Interestingly, well into the early 1960s, older
curmudgeonly fans still insisted that Ty Cobb was the better player
because his game was built around speed, singles, and other strategies of the pre-1920 dead ball era. These are the spiritual progeni-
tors of those announcers today who believe that such players as
Don Drysdale were better than Pedro Martínez because the former
pitcher had more complete games.

Led by Ruth, baseball pivoted away from the dead ball era, in
which players such as Cobb excelled, when high batting averages,
stolen bases, and bunting were the key to winning, to the modern
era, when the home run became king. When Ruth made his debut as
a pitcher in 1914, no active player even had 100 career home runs;
Ruth ended up hitting 714. In 1919, splitting his time between
pitching and playing the outfield, Ruth led the league with twenty-
nine home runs, the most anybody had hit in a single season up
until that that time. Until then, only two other players, Gavvy Cra-
vath in 1915 and Frank Schulte in 1911, had hit as many as twenty
home runs in one season since 1900.

The home run brought a new level of excitement to the game
and quickly became the most dramatic and anticipated event on
the field. Although many of the most intense fans still prefer a
good pitching duel, it is the long home run that has for decades
captivated most fans' attention. Even today, during the baseball
season, most television and Internet highlight shows largely
consist of, or have a special section dedicated to, players who hit
home runs that day; announcers have signature home run calls;

and home run hitters are still generally the most valued and best-paid players.

Off the field, Ruth was an extraordinary figure with a huge and likable personality, particularly because the reporters generally covered up, or made light of, Ruth's personal missteps, including his penchant for heavy drinking. The most famous example of this, of course, occurred in 1925, when Ruth missed a third of the season as a result of what was called a stomachache but was thought by many to have been gonorrhea.

During the 1920s and early 1930s, Ruth became the archetype of the sports celebrity. His on-the-field exploits included moments, such as his called shot in the 1932 World Series and the three home runs he hit in the last game of the 1928 World Series, that were better suited to the backyard or sandlot dreams of millions of American kids than to reality. He had also been a great pitcher before becoming the greatest hitter of his era.

Ruth also had the huge advantage of playing in New York, which was then and is now the media center of the country. The media liked him and not only covered up most of his foibles but also rarely failed to report on one of his visits to the hospital to see sick children or any of the Babe's many other genuine acts of kindness and charity. Ruth also barnstormed during many off-seasons, thus ensuring that at least some Americans could lay eyes on the man, and maybe even see him hit one out of some modest rural ball field, whom they mostly knew from the newspapers and the radio.

Ruth's contributions to the notion of not just sports celebrity but American celebrity in general rival what he did on the field. The Bambino may have been the first true baseball celebrity, but many came after him. The nature of celebrity in baseball changed over the first forty years or so after Ruth retired in 1935, but the basic outline had been created by the Babe.

Baseball celebrities or heroes have left a deep, sometimes confounding, impact on the American consciousness. After Ruth, such players as Joe DiMaggio, Bob Feller, Stan Musial, Mickey Mantle, Willie Mays, and a few others were viewed as American heroes. Jackie Robinson is in this category as well, but his contributions to the country were of greater significance than any ballplayer since the Babe, or maybe ever. Other players, such as Hank Greenberg, Sandy Koufax, and Roberto Clemente, were somewhat less prominent in the national consciousness than Mantle or Mays, but they achieved extraordinary levels of fame among Jews and Puerto Ricans, respectively.

Paul Simon sang of the relationship between baseball heroes and America in the mid-1960s, just as baseball was entering its fifteen-to-twenty-year nadir of popularity. In the song "Mrs. Robinson," Simon posed the question of where Joe DiMaggio had gone as a way to poignantly express the idea of a great nation losing its way, as one of its most well-known heroes had returned to a quiet life in his hometown.

We see this frequently in our own lives, as adults sometimes seem to revert to their youth at the mention of their favorite childhood star. I remember visiting my father around the time of his eightieth birthday in 2014. He had recently been hit by a car and had not been out of the hospital for long. At some point, I mentioned Stan Musial, my father's childhood hero. My father, who had last been to a big league baseball game in 1982, instantly said, "Stan the Man!" and imitated Musial's unique batting stance.

The concepts of celebrity and of its sometimes-close relative heroism are part of baseball's enduring appeal. People who grow up with a favorite player whom they deeply admire often remain fans for life. Players who become true celebrities help bring people to the ballpark on a regular basis. These dynamics also facilitate enduring fan support for individual teams. For a Royals fan born in the 1960s, passion for baseball and for the Royals is inseparable from the great George Brett. Yankee fans born in the 1980s feel the same way about Yankee immortals, such as Derek Jeter and Mariano Rivera.

The Changing Nature of the Baseball Hero

The nature of celebrity in baseball is, however, changing. More accurately, it is changing again. The golden era of baseball celebrity and heroism ushered in by Ruth continued through the 1960s and early 1970s. The last heroes of that group were Mickey Mantle, Willie Mays, and Henry Aaron. These stars enjoyed relatively unambiguously positive and often cooperative relationships with the media. They were held up as models of American manhood by a media that almost never saw fit to look into their personal affairs, political views, finances, or anything of that nature. Joe DiMaggio's 1949 book *Lucky to Be a Yankee* is an example of this kind of hagiography in which the player is uncritical of the media who, in return, are uncritical of the player. DiMaggio sums up his experience in a chapter called "Along Memory Lane," with the lines "Looking back, I've met some great people, played with some great ball players. . . . And, I'll have to say again what I've said before—I'm lucky to be a Yankee."[17]

Tom Meany's 1963 book *The Magnificent Yankees*, written just as the age of unflinching hero worship was winding down, features a foreword in which longtime Yankee announcer Mel Allen states: "The Yankees have never let me down. . . . I believe that there is something extra special about the Yankee uniform. . . . I know that . . . no athletic organization in any sport . . . boasted greater team spirit than the Yankees. And that goes for all Yankee teams—the Yankees of tomorrow as well."[18] Words such as these are still very occasionally written today, but usually in books for young children. But in the mid–twentieth century, such descriptions, for the most part, were the only way the media described baseball. Within ten to twenty-five years, Yankees and former Yankees Jim Bouton, Graig Nettles, and Sparky Lyle would write the books *Ball Four* (1970), *Balls* (1984), and *The Bronx Zoo* (1979), respectively, that would strike a very different tone about baseball and the Yankees.

In the late 1960s, a younger generation of journalists brought different ethics and mores to their professions. Players began to make demands on owners, challenging the economic foundations of big league ball and causing more rancor than in previous eras between players and managers. Players themselves began to view their role differently—and then in 1970, Jim Bouton published *Ball Four*, possibly the best baseball book ever written. In the almost fifty years since its publication, it has received awards, been read and reread by generations of fans, and even been listed as one of most influential books of the twentieth century by the New York Public Library. *Ball Four* takes the form of the memoir/diary that by 1969, the season covered by Bouton in the book, was relatively common in sports literature. Two things made *Ball Four* distinctive from any previous sports book. First, Bouton was not a star player. He was a fringe pitcher, a few seasons removed from his best years, trying to land a spot in the bullpen of the expansion Seattle Pilots and then attempting to hold on with the Houston Astros following a midseason trade. Baseball looks very different from where Bouton sat in 1969 than it does from the perspective of a star player. Throughout the book, Bouton is obsessed with fears of being cut or released, anger at not being given enough of a chance to pitch, and general worry about his future. Bouton was also an outsider who did not fit into the macho, conservative, and anti-intellectual culture of big league baseball. This stance made him well positioned to report on the absurdity, hypocrisy, and not-always-deliberate humor that has always permeated the game at the big league level.

This exchange between Bouton and bullpen coach Eddie O'Brien captures the absurdity of big league baseball that until then was rarely explored: "Today while we were sitting in the bullpen, Eddie O'Brien, All-American coach, said, just after one of our pitchers walked somebody in the ballgame: 'The secret to pitching, boys, is throwing strikes.' Gee, Eddie! Thanks."[19] That comment seems very tame today, but until *Ball Four*, players did not ridicule their coaches in print.

Bouton's book was also different because he more or less told the truth about what baseball players said and did. In 1969, this honesty was a big deal. Bouton wrote about baseball players' drinking excessively, cheating on their wives, and using profanities. He also did not hesitate to draw attention to the pettiness and sometimes sheer stupidity of not only players but also managers and baseball executives. Not surprisingly, MLB officials as well as many players, managers, and others around the game were very upset with Bouton after his book was published and sought to push him out of the game. Bouton, for his part, did not play much after the book was published. He had always been a marginal player, so management found it very easy to keep him out of the game. Bouton did have an extraordinary, but brief, comeback in 1978 with the Atlanta Braves.

Sportswriters, of course, also reacted to *Ball Four*. Those who had been part of the old guard, conservatives who were complicit in covering up the shortcomings (or worse) of American baseball heroes, savaged Bouton. None did this more aggressively than Dick Young of the *New York Daily News*. Young was fifty-two at the time Bouton's book was published, had been writing for the *Daily News* for more than thirty years, and was unambiguously on the other side of the generational and cultural divide from Bouton.

In May 1970, the season after *Ball Four* was published, when Bouton was still holding on as a reliever for the Houston Astros, Young reviewed *Ball Four*:

> I feel sorry for Jim Bouton. He is a social leper. He didn't catch it, he developed it. His collaborator on the book, Leonard Schecter, is a social leper. People like this, embittered people, sit down in their time of deepest rejection and write. They write, oh hell, everybody stinks, everybody but me, and it makes them feel much better.[20]

Interestingly, Bouton opens his 1971 book *I'm Glad You Didn't Take It Personally*, which discusses the reactions to *Ball Four*, with this quotation from Young. Bouton, in fact, dedicates that book to "Dick Young and [baseball commissioner] Bowie Kuhn and those other faceless heroes of the bloody war to protect America from the small truths about baseball revealed in *Ball Four*."[21]

While many older writers shared Young's assessment of *Ball Four* and its author, the newer generation of journalists saw Bouton's work as a call to change the nature of how baseball was covered. Since 1970, money, racial politics, and substance abuse have been integral to baseball coverage. Moreover, few players have gotten a free ride from the media comparable to those enjoyed by Ruth, Mantle, and others from previous eras.

In the early 1970s, this new generation of writers, nudged along by the popularity of *Ball Four*, found themselves in a baseball landscape that was rapidly changing on and off the field. In his 2012 book, Dan Epstein writes:

Drugs, fashion, political upheaval, black power, the sexual revolution, gay liberation—all of these things left their mark upon '70s baseball in ways that would have been unthinkable just a few years earlier. . . . For the first time in history, major league ballplayers felt comfortable letting their "freak flags" fly, sprouting bold Afros and wild facial hair and expressing their opinions about everything from drugs and sex to Richard Nixon and the war in Vietnam. Instead of clean cut heroes, there were flawed but talented players like Dick Allen and Reggie Jackson . . . [who] seemed as cool and/or crazy as the antiheroes then populating the nation's movie screens.[22]

The 1970s represented a stark transition, but there were still some stars in that decade who, unlike Allen or Jackson, could be seen as all-American heroes. These included Joe Morgan, Johnny Bench, and Pete Rose of the Cincinnati Reds; Tom Seaver of the Mets; and Steve Garvey of the Dodgers. Strikingly, after that decade was over, Rose and Garvey became embroiled in late or postcareer scandals, Rose for gambling and Garvey for extramarital liaisons.

In recent decades, baseball's greatest players have continued to be more like antiheroes than heroes. One way to see this is that since 1970, the three best players in the game, solely on the basis of what they did on the field, have been Barry Bonds, Roger Clemens, and Alex Rodriguez. These three have accumulated the most Wins above Replacement (WAR) since 1970, with Bonds at 162, Clemens at 139, and Rodriguez at 119. Rickey Henderson is fourth with 111.

WAR is an omnibus statistic that for nonpitchers seeks to aggregate offensive and defensive measures to determine how much better or worse a particular player is than a replacement player would be. A replacement player is defined as slightly below league average. A different formula is used to evaluate the overall contribution of pitchers. Because WAR takes into consideration such factors as ballpark and era effects, it is good for comparing across leagues and times. The details of the formula itself can be debated, but it is a very good heuristic measure.

Even without taking WAR into consideration, Bonds, Clemens, and Rodriguez have conventional numbers that speak for themselves. Bonds is the all-time home run and walks leader, won seven Most Valuable Player (MVP) awards, stole more than five hundred bases, and won eight Gold Gloves. Rodriguez won three MVP awards, during the first part of his career combined fearsome power with top-notch defense at shortstop, and will likely retire with the fourth, and possibly third, most home runs in baseball history and more than three thousand hits, making him one of three players with three thousand hits and six hundred home runs (the other two are Willie Mays and Henry Aaron). Roger Clemens was a seven-time Cy Young Award winner, has the third-highest number of strikeouts in history, and is ninth on the all-time win list.

But despite their awesome statistics, Clemens, Bonds, and Rodriguez are so intensely despised by baseball fans that many fans have probably had a tough time getting through these last two paragraphs without spitting out epithets about steroids. Clemens and Bonds are so widely disliked that during the three years they have each been on the Hall of Fame ballot, neither has received even 40 percent of the vote; 75 percent is required for election. Thus, the two best players of the last forty years have fallen very far short of being elected to the Hall of Fame.

The reasons for this are obvious to any baseball fan: all three of these great players not only have been associated with the widespread use of performance-enhancing drugs (PEDs) of the late 1990s and early 2000s but also have been embroiled in peripheral scandals involving perjury charges, court cases, testimonies, and the like. Additionally, Rodriguez, Bonds, and Clemens were not known for working well with the media. This toxic combination has meant that these three players of historic greatness are not even remotely considered heroes to anybody. Some Giants fans still like Bonds, but his memory has been pushed out by the 2010–2014 Giants' remarkable accomplishments. Rodriguez and Clemens are no longer even popular in the cities where they played, although beginning in 2015, Rodriguez began to rebuild his reputation, at least among Yankee fans. Thirty years from now, it is unlikely that many middle-aged or older men will be describing these players to their kids or grandkids as heroes.

Bonds, Rodriguez, and Clemens are the most dramatic examples of how the baseball hero has faded away in recent years, but they are not the only ones. The 1998 home run race between Mark McGwire and Sammy Sosa that was so celebrated at the time was soon also lost to controversy when the rather obvious, even at the time, fact that McGwire and Sosa were both using PED became broadly known. Other stars of the era, including Rafael Palmeiro, Jose Canseco, and Andy Pettitte, have also been linked to PED use.

Because MLB never fully confronted and eliminated PED use, its protestations to the contrary notwithstanding, the damage of that period to the concept of the baseball hero had even greater consequences. Great players such as Jeff Bagwell and David Ortiz saw their reputations tarnished not for PED use but for rumored PED use or guilt by association, on the basis of the belief that all big sluggers of the era were using PEDs.

In recent years, not just been PED use but other flaws have damaged the images of baseball stars, sometimes after they have retired. World Series heroes Curt Schilling and Lenny Dykstra encountered ugly financial problems a few years after leaving the game that left a trail of bad publicity. To fans under thirty, George Brett might be better known for a YouTube clip in which he recounts a story of losing control of his bowels at the Bellagio Hotel in Las Vegas than for being one of the greatest hitters of his era.

Steve Carlton, one of the best left-handed pitchers of the postwar era, was one of a relatively small number of stars who did not talk to the media during most of the time he spent playing big league baseball, an almost surefire way to guarantee poor press coverage. Given what he said when he finally spoke to the media, Carlton probably had the right idea for most of his career. Shortly after his election to the Hall of Fame in 1994, Carlton gave an interview to *Philadelphia Magazine* in which he revealed himself to be obsessed with bizarre right-wing conspiracies and to be an anti-Semite, alluding to the *Protocols of the Elders of Zion* and the "12 Jewish bankers meeting in Switzerland" whom Carlton believed controlled the global economy.[23]

Of course, not all great players of the past forty years have been surrounded by scandal. Greg Maddux, Randy Johnson, Mariano

Rivera, Joe Morgan, Mike Schmidt, Cal Ripken Jr., Derek Jeter, and Ken Griffey Jr. are among those great players from this period who have been able to maintain sterling public images. But the failure of most of these players, despite their good reputations, to break through as truly national celebrities or heroes speaks to the changing culture around media, celebrity, and baseball more than any personal shortcomings. These players never did anything wrong off the field, but they played at a time when the national culture was no longer receptive to the idea of baseball players as true heroes or celebrities beyond the confines of baseball.

Griffey and Jeter probably came the closest to achieving the celebrity status enjoyed by such players as Mantle and Mays thirty to forty years earlier. Griffey had the potential to be a national figure but was eclipsed by the steroid era as well as by his inability to sustain an elite-level performance after his prime years. Ironically, because he did *not* use steroids, his numbers were no longer among the best in the game by 2001 or so, thus dimming his star.

Jeter is an even more intriguing reflection of the state of celebrity in baseball. He spent his entire career playing a marquee position for the most famous team in baseball. Over the course of the twenty seasons he played in the big leagues, Jeter's Yankees played in the postseason sixteen times and won the World Series five times. Jeter was also a good-looking, media-savvy man who was never involved in a scandal of any kind, treated people respectfully, and was viewed by many as the face of big league baseball during the last half of his career.

Jeter clearly achieved celebrity status while he was playing. For many years, his jersey sold more than that of any other player.[24] By the end of his career, polling data from Saint Leo University showed Jeter to be the most popular player in the game. Interestingly, when asked who their favorite player of all time was, many respondents still named Babe Ruth, almost eighty years after he had played his last game and more than sixty years after his death. That is an extraordinary testimony to Ruth's enduring popularity.[25]

Jeter was also an extremely polarizing figure among baseball fans. The dominant narrative regarding the great Yankee shortstop was that he was beloved by Yankee fans and many others and respected almost universally by fans of other teams, including fans of the Yankees' biggest rivals, the Boston Red Sox. This was probably true to some extent but also tells only half the story.

For most of his career, there was also strong backlash against Jeter from fans who thought he was overrated, particularly his defense, and saw his all-American image as a media creation. For many years, particularly as he got older, Jeter was probably among the most beloved and simultaneously most disliked players of his era. There is little evidence that baseball heroes from the pre-1970 era were similarly divisive, except for perhaps Ted Williams, who was frequently booed by fans at Fenway Park, where he played all his home games.

The debate around Jeter's defensive ability was not just an argument about how well he could field; for years it was also one of the battleground issues between traditional fans, particularly traditional Yankee fans, and more quantitative-minded fans. In 2013, Ben Lindbergh discussed this tension:

> Jeter has long been baseball's most polarizing defensive player. In the right crowd—a mix of sabermetricians and the regulars at Stan's Sports Bar—it takes just three words ("Derek Jeter's defense") to touch off a debate between people who are equally convinced that the Yankees captain is either one of the best or one of the worst defenders of all time. The "best ever" argument is easy. Jeter has the hardware; only four shortstops can top his total of five Gold Gloves. . . . On the other side are the advanced statistics, which disregard Gold Gloves. . . . According to two historical play-by-play-based systems, Baseball Prospectus's Fielding Runs Above Average and Baseball-Reference's Total Zone, Jeter has cost his team more in the field than any other player in history, with both methods assessing the damage at 230 to 260 runs.[26]

The contrast between Jeter's reputation and the data is, as Lindbergh notes, extremely stark. Further evidence of this discrepancy is that in four of the five years in which Jeter was awarded the Gold Glove, he had negative defensive WAR. In lay terms, that means that in four of the five years when Jeter was voted the best defensive shortstop in the American League, advanced metrics showed that he was a worse defender than a typical backup infielder or a good shortstop in the high minor leagues.

Discussions about how good a player was are common, and debates about all-time great players do not necessarily diminish their celebrity. Most sophisticated fans also understand, for example, that Sandy Koufax's awesome pitching numbers were bolstered by pitching in a pitcher's park during a pitcher's era, or that sluggers of the 1930s, such as Jimmie Foxx, Mel Ott, and Lou Gehrig, benefited from playing in a high-offense era, but these qualifiers have done little to damage their celebrity, or even hero, status.

The backlash against Jeter was different because it was, to a great extent, a reaction to his clean image and celebrity status itself. Not surprisingly, this backlash reached its climax in 2014, Jeter's last season, when the great Yankee was endlessly lauded and celebrated in what Keith Olbermann referred to as the "forced adulation of a player . . . [who was] nowhere near an immortal."[27]

Early that season, Michael Gray wrote in the *New York Post*:

> The Myth of Derek Jeter is so well tended that it's blasphemy to suggest that he's anything but a humble paragon of a gentleman's game. . . . Despite his well-worn protests that it's all about the team, he was consistently the last one out of the dugout at the bottom of the inning, feeding the endless ovation that has followed him around the country. . . . At his retirement announcement, Jeter maintained he was giving a heads up before the season so that questions of his longevity didn't become a distraction. Right. Because there's nothing distracting about the ceremonies, the curtain calls, the gifts of surfboards and subway tiles.[28]

In 2011, Tom Mechin described Jeter as "arguably the most overrated athlete ever to play professional sports," adding that "Derek Jeter is merely a very good player who benefited greatly from being drafted by the right team, at the right time, playing in the right city."[29] At times even Jeter's fellow players have shared this view. In 2008, a *Sports Illustrated* poll of players showed Jeter to be the most overrated in the eyes of his peers.[30]

These are just some of the seemingly infinite articles and blogs that were part of the Jeter backlash during the latter part of his career. In 2014, Howard Megdal captured the dilemma of Jeter's celebrity: "It irritates the rest of us, that Derek Jeter can't simply be extolled for all the things he is, but also has to be celebrated for all the things he pretty clearly isn't."[31] Megdal is right in that nobody, other than perhaps Mechin, disputes that Jeter was a great player, but the constant attempts to make him into something beyond that are extremely annoying to many fans.

Megdal is referring to such writers as Richard Justice, who said of Jeter in 2014, "I've made the point that this might be the greatest player that ever lived—if you just look across the board, the way he played, the way his teams played, the way he represented the franchise."[32] This is a nonsensical argument. Anybody who thinks Jeter is the greatest player ever has a very tenuous relationship with baseball reality. Further descriptions of Jeter as "baseball's primary role model or the game's unofficial but leading ambassador to the rest of humanity"[33] or as the greatest Yankee ever (according to former teammate and longtime Yankee Jorge Posada) are similarly annoying to many baseball fans, even many fans of Jeter.

While it is easy to see Megdal's point about how some fans could resent the cloying and excessive coverage of Jeter, it is also not exactly Jeter's fault. Jeter did all the things a celebrity and baseball hero is supposed to do. He played hard on the field, had a handful of moments that made a lasting imprint on the memories of most baseball fans and all Yankee fans, stayed out of trouble, was polite to the media, and was very good looking and reasonably charming. Given all that, it is no surprise that Jeter enjoyed a level of fame and a positive public image greater than that of any player of his generation, even greater than those, such as his teammates Randy Johnson, Alex Rodriguez, and Roger Clemens, who were clearly better players than he was. Nonetheless, Jeter had his detractors and a small but vocal minority of fans who resented him and his image.

Ultimately, this dislike is more a reflection on the state of celebrity than on Jeter himself. Moreover, the negative publicity around

Jeter stemming primarily from the resentment of the treatment of him by the media does not bode well for the future of baseball celebrity and heroism. Further evidence of this attitudinal shift is the failure of any of the most recent group of young stars to emerge as genuine celebrities or baseball heroes.

Two players in particular should be able to become the next national baseball celebrities but have not achieved that level of national fame. Mike Trout plays center field for a Los Angeles team, excels at every aspect of the game, and has in his short career drawn comparisons to the likes of Mickey Mantle.[34] While Trout is a genuinely outstanding player and the consensus current best player in the game, he would not be recognized in most parts of the country, and his name is probably little known by people who are not baseball fans.

Buster Posey has been at the center of the revival of the San Francisco Giants. Three times in his first five years in the big leagues, he found himself catching and batting cleanup on the team that won the World Series. Posey is soft-spoken, polite, a great hitter, and a natural team leader, and he even has a pretty wife and twins—a boy and a girl, of course.

Significantly, after Jeter retired, MLB, feeling the player's absence, actually held a contest to determine the new face of baseball following the 2014 season. Posey won and became the official face of baseball. As a superstar-caliber player who is clean-cut, with an all-American look, he is well suited to the role. However, Posey is in no organic way the face of baseball. He does not enjoy anything approaching the national recognition of such players as Mays, Rose, and DiMaggio in previous generations. Outside the Bay Area, it is unlikely many people who are not intense baseball fans would recognize Posey if he were behind them in the checkout line at the grocery store.

The notion of celebrity in baseball began to crumble in the late 1960s and early 1970s, as changes in journalism and society more broadly made hero worship of the kind that had been common in the previous half century no longer possible. Currently, media and society are in the midst of another transition that is raising a second wave of challenges for baseball celebrities.

Today, thanks to newer forms of media, particularly social

media—most specifically, Twitter—sports stars and celebrities are expected to be available to their fans to a much greater degree than in previous generations. Demands for this kind of behavior from baseball celebrities will likely increase even more over the next few years. This requirement raises a particular challenge for baseball players, many of whom are not well educated, speak English as a second language, or come from a baseball culture that is, in many ways, out of sync with the fans, particularly younger fans, and the media.

Twitter is a great medium for connecting players with fans, but it also provides almost infinite opportunities for any celebrity, including baseball players, to tweet the wrong thing and almost instantly find themselves mired in terrible publicity or scandal. If John Rocker had used Twitter instead of waiting for *Sports Illustrated* to interview him almost twenty years ago, he would have gotten himself into trouble much more quickly

One does not have to imagine this scenario, because Rocker, who has tried to maintain his celebrity status, does have a Twitter account, and when he is not tweeting about sports, he frequently tweets offensive statements. In a single day in November 2013, Rocker tweeted, "Fact: God hates liberals," "Shouldn't u liberal dirt bags b at work today? U ALL can't b on welfare," and "In fact grow a pair of balls and stick a needle n Ur ass. Mayb u wouldn't all b such limp wristed ineffective pussies."[35]

Rocker's one-time teammate and likely future Hall of Famer Larry "Chipper" Jones has had an equally offensive and controversial, but even stranger, online presence. In February 2015, Jones tweeted, "So the FBI comes out and confirms that Sandy Hook was a hoax! Where is the outrage? What else are we being lied to about? Waco? JFK? Pff." Jones deleted that tweet but not before thousands saw it, leading to critical stories about the great third baseman. In June 2013, Jones showed his insensitivity to immigrants by tweeting, "Y'all think if they took all them gators they trap in Fla and La and put them in the Rio Grande, it wud stop the illegals from crossing? Jk." In November 2012, he revealed the depths of his vulnerability to bizarre conspiracy theories: "What a crock of crap! Oswald killed Kennedy? Seriously? Sorry, but I'm watching JFK. It's almost laughable what they want us to believe."[36]

To date, no active players have provoked similar controversy on Twitter, but it seems like only a matter of time until that happens. It is significant that Rocker and Jones ran afoul of the media by making, at least in part, far-right or racist statements. Many white American baseball players are from the South or other conservative regions of the country. Not a lot of white big leaguers grew up in Berkeley; San Francisco; Brownstone Brooklyn; Madison, Wisconsin; or the west side of Los Angeles, so conservative politics are not uncommon among these players.

The problem is not a political one of conservative players getting entrapped or pilloried by progressive media elites. Rather, it is one of players who are not media-savvy being forced to interact with media and directly with fans in new and potentially problematic ways. It is not just ballplayers who make mistakes on Twitter—Internet shaming can affect all kinds of celebrities as well as ordinary people—but ballplayers are particularly vulnerable.

The obvious solution for ballplayers is to use social media less frequently. This is, in fact, what many players do, but that approach will likely become more difficult over time as demands from the media and the public increase. As everybody from politicians to entertainers to writers has an online presence to build a brand and sell a product, it will be harder for baseball players to avoid doing the same, which will force the notion of baseball celebrity to take a different form.

The changing nature or even disappearance of the baseball celebrity is important because baseball's popularity, at least as much as that of any other sport, rests on the popularity of individuals and of the perception that those individuals are deeply special, even heroic, people. While this may be an inaccurate, and probably psychologically unhealthy, dynamic for everybody involved, it has proven to be a very lucrative one for MLB over the years.

If baseball players are not heroes, and increasingly not even marketable celebrities, much of the edifice of MLB will also become susceptible to doubt and questioning. The extraordinarily huge salaries paid to almost all players, the constantly rising costs of attending a game, and the big cable contracts are all vulnerable if fans begin to view players as very talented but also very ordinary people. That transition will take time, but once it starts, it will be very difficult to stop.

Big League Salaries in the Age of Income Inequality

When free agency began in the mid- to late 1970s and baseball salaries began to escalate rapidly, older fans often joked that reading the sports pages was more like reading the business pages. This was a reaction to the high salaries the players were making and the new ways that free agency, long-term contracts, and the like were beginning to affect the game.

For the past twenty years or so, it has been impossible to understand big league baseball, the chances and futures of specific teams, the value of players, and almost all player transactions without understanding the business of the game. To suggest now that money should be kept out of the sports pages, the way many fans did forty years ago, would be absurd. Free-agent signings are big news, but less obvious elements, such as the timing of bringing up a top prospect, also need to be understood in the context of baseball finances.

Terms such as *luxury tax*, *super two*, and *slot value* are essential to understanding any team's strategic decisions. Moreover, such issues as signing young players to large, but still under market, long-term contracts; avoiding free-agent contracts that inevitably include a player's decline phase; and international signings are all deeply part of baseball now. These concepts have given the game an additional strategic dynamic, as smart teams try to nail down their young stars and are hesitant to give too many years to players over thirty. They are also a constant reminder of the extraordinary salaries paid to baseball's top players.

There is nothing particularly new about baseball players' making more money than ordinary Americans. In the middle of the depression, from 1930 to 1934, Babe Ruth's annual salaries ranged from $70,000 to $80,000. That income did not include money from barnstorming or endorsements. In an era when unemployment reached as much as 25 percent in the United States, that was an enormous amount of money, but Ruth's salary was no more than $1.4 million in today's dollars.

Today, top players make between $25 million and $30 million a year, exponentially more, in constant dollars, than Ruth ever made. Moreover, Ruth was always a bit of an exception. In the early 1930s, other great stars did not make nearly as much as he did. Between 1930 and 1934, Lou Gehrig made $25,000 every year. Jimmie Foxx's top salary was $17,500. Foxx's teammate Lefty Grove, baseball's best pitcher during those years, made $45,000 in 1934, but other than that never more than $20,000 a year in a career that lasted from 1925 to 1941. Grove supplemented that salary substantially by barnstorming throughout the 1930s.

It is no longer true that the best and most famous player makes almost twice the salary of the second-highest player and three times as much as everybody else. Many players make more than $20 million a year, but more significantly, the average salary was more than $4 million in 2015, and the minimum salary was just over $500,000. In other words, in constant dollars, the average big leaguer today makes about three times what Ruth made at his peak, while the lowest-paid big leaguer makes more than any other player of that era besides Ruth.

The discrepancy between the salaries of almost all big league players and those of most of their fans is thus greater, in terms of real dollars. In March 2015, the median household income in the United States was $54,203,[37] roughly one-ninth the big league minimum and about one-seventy-third the big league average. This is a much higher ratio than at any time in the twentieth century.

Table 5.1 shows the average and high salaries for the first year of every decade from 1910 to 2010. The last column shows the average household income for years when that data are available. While the ratio in the first to the last column increases throughout the one hundred years in the table, the rate of increase is much higher in the more recent decades. Not only have the numbers changed; perceptions of income inequality have changed as well. Income inequality—or, more accurately, wealth inequality—has been a part of Americans' economic life for a very long time, but in recent years it has become a part of the policy debate and the public consciousness in ways not seen in the United States in many decades.

Such books as Joseph Stiglitz's *The Price of Inequality: How*

TABLE 5.1. BASEBALL SALARIES OVER TIME

Year	Average salary	High salary	Player	Average household income
1910	$4,210 (21)	$9,000	Ty Cobb, Nap Lajoie	N/A
1920	$5,000	$20,000	Ty Cobb, Babe Ruth, Tris Speaker	N/A
1930	$7,608 (227)	$80,000	Babe Ruth	N/A
1940	$7,328 (182)	$35,000	Hank Greenberg	$1,368
1950	$13,300	$100,000	Joe DiMaggio	$3,319
1960	$16,000	$80,000	Willie Mays	$5,600
1970	$29,303	$135,000	Willie Mays	$7,559
1980	$143,756	$1,000,000	Nolan Ryan	$16,354
1990	$597,537	$3,200,000	Robin Yount	$28,149
2000	$1,895,630	$15,714,286	Kevin Brown	$40,703
2010	$3,297,828	$33,000,000	Alex Rodriguez	$47,793

Today's Divided Society Endangers Our Future (2012), Thomas Piketty's much-discussed *Capital in the Twenty-First Century* (2013), Matt Taibbi's *The Divide: American Injustice in the Age of the Wealth Gap* (2014), and David Cay Johnston's *Divided: The Perils of Our Growing Inequality* (2014) reflect concern about growing income inequality and help ensure that the topic remains in the minds of many. Such politicians as Elizabeth Warren have built successful careers by focusing heavily on this issue, and Bernie Sanders's campaign for the 2016 Democratic nomination for president was waged largely around the issue of income inequality. Popular economists, such as Robert Reich and Paul Krugman, write frequent blog posts and columns about income inequality. Movements such as Occupy and efforts to increase the minimum wage also reflect the growing awareness of income inequality.

In an era when income inequality between CEOs and workers, the wealthiest 1 percent and everybody else, or teachers and hedge-fund managers is increasingly part of the political discourse, it may become less possible for the equally yawning gap between big league stars and the people who pay to watch them to continue to be ignored. It is, of course, true that owners are getting wealthier than most players and that big league ballplayers are at the very top of their profession, have short careers, and help produce massive amounts of wealth. Nonetheless, it is their huge salaries that are publicized, and they—not the owners—are the public face of the game.

Being a fan of any sport, including baseball, provokes a range of emotions. The happiness that people feel when their teams win a championship is real. Similarly, the despair when the other team hits a walk-off home run to win a play-off or a World Series game is genuine. In a less extreme sense, the feeling of comfort and happiness when arriving at a beloved ballpark is something to which many sports fan can relate. Joy, despair, comfort, frustration at a missed scoring opportunity, and hope when a new season begins are all part of the emotional range of most baseball fans.

Anger is also part of the emotional repertoire of many fans, although some embrace it more than others. The angry baseball fan reacts to his team's loss not with disappointment or sadness but with anger. Instead of understanding that sometimes in baseball, luck is with the other team, that a great pitcher can stop any team, or any of the realities that determine who wins and loses baseball games, the angry fan attributes his team's defeat to the manager's alleged stupidity, the belief that the players on the team are not trying hard enough, or to the players' being overpaid and therefore unwilling to do whatever it takes to win. For most of these fans, the enormous salaries paid to all players are a significant and constant source of anger.

Today, the angry baseball fan represents a minority of baseball fans, but if income inequality remains an important political issue, the sentiments expressed by angry baseball fans could become more widespread. Not all fans will respond to income gaps between players and fans with anger—and for decades, most have not—but many will begin to question why they are spending so much time and money watching and celebrating the actions of people whose salaries put them at the high end of the 1 percent. This perception could lead to declining interest in the game or perhaps even force the game to change so as not to alienate its fans.

In addition to these questions of perception, there is also the reality that baseball is expensive. The costs of attending a baseball game have steadily increased over the last several decades. According to Team Marketing Report, the average cost for a group of four to go to a game in 2014, including parking, tickets, one hot dog for each person, one beer for each of two adults, one soda for each of two children, and two programs was $179.39. Data compiled by the Society for American Baseball Research (SABR) show that a similar experience in 1991 was $77.89 ($135.38 in 2014 dollars) and in 2004 was $95.80 ($153.25 in 2014 dollars). That is an increase of 32.5 percent over the past twenty-three years and 17 percent over the last decade,[38] occurring at a time when wages for most Americans have been stagnant at best. Another way to think about this is that until the late 1990s, baseball was a relatively affordable form of entertainment that competed with movies or affordable restaurants. Today, baseball is priced to compete with concerts, theater performances, and fine dining, luxuries that most Americans can rarely, if ever, afford.

Rising prices are not, however, the only reason that being a fan is more expensive than ever. MLB seems ever more committed to, and more strategic in, its constant efforts to separate fans from their money. Thirty years ago, a particularly intense fan might own two caps, one jersey, and maybe a jacket and a few T-shirts from his or her favorite team. The caps and perhaps one of the T-shirts might have been freebies from a promotional day at the park. Today, equally intense fans might own three or more caps, several jerseys, and various other team-related paraphernalia from their favorite team. Teams, and MLB in general, are relentless in their efforts to produce more memorabilia of special products to market. Examples include several versions of a team cap, special caps for spring training and each round of the postseason and the All-Star Game, jerseys for great players from the past and present, and T-shirts sold to promote milestones, postseason series, anniversaries, and the like.

The cost of buying all these trinkets, caps, and articles of clothing as well as attending a few games is prohibitive for all but the wealthiest fans. Nonetheless, many fans make irrational economic decisions and spend this money, using funds that otherwise might be dedicated to paying down debt or saving for retirement. In this regard, excessive consumerism is not very unusual in a culture where that kind of behavior is ubiquitous, but it is still not rational. Should consumer behaviors evolve as economic gaps become more hardened, MLB will lose important revenue streams.

Conclusion: Can Baseball Adapt?

Over the past century or so, baseball has proven itself to be very good at adapting to changing media and other technological, demographic, and cultural variables. By integrating the Internet in so many forms into its product and by expanding and moving west in the 1950s and 1960s, MLB has been able to grow into the lucrative business that is the biggest, most profitable, and most famous baseball organization in the world.

MLB has also been lucky. As a sport that, more than any other major American sport, lends itself to radio, it was able to build a national brand before television was invented and became widespread. Similarly, its biggest celebrity, a figure who still looms larger than life in American history, played in the media capital of the world.

The challenge facing baseball is to remain a favorite form of entertainment despite a changing culture of celebrity; an aging fan base; a different economic climate than what existed during the middle of the twentieth century, baseball's era of greatest dominance; and new means of consuming entertainment that disrupt existing models for generating revenue.

Baseball cannot assume that cable contracts generating more than $1 billion per year, the backbone of the current era of MLB prosperity, will continue for more than a few more years. Efforts to make up this entire revenue stream from selling subscriptions to MLB.TV or similar excellent products are not at all guaranteed to succeed, particularly in a climate of stagnant wages for many and the expectation that entertainment is growing cheaper. Continuing to raise ticket prices to make up for this revenue is an equally risky strategy. This changing media culture also threatens the concept of baseball celebrity that, going back at least to the days of Babe Ruth, has been a central part of baseball's appeal to younger fans.

6

....

DIRTY KURT AND
BAM BAM

n 1976, Topps, which at that time was the only major producer of baseball cards, issued a fun card featuring Milwaukee Brewers' backup infielder Kurt Bevacqua, also known as "Dirty Kurt," as the "1975 Joe Garagiola/Bazooka Bubble Gum Champ." Baseball fans of a certain age may remember that card, although the identity of the runner-up, the late Johnny Oates, is less frequently recalled. The card shows Bevacqua straining to blow the biggest possible bubble. The photo appears to be taken just a split second before the pink sugary concoction collapsed onto Bevacqua's face. The card has become a favorite of collectors and those interested in the quirky side of our national pastime's history. Bevacqua somehow lasted fifteen years in the big leagues with the Indians, the Royals, the Pirates, the Brewers, the Rangers, and the Padres. He hit a very unimpressive .236 with only twenty-seven home runs over the course of his career but managed to hit .412 with two home runs as the designated hitter (DH) when his Padres team lost the 1984 World Series in five games to the Detroit Tigers. Interestingly, the owner of Bevacqua's Milwaukee Brewers when he won the bubble-blowing contest was none other than Bud Selig. A few years after the end of Selig's tenure as commissioner, the question of whether he left baseball facing another bubble, one with much weightier implications than those blown by Bevacqua, Oates, and others in 1975, cannot be ignored.

There are reasons to think Selig left the game in the best financial shape in its history, as ticket sales and television contracts are up, and great and exciting players come from many different countries, offering significant competition and more parity than many realize. Yet there are also reasons for concern. Most of baseball's revenue comes from a media model that may not work by the time the current cable contracts expire following the 2021 season and from selling expensive tickets that frequently go unused. Fewer young people are playing the game regularly, and for many families a trip to the ballpark is now an expense that they cannot really afford. If baseball is in the middle of a bubble and that bubble bursts, it will not mean the end of baseball, professional baseball, or even big league baseball, but it will change much about how the game is played at the highest levels.

Hensley Meulens shared Bevacqua's inability to hit well at a big league level but otherwise had a very different career in baseball. Meulens, known to many inside baseball as "Bam Bam," was one of the top prospects in the New York Yankees' system in the late 1980s. He was a hard-hitting third baseman who could also play first, left field, and right field. Baseball America listed Meulens among the Yankees' top prospects every year from 1987, when he was just nineteen years old, through 1991. He was ranked first among all Yankees' minor leaguers in both 1988 and 1989.[1]

Meulens never made it big with the Yankees. He played parts of five seasons, from 1989 to 1993, with the team but could never hit big league pitching, compiling a .211/.290/.344 line in 505 plate appearances over those years.[2] After failing to become a star with the Yankees, Meulens spent three seasons playing in Japan, where he established himself as a decent but not great power hitter. Meulens briefly returned to the big leagues in 1997–1998 but did not hit much during those years either. After that, he played very briefly in Korea and Mexico.

On the surface, Meulens's story is not that unusual. He was one of many players who were not quite good enough for Major League Baseball (MLB) but did fine and made a bit of money playing in

Japan, but that is not where Meulens's story ends. Since 2010, Meulens has been the hitting coach for the San Francisco Giants and has helped that team win three World Series. Meulens also demonstrates how global baseball can be. He is a native of Curaçao, his mother was Dominican, and he has served as a coach and a manager for the Dutch World Baseball Classic (WBC) teams. Meulens has also played in Japan, so he has strong ties to three traditional baseball strongholds as well as one of significant potential growth. In addition, Meulens speaks the three most important baseball languages—English, Japanese, and Spanish—as well as Dutch and Papiamento, a language spoken in Curaçao.

Meulens, who has been knighted in the Netherlands, has played a major role in the growth of baseball in Curaçao and in building links between that small island and the rest of the baseball world. Bruce Jenkins of the *San Francisco Chronicle* describes Meulens and his native country:

> Curacao has become a hotbed of baseball talent, and Meulens is largely responsible for the revolution. As the first from his country to reach the major leagues, he oversees the youth baseball leagues and conducts annual clinics that have helped develop Andrelton Simmons, Jurickson Profar, Didi Gregorious, Jair Jurrjens, Kenley Jansen and many others thriving in American pro ball—all of this from a 171-square-mile area with a population of around 145,000. Meulens managed the Netherlands' team to two shocking victories over Cuba in the 2013 World Baseball Classic, and most everyone thinks he's destined to manage in the big leagues someday.[3]

Meulens's broad international experience, relationships, and identities are illustrative of one possible future of baseball, one that is increasingly global and links the sport in the Caribbean, Asia, and North America.

If MLB in its current form—characterized by extremely high salaries; limited to twenty-six metropolitan areas, all in the United States and Canada; and holding a virtual monopoly on the world's

144 · CHAPTER 6

best players—cannot survive, it will adapt as it always has. The all-white version of big league baseball that was played only in the Northeast and the Midwest, and almost never televised, at the end of World War II could not have survived another twenty years, so changes were made. Similarly, the expansion of the play-offs and the introduction of interleague play that Selig implemented early in his tenure as commissioner also dramatically changed the game.

Big league baseball may be entering another period where it has to adapt to survive, but it could move in several directions as it adapts to evolutions in technology and media and to broader changes in society, the economy, and the culture.

Collapse, Survival, and Change

If an American from not that long ago—say, 1982, the season after baseball's first major strike, when the Cardinals beat the Brewers in the World Series and when cocaine was about to become a major problem in baseball—woke up from a thirty-four-year nap, she would be amazed by, among other things, such new technologies as cell phones and the Internet and puzzled by such social changes as marriage equality and medical marijuana. However, she would probably be equally struck by the absence of many things from American society. Institutions that were central to the fabric of American life in the early 1980s, including newspapers, retail stores, malls, and the nightly news, are all either disappearing or at the periphery of American life. The time traveler would also be struck by the dramatic and ongoing changes in our education and health care structures. Once she figured out how to read the papers on her new phone or tablet, she would be most amazed to learn that the Soviet Union, which in 1982 was the second-most-powerful country in the world and the chief rival to the United States in all political and military matters, had also ceased to exist. To many Americans today, these developments seem like the inevitable result of new technologies, new economies, and political evolution, but the journey from unimaginable to inevitable is often very brief. History, particularly recent history, is riddled with institutions that once seemed eternal but whose subsequent collapse seemed unavoidable only a decade or so later. Baseball might be no different. The complete collapse of MLB is extremely unlikely, but it cannot be ruled out entirely. MLB is an unusual entity, as it is a company, an industry, and a cultural institution rolled into one. That position is extremely valuable to MLB, but it can also be somewhat precarious, as it makes MLB potentially vulnerable in many different ways. MLB, for example, could lose its antitrust exemption, making it possible for other leagues and teams to form. This would not happen immediately, but being forced to play by the rules of normal competition could have an effect on player contracts, collective bargaining, and particularly the minor league system.

It is also possible that the next economic downturn could be severe enough and sufficiently poorly timed that it could cause great economic distress to a few teams. Baseball escaped relatively unscathed from the recession that began in 2008, but it raised problems for some teams. The Mets' owner Fred Wilpon, for example, lost millions of dollars investing with Bernie Madoff, who fleeced investors through a Ponzi scheme. Additionally, the Wilpons were accused of continuing to do business with Madoff despite knowing that he was fleecing others, and they even structured Mets' contracts so that deferred payments would be invested with Madoff.[4]

The Mets, and the Wilpon family's ownership of the Mets, survived this scandal, but had it been much worse, it would have created significant challenges for the Mets. As it was, the Mets had to cut payroll and were unable to compete for free agents, or do much on the field, from about 2009 to 2013. Had even three big league teams been hit at the same time by Madoff or any of the other economic problems around the great recession, the functioning of MLB could have been threatened.

Baseball could also collapse as a result of the acceleration of the trends discussed earlier in this work, including the decline of cable, the changing nature of youth sports, the inability to attract young fans, an unsustainable price structure, and the like. If that should happen, the way MLB responds will be of great import. If MLB handles it the way it integrated baseball and adapted to new Internet technologies, baseball will be fine. If, however, MLB responds to

146 · CHAPTER 6

these changes the way it responded to the problem of performance-enhancing drug (PED) abuse, baseball could be imperiled.

Jared Diamond's 2005 exploration of why societies collapse posits that "failures of group decision-making on the parts of whole societies or other groups" have contributed to collapses of various different societies over the course of history. Diamond fleshes this theory out with a "road map of factors contributing to failures of group decision-making." He then describes the four factors: "First of all, a group may fail to anticipate a problem before the problem actually arrives. Second, when the problem does arrive, the group may fail to perceive it. Then, after they perceive it, they may fail even to try to solve it. Finally, they may try to solve it but may not succeed."[5]

MLB's response to PED usage in particular fits this structure. PED use was not anticipated in the early 1990s, when baseball was still recovering from the drug scandals of the 1980s, nor was it noticed when it first arrived, as PED users, most notably Mark McGwire and Sammy Sosa, were celebrated well into the late 1990s, when PED abuse was already a big problem. Once it was finally perceived, efforts to solve the problem were not successful. Stop-and-go and incomplete approaches have contributed to the lack of closure on the issue. On the other hand, by almost any measure, PEDs are much less of an issue today than they were five, ten, or twenty years ago. More significantly, despite responding to the crisis so badly, baseball did not collapse. On the contrary, by most criteria, it is now in better financial shape than it was when the PED problems first started.

PED abuse did not lead to the collapse of MLB, but there is never a guarantee that the next battery of problems will not be misplayed with more dire consequences for the game. While it is possible to imagine that baseball could be blindsided and thus radically mishandle the problems raised by the current changes in society, media, and culture, recent evidence suggests this is unlikely. Moreover, MLB's survival of the PED period despite initially ignoring it and then never quite crafting a holistic strategy for confronting it suggests that MLB is too resilient to collapse entirely anytime soon. Complete collapse is thus an unlikely scenario, but this does not mean everything in baseball will stay the same. It is likely that baseball will evolve and change, surviving in one form or another. The question of whether that evolution will constitute survival of MLB as we know it remains subjective.

Below are five scenarios for baseball's future. These scenarios are based on the changes in society, economics, and media that will have an impact on baseball in the next decades. These are not proposals on how to fix baseball's problems, because baseball is not yet broken in any profound sense, nor is it in need of rescuing. But it finds itself in a period of changes, many of which cannot be controlled from the commissioner's or any other baseball office.

Scenario One: Baseball Becomes Smaller

For most of its history, baseball may have played a major role in the public consciousness, but it was not always a big industry in the way it is today. Until almost the twenty-first century, few regular season games sold out; players were accustomed to playing in half-empty stadiums; most games were not televised; salaries were high, but not exponentially higher than those of ordinary Americans; and MLB was not a magnet for international baseball talent. Many of the best young American athletes, particularly in the second half of the twentieth century, focused their attention on other sports. Baseball during that time was a smaller sport. Today it is likely that of the thousand or so best baseball players in the world, around 90 percent are either playing in MLB, in the high minors, or in college waiting to be drafted, but that number was lower before top Asian players found their way to MLB beginning in the mid-1990s. It was, of course, much lower before 1947, when segregation kept African Americans and dark-skinned Latinos out of the big leagues.

While baseball, like anything else, cannot go backward in time, the industry could become smaller in the coming decades. If baseball is unable to maintain its fan base because of competition from other or new sports, pricing itself out of some markets, or a breakdown of intergenerational fan development, it could find itself having to downsize. If baseball were to lose its mass fan base, it would have to make financial adjustments, but it would also have strengths on which to draw. Probably more than any other sport, baseball has a deeply dedicated group of supporters who love the game and are willing to spend money and time to support their baseball habit. This fan base could form the nucleus of support for baseball's next iteration as a niche sport. A Harris Poll from January 2015 shows that "pro football is the top pick among 32% of sports fans, while baseball only garners 'favorite' status among half as many Americans (16%)." The poll also outlines, in very broad terms, the demographics of baseball fans:

> As for those who believe home runs are number one, the largest percentages can also be found among Easterners (23%), Liberals (22%)[,] and Baby-Boomers (20%). Meanwhile, those who consider baseball their favorite sport are less abundant amidst Midwesterners (12%), Millennials (12%), and adults with children in their households (10%).[6]

While these numbers may not look encouraging for baseball, they also do not tell the whole story. The depth of baseball fan culture is much greater than that of other sports. One indicator is the sports section of any American bookstore, where the number of baseball books is usually at least twice the number of all other sports books combined. No other American sport has trading cards, card collectors, memorabilia, and the like at the level of baseball. The Society for American Baseball Research (SABR) is an organization of scholars of baseball that produces a journal that would meet most rigorous academic standards, with a wide variety of articles on baseball as it relates to history, economics, law, and other topics. Baseball may have a smaller mass market, but the market it has is more intense and has deeper pockets than that of any other sport—at least, that is the assumption upon which baseball would have to operate if it were to continue losing its mass appeal.

In this scenario, baseball would pivot away from maintaining a mass fan base, something that for the most part no longer exists in the television market anyway, and focus more on devising strategies about how to most effectively monetize the deep passion for the game held by a smaller number of Americans. This could mean selling higher-priced advanced media products to some fans that would give access to, for example, more in-depth analysis, minor league games, archival footage, and, if baseball wanted to get more creative, oral histories and old highlight reels. It could also mean devising other ways of marketing the game's history and cultural significance. The grandpa demographic may be small and aging out, but it is also affluent and willing to spend money. There is currently a lot of money in baseball-related commodities, such as memorabilia, that does not directly enrich MLB at all. That could change in this scenario.

If MLB became smaller, player salaries and team profits would be curtailed as a result of declining lower attendance, declining cable contracts, and the inability of MLB to replace that revenue through its own Internet-based products. For fans, however, the impact would be less clear. A smaller MLB would probably mean more affordable tickets and continued access to the same new technology that has added so much to the game in recent years. For the average fan, of course, the knowledge that the top star was earning only $25 million as opposed to $30 million, that attendance figures were decreasing, and that wealthy owners were getting only a little bit wealthier would not be significant.

The only way this would affect fans would be if declining revenue led to salaries that declined enough to affect talent on the field. If the best young American athletes were a little less drawn to baseball than to basketball and football and the best players from affluent countries, such as Japan and Korea, did not have the opportunity that they now have to increase their income by coming to MLB, the quality of play on the field would suffer.

But unless revenue shrank by a very significant amount—say, 30 percent or more—this decline would be only slightly perceptible even through the highly sophisticated tools some fans use to analyze the game. For example, it is possible that over time the average speed of a fastball would be slightly reduced or that the number of pitchers able to throw more than one hundred miles per hour would shrink in a similar manner. However, for most fans, particularly those watching the game with the naked eye, it would be almost impossible to notice these changes.

Moreover, the extent to which the chance of making perhaps 10 or even 20 percent less money than players today make would have any impact on the decisions of young athletes is not clear. Even in a smaller and less affluent MLB, salaries would still be much higher than that of the average worker and would still provide extraordinary financial incentives to pursue a career as a baseball player. It is hard to imagine an aspiring young ballplayer in Japan, the Dominican Republic, or California thinking to himself, "Well, the top pitcher got only a seven-year, $140-million contract last year as a free agent, so I think I'll give up baseball."

If MLB becomes smaller in this way, its position within the global baseball context might change. It would probably be less global, continuing to draw top talent from Venezuela, the Dominican Republic, and elsewhere in Latin America, but perhaps it would no longer compete as much for the best Korean and Japanese players. Those players might find it equally lucrative to remain in their home countries.

Similarly, a smaller MLB that had fewer resources to commit to expanding to new markets might put less emphasis on, for example, playing some games in Asia or Australia, developing new markets for talent and fans in parts of the world where baseball has not traditionally been popular, and even in continuing to promote the WBC.

In this scenario, the basic structures framing the game—two leagues, a long regular season followed by a month or so of postseason play, no barnstorming, and no North American leagues competing with MLB—would continue, but there would be less money in all of these things, which would help ensure that baseball would maintain its unique role in American culture and its continuity of stories, records, and history.

Baseball's ascendancy in the larger American culture and the story of the consolidation of dominance by MLB were never the same thing. The former occurred independently of the latter and predated the latter by around a half a century. Baseball's role in Americana, as a symbol of hope, lost youth, aging, relations between fathers and sons, and pretty much everything else in the American gestalt, will not be threatened or undermined by the Philadelphia

Phillies' or the Seattle Mariners' paying less for their top players and receiving less money from cable contracts.

A smaller big league baseball would also be a more normal, in a historical sense, environment for the game, one consistent with how MLB functioned for most of the twentieth century. The economic reasons for this scenario are clear: if revenues shrink slightly but noticeably, baseball will be overextended, and the easiest and safest response will be to trim baseball's sails a bit without significantly changing how the game is played on the field or experienced by fans.

Although this scenario may be the simplest and easiest to achieve, several strong factors will make it difficult for baseball to pursue this course. First, it would require baseball to pursue more modest goals and a more risk-averse approach to the future. The billionaires who own baseball teams and determine their futures are very unlikely to embrace such an approach after decades when the mantra of growth and expansion has been unquestioned.

Second, becoming smaller is, at least in part, an effort to turn back the clock. Baseball already has a complex relationship with its past. The game can seem burdened by a degree of nostalgia that is at times excessive, unhealthy, and bizarre. For decades now, former ballplayers have told us that the game was played better when they were playing. Sepia-toned montages from years ago precede many televised big games and are reasonably common on stadium screens, particularly for such teams as the Cardinals, the Red Sox, the Giants, and the Yankees that have storied histories.

There is also a strong strain of denial that is part of baseball's relationship with its history. Jackie Robinson is celebrated every year, but the segregation that Robinson ended is rarely examined. The 1950s are frequently referred to as the Golden Age of baseball, but the poor attendance figures from those years are rarely mentioned. During those years, few teams ever drew more than 1.5 million fans in a year. Some, such as the Senators, the Reds, and the Braves before they moved to Milwaukee, rarely drew half that. Even the Yankees, the dominant team of that era, drew more than two million only once in the 1950s.

The Brooklyn Dodgers won six pennants between 1947 and 1957, their final eleven years in Brooklyn. Their best attendance during that time was 1,807,526 in 1947, during Robinson's historic rookie season. However, the Dodgers did not come close to drawing 1.5 million any year after 1949, before they moved to Los Angeles following the 1957 season.

Nobody around baseball is going to advocate for moving the game back to what it was a few decades ago, particularly as doing so would mean lower revenues for owners and lower salaries for players, but it could happen anyway. In the long term, it could also stabilize the relationship between fans and their teams, advance the long-term financial stability of the game, and largely enhance the quality of the product, but those would be secondary considerations for many baseball people.

Scenario Two: The Next Level for International Baseball

Most baseball fans, and perhaps most Americans, who travel abroad invariably get asked, "Why is it called the World Series if only American teams compete?"[7] Sometimes this question is asked out of genuine curiosity, sometimes as a way to argue that baseball is a uniquely American pastime, and sometimes simply as a critique of American arrogance. It is a good story, but not true, that the World Series was named after the old *New York World-Telegram*, a now defunct newspaper. It is not known for certain why it was first called the World Series, but that is what it has been called for well over a century.

The question, while annoying and petulant, still has some legitimacy. One answer is that the best baseball, and the best baseball players, are playing MLB in the United States and Toronto, and that since the nineteenth century, the highest quality of competitive baseball has been played in the United States. The leagues in Japan, Korea, Venezuela, and elsewhere are good, but the best teams in those leagues are not as good as the best, and in most cases the worst, American and National League teams. The WBC has become the biggest and most enduring international baseball tournament, but it still does not draw all the best players, and it is a tournament between countries, not teams.

If the globalization that has changed the game so much, and so positively, in the past twenty years continues, baseball may have to adapt to being a qualitatively different kind of international game than it is now. Thus, the second scenario for the future of MLB is for baseball to become more international, expanding to cities outside the United States and drawing more of the players, fans, and revenue in those countries.

If size, wealth, infrastructure, interest in the game, and political constraints are taken into consideration, five to ten cities outside the United States and Canada would be excellent places to locate a big league baseball team. These include San Juan, Puerto Rico; Santo Domingo, Dominican Republic; Tokyo, which could easily host two teams, and Osaka, Japan; Taipei, Taiwan; and Seoul, South Korea. Political issues make the idea of big league baseball in Havana, Cuba, or Caracas, Venezuela, difficult, but if the politics change, those two cities would also be good places to eventually host big league baseball.

The idea of expanding big league baseball in this way is dramatic and would not happen easily. Nonetheless, it is also a natural extension of what MLB has been doing over the last decades and of the general trends toward globalization in baseball and elsewhere. In the twenty-first century, most businesses are not limited to one country, particularly in the fields of tech and entertainment, the intersection at which MLB increasingly lies.

As baseball writer Joe Sheehan points out, such cities as "Milwaukee, Cincinnati, Detroit—cities that were large cities two generations ago are small markets now and they're not getting any bigger. . . . Baseball has to figure out where it needs to put baseball teams to best maximize interest and revenue." Sheehan also notes, "I don't think there are any markets left in the United States that you can go to without having the same problems you have in Milwaukee or Kansas City." Although Sheehan is skeptical about the possibility of MLB's becoming a global league anytime soon, the problem of where to go for the next big baseball market is real, and the only answers may be outside the United States.[8]

As baseball becomes more popular outside the United States, in traditional strongholds and in newer baseball-playing countries, the feasibility and logic of having the game at its most elite level played in two countries (but mostly one) will break down even more. Fans in the Dominican Republic, the country that on a per-capita basis produces the most and best baseball players in the world, or in Japan, a country with a huge population and one of the world's largest economies, will not remain satisfied with seeing the best players from their country go to the United States or with seeing baseball in their country as, in a global sense, second tier. This problem will become even more acute as countries such as the Dominican Republic—and, if the politics change, possibly Cuba and Venezuela—continue to grow economically, thus increasing the market appeal for MLB and the demands from middle-class fans in those countries.

Making MLB truly international in this way would raise innumerable logistical questions, but if MLB addressed these questions the right way, it would revolutionize how baseball is played and potentially blaze a path for other professional sports in the twenty-first century. Moreover, figuring out how to resolve these logistical questions would lead to new markets and increased revenue, but doing so would also force MLB to change dramatically and ultimately not survive in its current form.

If MLB had teams in East Asia and the Caribbean—perhaps only in Korea, Japan, Puerto Rico, and the Dominican Republic at first—it would be the only truly international league. International competition in other sports is mostly oriented around specific tournaments, such as the Euro Cup, the World Cup, and the Olympics, as well as numerous lower-profile events, such as the Pan American Games. A league that played a regular and extensive schedule, drawing on players from twenty or more countries, with teams in at least four countries and possibly three continents would be a newer and much more significant development. This change would put MLB on the cutting edge of international sports and, correspondingly, position it to access unprecedented revenue.

The first, and perhaps most obvious, obstacles this type of league would face are those of distance and time zones. This problem would be particularly acute if MLB expanded to Asia. Tokyo, Taipei, and Seoul are a long way from the West Coast of the United States and even farther from the rest of North America. Flying there is expensive, although given how much teams spend on travel, this is a nonissue. More importantly, such travel requires a great deal of time and would force players to wrestle with a degree of jet lag that is much more severe than the kind players now get from a season of flying around North America.

This scenario raises particular problems for baseball that are different from those of other sports, because baseball has a long season that requires teams to play almost every day for six months. As Sheehan points out, "You can't give a team a week off," as the National Basketball Association (NBA) and the National Football League (NFL) do after their teams travel abroad for games. These problems can be ameliorated but not eliminated. One way to address this problem would be to expand to two cities in both the Latin America region and in Asia. These expansions could occur at the same time or a few years apart, but the key would be to add more than just one city at first in each of these regions.

If, for example, MLB added teams in Seoul and in Tokyo, or in Tokyo and in Osaka, visiting teams could play both those teams during one trip. Thus, the flight to Asia would be for an eight-game or possibly even ten-game set, played over a period of about twelve or fourteen days. This scenario would help players experience jet lag and other travel-related logistical problems less acutely. For teams from the West Coast, this trip would be very manageable; for teams from elsewhere in North America, the Asia road trip could be tacked on to a West Coast road trip to make it easier for the players and to use the travel time more efficiently. Teams outside the West Coast could rotate so they would not have to make this difficult and distant journey every year. As more teams were added in Asia, the length of the Asia road trips for North America teams could be expanded.

Traveling would be a bigger problem for the Asian teams, as they would be at a disadvantage if they had to frequently fly to North America. This problem could be addressed by scheduling those teams for longer home stands and fewer, but longer, road trips. This could make for a more arduous schedule, but the advantages of long home stands would balance that out.

A similar approach could be taken for teams in the Caribbean. The travel-related logistics would be much less severe as such countries as the Dominican Republic and Venezuela, or even Mexico and places like Puerto Rico, are much closer to the United States than Asia is. However, for teams from the West Coast, it would necessary to visit all Caribbean cities in one road trip, probably as part of a longer East Coast trip.

Because baseball is already somewhat international, many of the financial and legal issues that would confront greater expansion have already, to a lesser degree, been addressed by MLB. Teams are familiar with how to secure visas for players. Issues of Canadian tax law, for example, are familiar to all agents and many players. However, expanding to more cities in more countries outside the United States would make these challenges exponentially more difficult. Questions such as how to get a visa for a Panamanian player to play in Taipei, in which currency Japanese players playing in Santo Domingo or American players in Seoul would be paid, which countries would tax which players, and the like will create ample challenges for MLB's lawyers and accountants as well as those for each team. That said, these complicated questions are no more complex than those confronted by any multinational corporation or industry in which labor and capital are both mobile and transnational.

Another battery of logistical issues are more specific to baseball and baseball players. Today, while big league baseball is, in many respects, a global enterprise, it is also primarily an American one. A majority of players are American. The game's biggest fan base, by far, is American. Although Spanish is clearly baseball's second language, big league baseball is still conducted in English. Expanding big league baseball to cities outside the United States and Canada would challenge this status quo.

A global MLB would raise a lot of structural baseball-related issues. For example, currently amateur and youth players are treated differently, depending on where they live. Americans and Puerto Ricans are drafted by big league teams. Players from Japanese and Korean teams are part of a posting process, while Latin American players are eligible to be signed at sixteen years of age and are not subject to meaningful limits on spending or other constraints from big league teams. Players from Taiwan can come to the United States as essentially free agents.

Similarly, while players from all over the world have generally been happy to come to the United States and play in the big leagues, it is possible that American players would be less enthused about playing for teams in Tokyo, Santo Domingo, and other foreign cities where it would be hard to learn the culture, bring the family, and the like. For a young American player who was not well traveled, the idea of playing in Santo Domingo, Tokyo, or Caracas could be quite unsettling. In some cases, there would also be concerns about safety. Yet for many young players, the money and the opportunity to play big league ball would probably outweigh concerns about being based in a foreign country.

A related problem is that teams based outside the United States might have trouble signing veteran American players as free agents. However, the free-agent market has always played out in an unequal way. Big-market teams, such as the Yankees, the Dodgers, and the Angels, have long dominated their markets, while small-market teams, such as the Royals and the Brewers, sign fewer expensive free agents.

Some veterans, however, would be very happy to play outside the United States. For a Dominican player, being able to play in Santo Domingo, or for a Puerto Rican player, San Juan, would mean being closer to home, enjoying a lower cost of living, and not wrestling with a language barrier. This could lead to a global league in which the teams, despite drawing from the same pool of players, could each take on a local flavor. The back end of the Tokyo team's bullpen might be largely Japanese, while the utility infielders in teams in Latin America would probably come from that region.

If baseball expanded in this way, it would be almost impossible to continue the dominance by Americans—specifically, white Americans—in management and executive positions in the game. Teams in foreign cities would probably be owned by people from those places who would bring in baseball people with whom they were comfortable. This would mean that American players would have to grow comfortable playing for Japanese or Dominican managers in a way that has never been the case before. The possibility of cultural clashes or ethnic tensions would be very real and an issue baseball would have to be prepared to confront, but again, the payoff for getting it right would be very high.

Countless other baseball questions would have to be addressed that are less logistical and more structural. First, MLB already has a long season and thirty teams. Adding teams would create scheduling problems, as the season would have to be lengthened to give more teams the opportunity to play each other, shortened to allow for more travel and an expanded postseason, or restructured so that traditional rivals could continue to play each other frequently, while teams from other divisions or league played each other less frequently.

The first option is extremely unlikely to happen—there is almost no support for lengthening an already very long season. No team wants to play 180 regular-season games, begin the season two weeks earlier, or end it two weeks later. This change would be exhausting for the players, wreak havoc on the record books, and create major climate-related scheduling problems, as it is rarely possible to play baseball in the Northeast or in the Midwest before early April or after late October.

There would be much more support for shortening the season and expanding the postseason. Some have already called for this. In one of his first interviews after becoming commissioner in 2015, Rob Manfred said, "I don't think length of season is a topic that can't ever be discussed. I don't think it would be impossible to go back to 154 [games]."[9] Shortening the season would allow for a more expanded postseason and more rest for tired players, particularly pitchers, but it would in no way address the problems related to travel or expansion. If baseball were to expand to foreign countries, shortening the season would only exacerbate the ample logistical problems already associated with this possibility.

The simplest solution for baseball would be to rework the schedule and alignments so that teams played within their divisions most of the time and had fewer games outside their divisions. If, for example, baseball added four teams in Seoul, Tokyo, San Juan, and Santo Domingo, one league could have three divisions of six teams, while the other would have one division with six teams and two with five teams. As more teams were added, these numbers could be equalized. Traditional rivals, such as the Yankees and the Red Sox or the Giants and the Dodgers, would be kept in the same divisions. The details would be flexible, but this general framework is probably the only workable one.

The postseason would become difficult because of travel and distance. A League Championship Series (LCS) or World Series between the Cardinals and Seoul or the Yankees and Tokyo would require a lot of travel for a short series and necessitate spreading a seven-game series over at least eleven games. This would change the nature of the postseason, as it would allow teams to rely on only two starting pitchers for most of the postseason. Breaking up the travel differently so that a seven-game series was conducted in a four-and-three format rather than a two-three-two format, necessitating only one trip between cities per series, would help address this problem.

Placing big league teams in such cities as Tokyo, Seoul, and Santo Domingo would be an unmistakable assertion of MLB's hegemony, one that would have severe implications for existing teams in those cities and leagues in such countries as Japan, Korea, and the Dominican Republic. The steady expansion of MLB and the consolidation of all professional baseball in the United States under that framework has already led to the decline of barnstorming and semi-pro ball as important parts of the baseball landscape in the United States. It has also contributed to the end of the Negro Leagues and of vibrant, semi-independent minor leagues, most prominently the Pacific Coast League (PCL) as it once operated.

The Nippon Professional Baseball (NPB), Korean, Taiwanese, and Dominican Leagues could face similar prospects if MLB were to expand to become truly international. These leagues, and the owners and players who are making a lot of money through them, would likely resist this change. Leagues in the Caribbean could still coexist with an expanded MLB, because they include high-profile winter leagues that play when it is too cold for baseball in most of the United States or East Asia.

MLB has already begun to weaken these leagues by luring away many of their best players. For decades, Caribbean baseball has been primarily a winter event, allowing the best players from Puerto Rico, the Dominican Republican, and Venezuela who spend their summers playing in North America to participate. Asian baseball leagues have been less affected, but the presence of such stars as Ichiro Suzuki, Hideki Matsui, Masahiro Tanaka, Yu Darvish, Hee-Seop Choi, Chan Ho Park, and Chien-Ming Wang in MLB has weakened baseball leagues in Asia over the past ten to twenty years. The departure of these prominent stars as well as numerous other players from their Asian leagues to MLB has affected the quality of play, but it has not undermined the leagues more generally.

Putting an MLB team in Tokyo might have a different effect. There are already five teams in greater Tokyo,[10] a metropolitan region of more than thirty-five million. One more team would not put the other five out of business, but it would create competition for them. MLB teams in such countries as Korea or Taiwan would draw top players from those places and would inevitably sap fan enthusiasm and interest for existing leagues. The MLB teams would probably become the highest-profile teams and generate the most fan interest, but they would not offer enough baseball to meet the needs of an entire national or metropolitan fan base. A team in Seoul, for example, would not be enough baseball for all the fans in Korea. Thus, these nationally based leagues could probably survive by also functioning as high minor leagues, producing talent for the expanded MLB.

Clearly, these baseball-related questions are not simple, but baseball has addressed similar questions in the past. In the middle of the twentieth century, travel to the West Coast seemed very daunting. The PCL never was the same after the Dodgers and the Giants moved west, but it transitioned into a successful, but not at all independent, minor league. Night baseball, the introduction of new technologies, and other innovations have also required baseball to adapt and make major changes.

The scenario of making MLB more genuinely international by putting franchises in major cities of countries with strong baseball interests, such as the Dominican Republic and Japan, could lead to a larger international presence for baseball. If baseball's popularity continues to grow in a small handful of European countries, it is possible that in twenty to thirty years, MLB could award a franchise to Amsterdam, to a major German or Italian city, or to cities in other countries, such as Australia and China, where baseball is growing rapidly. Expanding beyond the baseball belt to sports-crazy countries, such as Australia; secondary baseball markets, such as the Netherlands; or China, the world's most populated country and a still-expanding economic powerhouse, would make baseball a truly global sport.

This scenario of a truly global MLB is, at best, several years in the future, but it is not impossible. Moreover, it may be the only direction in which big league baseball can move if it is to remain a major economic force and a cohesive league. The option of trying to contain MLB in the United States and Canada, maintain enormous revenue and a global talent base, and limit competition from older and newer baseball countries is probably even less likely.

Scenario Three: MLB Loses Its Hegemony and Becomes a Hybrid

During the last two or three decades, MLB has dominated professional baseball in the United States, and even internationally, to a much greater extent than ever before. The early and mid-twentieth-century baseball quilt of winter barnstorming; independent minor leagues; strong semipro teams about whom many people cared; Negro Leagues; third major leagues, such as the Federal League; rumors of new leagues, such as the Continental League, that existed alongside the big leagues; and affiliated minor league teams has not existed for half a century or more. The best talent in the world is now more likely to be found on big league ball fields than at any time in the past, a fact that may become even truer if Cuba opens up more to the United States.

This system works well now—fans get a great product, and MLB ownership and players are able to make unprecedented amounts of money. However, as changes inside and outside baseball begin to threaten this setup, it is possible that new revenue sources will become available to baseball players and even team owners, or that baseball will become sufficiently strong and lucrative in other countries to force MLB to do something. Thus, a hybrid of MLB and other baseball leagues and activities, much like what characterized the first half of the twentieth century, could reemerge.

This hybrid would, of course, not look the same as baseball from the 1920s or 1940s. Segregation would not return, teams from neighboring towns and factories would not play against each other in front of large crowds, and Mike Trout and Clayton Kershaw would not face off against each other in dusty fields in Oklahoma or Nebraska. Nonetheless, MLB's supremacy could slowly give way to modern-day equivalents of this kind of baseball.

One way to envision this possibility is through the WBC. The WBC has largely been a success, but many of the game's best players, particularly the game's best pitchers, do not participate. For example, of the pitchers with the ten highest Wins above Replacement (WAR) in 2012, only two, R. A. Dickey and Gio Gonzalez, participated in the WBC in the spring of 2013. The National League (NL) Most Valuable Player (MVP) from that year, Buster Posey, also skipped the WBC that spring. These individual decisions all made sense. Pitchers need to be very careful about avoiding arm injury; Posey had caught a lot in 2012, and his team, the Giants, was concerned about putting too much stress on the leg he had broken in early 2011.

In a 2013 article, Jon Michaud describes the problem of having so many top players miss the WBC:

> W.B.C. organizers are touting the array of major-league stars who will be participating, including triple-crown winner Miguel Cabrera (Venezuela), Joey Votto (Canada), Adrian Gonzalez (Mexico), Jose Reyes (Dominican Republic), Carlos Beltran (Puerto Rico), Gio Gonzalez, Giancarlo Stanton, Ryan Braun, and David Wright (U.S.A.). It's an impressive list, but the roster of players passing up the opportunity to don a national uniform this spring is even stronger. Buster Posey, Felix Hernandez, Justin Verlander, Albert Pujols, Ichiro Suzuki, Clayton Kershaw, Stephen Strasburg, Johnny Cueto, and Johan Santana are all giving the W.B.C. a pass. Those big-name deferrals are a major

reason why the W.B.C. still lags significantly behind the international tournaments of other sports in generating fan passion and television ratings.[11]

In previous WBCs, a similar dynamic emerged. Because so many top players skip the WBC, generally with support from their teams—and often at the insistence of their teams—the WBC itself has been stunted. While it may be the best and most successful international baseball tournament ever, it is still not a genuine international tournament comparable to the World Cup or the Olympics, nor will it be until the best players participate. The best players, in turn, will not participate, nor will MLB owners let them, until the economic equation changes.

Solving this problem is essential for making the WBC a more successful and lucrative tournament. In his article, Michaud argues in favor of moving the tournament to November after the World Series, but this change would not help with the issue of tired pitchers, particularly those from the two World Series teams, who would need to rest their arms.[12] In a 2009 piece, Jayson Stark proposes a more multistep tournament that would culminate in the WBC finals and semifinals during the big league All-Star break.[13] These are both intriguing ideas, but they still exist within a framework of the WBC's being essentially secondary to MLB. For longtime American baseball fans, it is hard to imagine any other relationship between the WBC and MLB. From their perspective, the former is a fun tournament, while the latter is real baseball.

This perception will change only if the WBC has enough money to lure the best players. That money may have to come from outside MLB, but it is also possible that MLB could see a genuine international tournament as being sufficiently lucrative to shorten the season, require participation in international tournaments as part of all contracts (or at least all contracts for nonpitchers), or similarly facilitate the growth of the WBC.

The WBC is only one way that MLB could develop into more of a hybrid. If baseball continues to become a global sport, there will be other demands and opportunities for the best baseball players. This could mean a series of international tournaments, one-time barnstorming opportunities, or other exhibitions. The demand for barn-storming no longer exists in the United States, where most fans can get to a big league ballpark without much trouble, but baseball fans in Japan do not get a chance to see Clayton Kershaw, Mike Trout, Bryce Harper, or Giancarlo Stanton very frequently and would prob-ably pay good money for that opportunity. Should baseball grow in popularity in China, the opportunity for elite players to make money barnstorming China, or even just playing in a few exhibition games, would be substantial. This possibility is, of course, several decades away, but it cannot be ruled out.

Although baseball in China remains in its infancy, further devel-opment of the game there could have dramatic impacts on MLB. If baseball ever meaningfully takes root in China and becomes one of the country's five most popular sports, the international structure of the game could change. Given how much money is in China, there are many ways this could play out.

Chinese teams or leagues could emerge as a direct competitor to the NPB, offering a level of play one or two levels below MLB, sending their best players to the United States, and competing with the NPB for older players from the West or for prospects who just missed making a career in MLB. This scenario would work well for MLB and reinforce the existing way the game is structured.

There are, however, other possibilities—for instance, a Chi-nese Jorge Pasquel could emerge. Pasquel was the wealthy Mexi-can behind efforts to lure such players as Sal Maglie and Mickey Owen to the Mexican League in the 1940s. This did not end well for the players, who were banned from the big leagues, although some of those bans were lifted, or for Pasquel, who ended up losing his money. Given the wealth that some have accumulated in China, a Chinese Pasquel would have much deeper pockets and be less sus-ceptible to bankruptcy.

On the other hand, as Sheehan argues, there is simply too much money in baseball today for something like what happened in the 1940s to occur now.[14] It is unfathomable that a top player would walk away from a multi-year contract worth more than $150 mil-lion to play in a foreign country, or that a player about to become a big league free agent would make a similar decision. However, a

Chinese baseball league could have sufficient funds to pay players who would be fourth outfielders or middle relievers in the United States more money and give them more opportunities to play. This option might be less of a direct threat to MLB, but it would slowly take some of the top players out of MLB and change the global baseball talent balance.

Less dramatically, if baseball catches on in China, the demand for baseball and for seeing big league stars might be too great to be met by a single series in April between two big league teams. This scenario would create a very lucrative market for barnstorming in China, international or other tournaments there during the off-season, or other potential competitors for MLB. In this scenario, barnstorming would probably be organized by MLB and take the form of lucrative tours in the off-season, or perhaps tournaments between Chinese and MLB players. This scenario could occur alongside or as a kind of predecessor of MLB's expanding to Asia, because the opportunity to capture more of the revenue in Japan, Taiwan, Korea, and—if baseball catches on there—in China would be too enormous for MLB to ignore.

Today, it is hard to imagine baseball becoming popular in China, especially given the growing rivalry between the United States and China. It seems unlikely that at a historical moment when China is beginning to challenge the United States, at least in the eyes of Beijing, for global supremacy, the country would embrace a sport that is so deeply identified with the United States. However, there are precedents that are relevant here. First, baseball has a history of becoming very popular in countries outside the United States, often at a fast pace. Today, baseball is probably more popular and of roughly equivalent, if not greater, cultural significance in Japan and in the Dominican Republic than in the United States. In 1900, few could have predicted that would be true by 1940 or so, but that is what happened.

The case of Japan is particularly relevant here, because the period of baseball's most significant and conclusive ascendancy in that country coincided almost precisely with the interwar period when U.S.-Japan tensions were rising and ultimately led to the Japanese attack on Pearl Harbor and a major war between the two baseball-loving countries. By the early 1930s, baseball was so popular in Japan that it was a major destination for barnstorming American All-Star teams in the off-season.

The most famous of these barnstorming tours occurred in 1934 and included stars Lou Gehrig, Jimmie Foxx, and, most famously, Babe Ruth. However, three years earlier, a team of American stars that included Gehrig, Lefty Grove, and catcher Mickey Cochrane also barnstormed Japan. Ruth, the biggest baseball star anywhere at that time, did not participate in that trip, yet despite his absence, the tour was still a tremendous success.

In his 2002 book, Joseph Reaves describes the success of the seventeen-game tour and puts it in perspective:

In all, 450,000 Japanese paid to see the barnstorming Americans play in November 1931. That was more fans in a month than seven of the sixteen Major League teams drew during the entire 1931 season. The U.S. professionals pulled more people through the gates in seventeen games in Japan than the Pittsburgh Pirates and St. Louis Browns *combined* drew in 155 home games that year.[15]

The success of that trip reflected the growing popularity of baseball in Japan and contributed to the creation of a Japanese baseball league. In the twenty-first century, in a different geopolitical setting with a more global economy, a wildly successful barnstorming trip such as that to, for example, a China that is falling hard for baseball would very likely convince MLB not to simply let China develop its own baseball structures but to find a way to consistently plug into that new, huge, baseball-loving market. That could easily lead to more barnstorming and the hybrids described in this scenario.

If MLB does not expand to become truly international, as outlined in the previous section, the hybrid scenario may become inevitable. Growing numbers of baseball fans outside North America will want to see not only the best players but also the best competition. Moreover, as baseball becomes more popular in countries outside the United States, the movement of the best players to MLB from other countries' leagues may begin to reverse itself. If more countries produce more good players, salaries and the quality of competition in these other countries will increase, making MLB less tempting to players from Korea, Japan, and emerging baseball countries. This will drive demand for more international tournaments and other forums, including barnstorming. With modifications to MLB, particularly in the area of scheduling, these events could exist alongside an MLB that operates much as it has for the past few decades.

Scenario Four: Baseball Stays the Same, Kind Of

The history of big league baseball is, in many ways, one of change and of a contradictory-seeming fear of threats to the game. The current historiography and the passage of time obscure that view for many followers of the game, but it remains largely true.

In the 1910s, the Federal League threatened the structures of MLB. In the early 1930s and again in the early 1970s, low attendance was a major worry for the people who ran MLB. As recently as the late 1990s, MLB worried about the health of some teams so much that contracting the leagues was considered. The likely teams that would have been dropped were the Minnesota Twins, the Florida Marlins, and the Montreal Expos.[16] In the 1940s thru the 1970s, teams worried that radio and later television would rob them of their revenue. The period from roughly the late 1960s through the early 1980s was characterized by labor strife and concern that enormous increases in salaries would destroy the game and competitive balance. This concern lingered into the 1990s, when a major strike in 1994 cost MLB a third of the season and the entire postseason.

Similarly, MLB has been in a state of change and evolution for more than a hundred years, since the upstart American League (AL) first challenged the supremacy of the NL in the early 1900s. The introduction of the live ball and the home run remade how the game was played on the field in the 1920s. The development of affiliated minor league systems in the 1930s and 1940s, integration of the game in the years immediately following World War II, and expansion and franchise movements had massive impacts on MLB in the middle part of the twentieth century. The introduction of the DH, free agency, interleague play, expanded play-offs, and steroids kept baseball in a state of more or less constant flux between about 1973 and 2010.

Given this history, it is extremely unlikely that MLB will stagnate or that it has reached its final level of development, so there is almost no scenario in which baseball simply stops changing. Inevitably, there will be more expansion. Slight changes to the rules, such as expanded rosters, adjustments aimed at speeding up the game, or other modifications of how baseball is played, have always occurred periodically and will continue to do so. MLB may even include larger changes, such as shortening the season and adding another play-off round. This scenario assumes minor or nonstructural changes but also assumes that they will be the extent of the changes to MLB.

There are several ways in which this scenario could come to pass. First, it is possible that baseball will not continue to grow internationally, that MLB will be able to replace declining cable revenue with income from streaming and other Internet services, and that baseball will somehow reverse the problem of an aging fan base that threatens the game's future. If that happens, baseball will be able to remain more or less in its current form for at least the next ten or twenty years. But this is not likely, for all the reasons explained in the preceding chapters.

It is also possible that MLB could craft a strategy, or see it as the best available strategy, to try to keep the structures that currently exist in place and mostly unchanged. The biggest difficulty here would be to replace the cable television revenue without turning to more global or other sources of revenue that are considered unconventional today. The best way to do this would be through existing MLB platforms, such as MLB.TV, but the economics of that would not be easy.

An additional challenge baseball will have to resolve if it wants to keep the current basic structure of the game is the careful management of the increased internationalization of MLB. If MLB intends to keep drawing the best ballplayers in the world to the United States while also becoming more popular globally, it will need a strategy for resolving demands based on logistics, lucrative foreign markets, and millions of fans in Asia and elsewhere. Thus, this last scenario at first glance may seem like the most likely, because it requires the least amount of change and is the easiest to imagine. It is somewhat counterintuitive that achieving it will also be difficult and will demand deft handling of a range of developments that have their roots in the last decade or so of MLB's history.

Scenario Five: The Question of Collapse Revisited

Big league baseball has endured in a recognizable form for more than a century and has survived two World Wars, a civil rights revolution, globalization, PED scandals, gambling scandals, the DH rule, economic and demographic transitions, and massive technological changes. The game's extraordinary synergy between resilience and adaptability has facilitated this survival. Therefore, the chances of complete collapse are quite small but are also not zero.

The precedents for this kind of collapse are not only American institutions, such as the printed newspaper or brick-and-mortar shopping, that have been pushed to the edge of irrelevancy and financial ruin by the Internet revolution; they exist in the world of sports as well. For most of the twentieth century, boxing was an enormously popular sport. In the early and middle years of that century, such boxers as Joe Louis, Sugar Ray Robinson, and Jack Dempsey were huge stars whose fights were major media and athletic events. The fights between Louis and the German heavyweight Max Schmeling were among the most important sports events of the late 1930s. Even as late as the 1970s, such boxers as George Foreman, Ken Norton, Leon Spinks, Roberto Duran, and Sugar Ray Leonard were as well known as the baseball, football, and basketball stars of the era. For much of the period from about 1965 to 1985, Muhammad Ali was the most famous athlete in the United States and probably the world. A BBC report from 2012 argues that in the mid-1970s, Ali was not only the best-known athlete in the world but also "the most recognizable person on the planet."[17] That may be an overstatement, but Ali was at that time a global figure in a way no baseball, football, or basketball player, including Michael Jordan, ever has been.

Today, boxing is on the fringes of American sports. Polling done by Harris between 2009 and 2014 revealed that boxing was never, in those years, the favorite sport of more than 2 percent of the population.[18] An occasional big fight will generate a large pay-per-view television audience, but boxing is no longer a sport that the American people follow, discuss, or pay attention to in a way that is comparable to how they did thirty, fifty, seventy, or one hundred years ago. Boxing's decline came from a combination of changing cultural views about violence, the growth of other sports, questions about the financial arrangements around boxing, and several other factors.

This decline may seem of questionable pertinence to baseball, because the sports are so different. Baseball is a team sport with little violence, and it largely eliminated any ethical or gambling-related problems by the early 1920s. Moreover, unlike boxing, baseball is organized into a powerful league with franchises in many large cities and consistent revenue streams. For this reason, football might be more comparable to boxing. Football is still wildly popular, but few fans, journalists, players, coaches, or league officials twenty years ago could have anticipated the threat that concussions are raising for the future of the sport. Although football continues to thrive, as more parents forbid their sons to play because of fear of injury and more professional players retire early because of fear of injury, or because of actual injury, football will have to adapt, or its future could be threatened. Adapting will not be easy, given the nature of the game and the unavoidability—and, among fans, popularity—of hard hits.

If baseball suffers a collapse in popularity and relevance comparable to the one experienced by boxing over the past thirty years or so, it will be due to a different set of causes. The potential causes include revelations about ongoing PED abuse that are much greater than previously assumed by many; the financial implosion of a handful of teams that could, if timed right, threaten the overall financial health of MLB; and (much harder to predict and less directly related to baseball) such developments as widespread financial instability or terrorist attacks at a few ballparks.

This scenario is, by far, the least likely of the five. There are too many financial incentives for MLB to continue and a fan base that, while providing some reasons for concern, still represents and enormous market. Nonetheless, this option cannot be ruled out entirely.

Moving Forward

Each of these scenarios seems both plausible and a bit far-fetched. MLB's going back to the scope it had in the 1960s or 1970s; expanding to Tokyo, Santo Domingo, and beyond; combining a regular season with an extensive schedule of international tournaments and high-profile exhibitions; or even, despite all the changes inside and outside the game, entering an unprecedented period of very little change raises obstacles and challenges that will not be easy to overcome. Yet something has to happen, as MLB is not going away.

Achieving any of the more positive outcomes requires not only strategy but vision. Most obviously, making MLB truly international requires a vision and a plan that extends for at least twenty years. Baseball may be about halfway there now, as it has been actively pursuing a strategy to make the game more global.

The other scenarios, perhaps less immediately, require thoughtful visions as well. If baseball becomes a hybrid, finding a way to generate meaningful amounts of revenue from extraseasonal baseball events while not compromising the season itself will not be easy. Similarly, if the game suffers economically, preserving it in a holistic but smaller form will require forethought and vision. Even MLB's staying more or less the same is not the default setting and will not occur simply by the organization's doing nothing.

7

JOAQUIN ANDUJAR

The first great Dominican pitcher in the big leagues, as every fan knows, was Juan Marichal. Marichal was the ace of the San Francisco Giants, where he played alongside Willie Mays and Willie McCovey for more than a decade. His 243 victories are still tops among Dominican-born pitchers. Marichal, the first Dominican elected to baseball's Hall of Fame, had a career 2.89 earned run average (ERA) with a remarkable fifty-two shutouts. Perhaps the most extraordinary of Marichal's accomplishments, and a strong indicator of how much the game has changed since the 1960s, is that Marichal had one more complete game, 244, than career victories. Pedro Martínez, a better pitcher in a higher-scoring era, has eclipsed Marichal as the greatest Dominican pitcher ever, but the former Giant was nonetheless a trailblazer and an important figure in baseball history.

One of the best Dominican pitchers in the period between Marichal, who retired in 1974, and Martínez, who began his career in 1992, was a lesser-known player named Joaquin Andujar.[1] Andujar had a thirteen-year career and was a four time All-Star, pitching for the Astros, the Cardinals, and the A's. His best season was in 1982, when he won fifteen games as the ace of the pennant-winning Cardinals and pitched well enough in the World Series to pick up two wins, including the seventh game.

Andujar was renowned for being a bit of a character, mastering several different pitches, and frequently clashing with umpires. He was thrown out of Game Seven of the 1985 World Series for vociferously arguing balls and strikes, and he refused to participate in the All-Star Game that year when it became clear he was not going to be named the starting pitcher. He also was good with reporters, freely giving interviews about, for example, his collection of rocking chairs[2] and referring to himself, not inaccurately, as "one tough Dominican."[3]

Andujar, who, died in 2015, had a life and career that were filled with unforeseen turns, bad breaks, and strokes of good luck, frequently said that his favorite word in English, a language he had picked up only after becoming a professional ballplayer, was "youneverknow."[4]

A Changing Game in a Changing Context

When thinking about baseball's future and the larger question of whether big league baseball will survive, it is useful to remember Andujar's favorite word. There is a great deal of uncertainty about baseball's future, but there are also some things we know to be relevant to the question.

Big league baseball has never been stagnant or unchanging, and it is unlikely to take on those characteristics in the near future. Additionally, the game continues to evolve in very significant ways. For example, MLB is becoming more global as it continues to lose its grip on younger American fans. At the moment, these two trends have reached a kind of equilibrium, where the growth of the game internationally has helped generate foreign revenue and has drawn many great non-American players to the game, yet the U.S. fan base is still large enough to sustain large cable contracts, generally good attendance, and a high level of interest in the game.

On their own, the rising cost of attending games; the number of unused tickets at many games, particularly those of baseball's most famous and storied franchise; the declining number of young people who are playing baseball; or the growth in popularity of such sports as skateboarding, snowboarding, and lacrosse that a generation ago were either barely played in an organized way or on the fringes of youth culture would be unequivocally bad news for MLB.

These structural problems facing the game are not, however, occurring in isolation; they are occurring alongside unprecedented international growth of baseball, particularly in countries that some generations ago had very few people familiar with the quirky America game. They are also occurring as Major League Baseball (MLB) keeps producing top-quality products to help the game thrive in the Internet era. Thus, the problems of baseball and the possibility of a solution to those problems are both reasonably clear. The major question is what form that solution will take.

MLB also has to wrestle with other societal changes, in addition to the changing dynamics of youth sports, as it contemplates its future. The changing patterns of television viewing as cable and broadcast give way to streaming and on-demand services; the cultural changes around ideas of heroism and celebrity, notions that have long been central to baseball's appeal; and a growing consciousness of the extent of, and problems related to, the enormous, and increasing, economic gaps between the wealthy and everybody else all raise concerns about baseball's future. These non-baseball-related issues will make it extremely difficult for MLB to survive if it cannot adapt.

Staying Ahead of the Changes

In the long, complex, and often misunderstood history of baseball, a clear trend has emerged: baseball is at its best and its most successful when it gets in front of the major changes facing the game and society. One illustration is the successful integration of modern baseball following World War II. Jackie Robinson is recognized as a genuine baseball hero who stood up to bigotry, name calling, threats of violence, and more as the first African American MLB player of the twentieth century. Robinson changed the game forever, making it finally possible for the best players in the United States to play America's pastime regardless of their skin color. Robinson was also a great player whose accomplishments as a pioneering African American player have frequently overshadowed just how good he was.[5]

Given Robinson's impact on the game, this perception is entirely appropriate. However, Robinson is not just an important baseball player; he is an American hero and a major American historical figure. In 1982, Robinson became the first baseball player to appear on a postage stamp. He was awarded the Presidential Medal of Freedom in 1984 and the Congressional Gold Medal in 2005. When he awarded Robinson the Medal of Freedom posthumously (Robinson died in 1972), President Ronald Reagan, hardly a radical civil rights activist, said that as "an individual of courage and conviction, and as a skilled and dedicated athlete, Jackie Robinson stood tall among his peers. . . . [H]e struck a mighty blow for equality, freedom, and the American way of life. Jackie Robinson was a good citizen, a great man, and a true American champion."[6]

At the time of Robinson's death in 1972, President Richard Nixon, a man with whom Robinson shared a complicated history,[7] reflected the views of many Americans when he said:

> I am deeply saddened by the death of Jackie Robinson. His courage, his sense of brotherhood, and his brilliance on the playing field brought a new human dimension not only to the game of baseball but to every area of American life where black and white people work side by side. This nation to which he gave so much in his lifetime will miss Jackie Robinson, but his example will continue to inspire us for years to come.[8]

Robinson's contribution to baseball is of national importance in no small part because it occurred in 1947. Baseball, it should be remembered, integrated several years before *Brown v. Board of Education* (1954) and the Montgomery Bus Boycott (1955–1956) and well over a decade before the Greensboro Sit-Ins (1960), the Freedom Riders (1961), or the Civil Rights Act (1964).

Baseball also benefited by being able to manage the integration of the big leagues on its own terms. While this was done slowly by some teams, such as the Boston Red Sox, which did not have an

African American player until Elijah "Pumpsie" Green joined the team in 1959, and hesitatingly by most teams, the result was that within a few years of Robinson's debut, the Negro Leagues were finished and the best African American players were playing in MLB. This situation could not have worked out better for MLB in the years following 1947.

Robinson's joining the Dodgers was one of the first blows struck by the civil rights movement. This change gave baseball the ability to claim that it led, rather than followed, on matters of racial equality. This is also largely why Robinson is a national figure beyond baseball who has also helped baseball deflect attention from its own apartheid past.

As the years went by, two things happened that were very fortunate for baseball. First, the civil rights movement gained momentum, ultimately bringing about enormous, although far from complete, changes to American society. This made baseball seem prescient, despite the widespread opposition to Dodgers' president Branch Rickey's decision to bring Robinson to Brooklyn. In a 1997 biography of Robinson, Arnold Rampersad states that shortly before Robinson's debut, "Rickey . . . was aware of the deep opposition to Jack's promotion among the single most important group in baseball—the team owners, who in a secret ballot had voted fifteen to one (with Rickey alone dissenting) against integration."[9]

More than a quarter century before Robinson came to Brooklyn, baseball found itself in a transitional moment of a different kind, when the 1919 World Series was thrown by the Chicago White Sox to the Cincinnati Reds. That incident is relatively well known, but the Black Sox scandal, as it came to be known, was more of a culmination of the previous two decades, when gambling and dishonest ballplayers were a persistent, if usually minor, problem than a sui generis event. For example, Hal Chase, a talented first baseman who played from 1905 to 1919, was known to be connected to gamblers and faced charges of throwing games throughout his career. Martin Kohout describes Chase as "the most notoriously corrupt player in baseball history."[10] Jacob Pomrenke sums up the role of gambling in the early part of the twentieth century:

It's impossible to understand the Black Sox scandal without taking into consideration the intimate relationship between baseball and gambling during that era. Fixing games, betting on games and bribery offers were common practices during baseball's Deadball Era in the early 20th century. . . . Baseball's powers that be implicitly encouraged this behavior because attendance was soaring. Even when their own players were involved with game-fixing, baseball executives looked the other way.[11]

Since the early 1920s, however, gambling and charges of throwing games have been extremely rare in baseball. The highest-profile gambling issue since 1919 involved a famous player and manager, Pete Rose, who was accused of, among other things, betting on his team to win. Rose's lifetime ban from baseball, including from being elected to the Hall of Fame, has been controversial, but it reflects the unambiguous position baseball has taken on gambling since the 1919 World Series was thrown.

In the early 1920s, MLB, led by its first commissioner, Judge Kenesaw Mountain Landis, banned the eight players involved in throwing the 1919 World Series for life and threatened similar punishment for other players who became involved in gambling. This stance changed the tone of baseball significantly and all but eliminated gambling and concerns about other forms of corruption. In the nearly one hundred years since then, when such sports as college basketball and boxing have had problems associated with gambling, baseball has had almost no problems of that kind. In the early 1920s, Landis modernized the game and proactively implemented a gambling policy that set the tone for the next century. Landis was vindictive and probably overly harsh in lumping together all the White Sox accused of gambling, and he later became a staunch defender of segregation in baseball, but his actions following the Black Sox scandal ensured that baseball got in front of the gambling problem before it weakened the game's potential for further growth.

A quarter century later, baseball faced a different set of challenges, as the demographic changes in the two decades following the end of World War II remade America, with the country becoming less urban and more suburban:

> From 1940 onward, suburbs accounted for more population growth than central cities and, by 1960, the proportion of the total U.S. population living in the suburbs (31 percent) was almost equal to the proportion of the population living in the central cities (32 percent). From 1940 to 2000, the proportion of the population living in central cities remained relatively stable, while the suburbs continued to grow substantially. By 2000, half of the entire U.S. population lived in the suburbs of metropolitan areas.[12]

More generally, people moved away from the Midwest and the Northeast and toward the South, the Southwest, and the West. In 1950, 55.7 percent of the U.S. population lived in the Midwest or the Northeast; by 1970, this number had declined to 52.6 percent, and by the end of the twentieth century, it was only 41.9 percent.[13] Frank Hobbs and Nicole Stoops describe this movement of population that characterized the twentieth century:

> Combined, these two regions [the South and the Southwest] increased by 471 percent during the century, compared with the combined increase of 149 percent for the Northeast and Midwest. Between 1900 and 2000, the combined increase of 135 million people in the South and the West represented 66 percent of the U.S. population increase of 205 million people.[14]

As an industry based entirely in the Midwest and the Northeast, with no franchises south or east of St. Louis and fully seven out of sixteen located along the eastern seaboard between Philadelphia and Boston, baseball had to adjust or risk losing its national primacy. The movement of franchises in the early and mid-1950s helped address this issue, as teams moved to Kansas City and Milwaukee from Philadelphia and Boston and, less geographically significantly, to Baltimore from St. Louis. But it was the relocation of the Giants and the Dodgers from New York to California that remade baseball and positioned MLB as a truly national organization.

The departure of the New York Giants and Brooklyn Dodgers, to San Francisco and Los Angeles respectively, following the 1957 season represented the birth of modern big league baseball. When these two famous and successful franchises left New York, it marked MLB's biggest step toward being a national organization and accelerated a period of franchise movements, expansion, construction of new ballparks, and televised baseball that still defines the game. The relocation of these two franchises was also the death knell for the Pacific Coast League (PCL) and for high-level independent baseball more generally. Even when looking at baseball videos from the past century, it often seems like 1958 is the year for which color video first became available.

The Dodgers and particularly the Giants in their new homes also began to aggressively scout Latin America, leading to further integration of baseball. This change also gave baseball the Latino feel that has helped define the game for several decades now. In 1957, there were only twenty-five Latino players in the big leagues from Cuba (14), the Dominican Republic (1), Puerto Rico (7), and Venezuela (3), the four polities in Latin America that have produced the most baseball players. By 1962, after the Dodgers and the Giants had been playing on the West Coast for five years, this overall number had almost doubled to forty-seven. The number of Dominicans alone had increased to nine, four of whom played for the Giants that year.[15]

The departure of the Giants and the Dodgers from New York also facilitated and accelerated the emergence of another aspect of the modern baseball era—middle-aged men pining for the baseball of their youth. The Dodgers' leaving Brooklyn is a constant source of this type of nostalgia, although oddly enough, few residents of Harlem, even decades ago, ever spent comparable effort bemoaning the Giants' leaving. In addition to being voiced by the many current residents of the borough—who well into the twenty-first century speak as if the Dodgers' going to Los Angeles was a personal insult that occurred just yesterday—this sentiment, deeply rooted in a nostalgic, sugar-coated version of Brooklyn in the 1950s, has appeared in other parts of the culture as well.

The 1981 novel *The Man Who Brought the Dodgers Back to Brooklyn* is an entertaining if bizarre story of the Dodgers' coming back to Brooklyn and making it all the way to the World Series, only to lose to the Yankees, as author David Ritz phrases it, "for the seventeenth millionth time."[16] Dan Bern's song "If the Dodgers Had Stayed in Brooklyn" expresses a similarly schmaltzy approach to the beloved franchise's departure to Los Angeles:

> If the Dodgers had stayed in Brooklyn maybe Watergate would be some obscure hotel
> Tiananmen Square would be a square and Vietnam a vacation spot that travel agencies would try to sell
> Maybe Jesus would have come for the second time by now or for the first time, depending on how you feel about that stuff
> If the Dodgers had stayed in Brooklyn and decided that Ebbets Field was enough.[17]

While many Brooklynites who now must be in their eighties might still like to "shoot O'Malley twice,"[18] with the benefit of sixty years of hindsight, it is clear that the Dodgers' and the Giants' leaving New York was one of the best things ever to happen to the game.

After the Giants and the Dodgers moved to California, the expansion and franchise movement continued so that by 1970, with teams in Los Angeles, San Diego, Houston, Dallas–Fort Worth, and Atlanta, baseball had demonstrated its ability to stay ahead of the demographic changes with regard to geography and the increasing Latino presence that were remaking America at that time.

In more recent years, baseball has embraced the Internet revolution to provide customers with an enhanced and better product. Again, rather than see these new technologies as a threat to baseball, although they may well have been, MLB created new ways for fans to enjoy the game, began to find ways to monetize those innovations, and demonstrated that it was not going to be left behind by new technology related to how people consume entertainment. The question of whether baseball can transition into what will likely be a postcable age remains unanswered, but MLB must get credit for working to keep up in this area.

In a 2012 *TechTarget* article, Albert McKeon summarizes baseball's approach to the current technological environment:

> Take me out to the ballgame.
>
> And while you're at it, I prefer bleacher seats for Wednesday night games, want an IPA to wash down a plate of lemon chicken, hope to win a retro T-shirt in the next team trivia giveaway and I might make a comment on Facebook about overpaid athletes after reading the star centerfielder's derisive tweet about playing day games.
>
> That's a grand slam of expectations from a customer, but with a solid social CRM [Customer Relationship Management] strategy in place, Major League Baseball (MLB) wants to hear from the peanut gallery. MLB teams want to understand, and try to meet, the expectations of their fans, because they otherwise risk losing them.
>
> They know fans can't put down their smartphones, tablets and laptops and that they expect an intense electronic relationship with their favorite baseball teams. Fans want personalized updates about seats, food, promotional contests, player transactions and the score of tonight's game.
>
> Not wanting to lose a sports fan's disposable income to NASCAR or some other summer pursuit, MLB uses social CRM tools to readily provide that connection—by doing all but letting its customers sit in the dugout.[19]

This positive evaluation reflects baseball's success in responding to the new technological environment and providing fans with new ways to enjoy the game in a context where people are increasingly turning to their phones, tablets, and computers for entertainment of all kinds. Baseball's history is not, of course, just a series of clever strategic decisions that allowed MLB to keep abreast, or even in front, of a changing game and society. There are several areas in which baseball was slow to adapt or to address problems. These missteps and slowness have damaged the game and may continue to threaten its future.

Although baseball successfully rid itself of gambling and of the attendant rumors of gambling that frequently undermined the integrity of the game following the scandal around the 1919 World Series, baseball had allowed gambling to corrode the game so much that a World Series was thrown, threatening the future of what was then only a nascent American institution. In its earliest years, MLB was timid about seeking to actively combat gambling. This was a very poor decision that, if it had not been reversed by Landis, could have destroyed big league baseball before it had a chance to meaningfully institutionalize itself in American society.

Baseball was similarly slow to embrace television. While MLB saw the opportunities to enhance revenue from the Internet and the inevitability of its becoming a powerful part of American life, the same cannot be said of television. In 2008, Walker and Bellamy asserted that "from the beginning, baseball saw television as a threat," adding that "complaints about the negative effects of television games would grow in the 1950s."[20]

More recently, the now more than twenty years old, and still ongoing, blunder that has been baseball's response to performance-enhancing drug (PED) abuse has been damaging to baseball and stems from MLB's unwillingness to be meaningfully proactive on this issue. The steroid period, which began in the early to mid-1990s, reached its high, or low, point in 1998, when two PED abusers, Sammy Sosa and Mark McGwire, battled to break Roger Maris's single-season home run record of sixty-one, set in 1961. This race was so exciting and generated so much interest and revenue for baseball that MLB ignored the anecdotal evidence, including the bizarrely bloated musculature of the two players, as well as the physical evidence, in the form of a bottle of androstenedione spotted in McGwire's locker that season.

MLB's failure to respond to this crisis in the late 1990s led to the growth of a problem that has never gone away. The history of the steroid era has been told elsewhere,[21] but the legacy of that period includes evidence of steroid use by many of the game's biggest stars, bungled congressional testimonies, accusations of perjury, suspensions, bans, debates about whether PEDs actually helped players, scapegoating of high-profile stars, a Hall of Fame voting procedure that has no steroid policy, and strong doubts that baseball ever caught or identified all the steroid users.

During these years, no attempt by MLB to address the PED issue, whether through the study commissioned by MLB and executed by former Senate Majority Leader George Mitchell, known as the Mitchell Report; steroid policies with stronger punishments; new revelations about steroid use; or occasional declarations that the steroid problem had been solved, was effective. In January 2010, Bud Selig commented, "The so-called steroid era—a reference that is resented by the many players who played in that era and never touched the substances—is clearly a thing of the past, and Mark's [McGwire] admission today is another step in the right direction."[22] This comment was made before the Alex Rodriguez case had begun, which eventually led to a one-year suspension for one of the game's greatest players ever, and during the time ballots were being counted for Jeff Bagwell's Hall of Fame candidacy. Bagwell, a slugger deserving the honor, has seen his Hall of Fame hopes damaged by unproven rumors of PED abuse. The years following that statement also saw more PED suspensions for such players as Nelson Cruz and Jhonny Peralta.

Five years earlier, when announcing baseball's then-new steroid policy, Selig made a similarly definitive proclamation: "In the end, what is important today is, we had a problem, and we dealt with the problem."[23] Making this statement in early 2005, when the PED era was in many respects still in full swing, demonstrates just how unable, or unwilling, Selig was to address this problem. Selig's frequent comments aside, the PED era is still not over. Because of the failure of MLB to either comprehensively identify all steroid users or to craft sound and consistent policies on, for example, the record books and the Hall of Fame, the legacy of steroids will be with MLB for years to come.

Baseball has survived the PED period, but not without sustaining significant damage. One of the casualties of the mishandling of this problem may be the Hall of Fame. By failing to act decisively on steroids, Selig passed the buck to Hall of Fame voters, who have generally voted against any players even rumored to have been involved with steroids. Thus, a generation of the game's greatest players, such as Barry Bonds, McGwire, Roger Clemens, Bagwell, and others, have not been elected, leading to a backlog on the ballot that has the effect of raising the standards for the Hall of Fame to new heights every year. Additionally, by keeping such people as Clemens and Bonds out, the Hall of Fame, and the Baseball Writers' Association of America (BBWAA) that votes on who gets into the Hall of Fame, has written two of the game's greatest players partially out of baseball history. The Hall of Fame is not part of MLB, but that is precisely the point: by never getting ahead of the PED issue, MLB has kicked the problem down the road to, among others, the baseball writers who vote for the Hall of Fame.

There is a historical basis for this deflection as well. Currently, two of the top four home run hitters of all time, Barry Bonds and Alex Rodriguez; owners of the three highest single-season home run totals, Bonds again, McGwire, and Sosa; and numerous other lower-profile but still significant milestones in total bases, home runs, and slugging percentage belong to players rumored or known to have used PEDs. Moreover, several World Series winners, such as the Red Sox in 2004 and 2007 and the Yankees in 2009, were known to have several PED users. Baseball's failure to address the PED issue when it first emerged allowed the problem to get much worse and to have a much larger impact on the game's history.

The absence of a policy in recent years leaves no clear indication of how baseball should respond when these records are threatened in the future. If a high school slugger today is in twenty years a big league star trying to break a home run record, MLB has ensured there will be a controversy over whose mark he is trying to reach— the one belonging to Barry Bonds or to Henry Aaron. Selig himself has contributed to this conundrum by handling relevant questions this way: "Speaking with reporters after the ceremony, Selig was asked about Aaron being called the true home run king. 'I'm always in a sensitive spot there, but I've said that myself and I'll just leave it at that,' Selig said."[24]

This statement by Selig reflects the confusion, and some might say hypocrisy, of a man who presided over widespread steroid use, said little until the problem was known to everybody and more or less out of control, and then still sought to retain the moral high ground on the issue. Selig also grew up in Milwaukee rooting for Aaron's Braves and has been friends with the great slugger for years. That connection should be irrelevant to who the all-time home run champion is, but apparently for Selig, it is not.

Conclusion: What and for Whom Is Big League Baseball?

MLB is a multinational, multi-billion-dollar, and multimedia industry. It offers a product, the best baseball in the world, to a large market based heavily, but not entirely, in the United States. It is governed by a complex set of rules and regulations ranging from on-the-field rules, to policies about player movement and rosters, to collective-bargaining agreements between players and management, as well as many others, such as policies regarding how decisions about expansion, player movement, and cable contracts are made. The players on the field are the most visible and popular people working for MLB, but thousands of others, including scouts, coaches, front office staff, media development people, attorneys, and lower-wage employees who may, for example, take tickets or sell beer, also draw their income from some part of MLB or one of its teams.

MLB is also something else. When many fans think about baseball, when historians or journalists describe the role of baseball in the American national gestalt, they are in many cases referring not only to MLB but also to something bigger. The legend of Babe Ruth, the grace of Joe DiMaggio, the courage and importance of Jackie Robinson, the poetry of Willie Mays, or the impact of DiMaggio, Hank Greenberg, Robinson, and Roberto Clemente for Italian Americans, American Jews, African Americans, and Puerto Ricans represent something real in American culture that goes well beyond the fortunes and future of one huge capitalist entity.

The question of whether, how, and in what form big league baseball will survive occurs in that context. MLB has long been acutely aware of its history and of how to turn that history into profit in concrete and more abstract ways. The former includes selling events and memorabilia commemorating historic events, while examples of the latter include marketing campaigns aimed at highlighting baseball's role as a bridge between generations.

The challenge for MLB, as it frequently has been in the past, is to adapt to a changing context without jeopardizing the special way that baseball fans see big league baseball's history and the continuity that defines big league baseball across the decades. These are very valuable commodities. If those dimensions fall away, the *raison d'être* for big league baseball, to a large extent, will as well.

Accordingly, the question of whether big league baseball will survive is linked to the question of what big league baseball is. The answer to that question is, however, almost entirely subjective. Fans under age fifty today do not know of big league baseball without the designated hitter (DH), anathema to an earlier generation of traditional fans, but they may think interleague play undermines the integrity of the game. Similarly, fans under age thirty know baseball only with interleague play and a multitiered postseason, but their grandfathers may have thought big league baseball lost an integral component when it broke the two leagues into divisions. This discourse can be traced at least all the way back to the 1920s, when older fans thought the home run was ruining the game.

Baseball's durability is grounded in its flexibility. Had MLB insisted on remaining all white, pushed away Spanish speakers, or stayed in the Northeast and the Midwest into the 1960s, it would have lost much of its stature fifty or sixty years ago. Similarly, expanding the play-offs has heightened fan interest in the postseason, despite being a somewhat radical break with big league baseball's past.

These and other decisions have all strengthened baseball economically while pushing away, although usually only initially, some fans. It is very likely that broad dynamic will continue to characterize MLB's evolution. Older fans will get angry and threaten to quit the game as it responds to a changing social, media, demographic, and economic environment, as it always has.

Baseball's adaptability will likely be tested in the coming years in more challenging ways than in the past. Between about 1947 and

2000, baseball's primary challenge was how to take advantage of expanding markets, pools of players, and technologies. In general, MLB handled these challenges well, but they were not particularly difficult. Moreover, they all were reflections, in one form or another, of growth. Baseball successfully positioned itself to benefit from that growth, but that is largely all that it did.

In the coming years, baseball will have to navigate a more fundamental change. Macrovariables in the next decades, such as changing forms of media and declines in youth baseball participation, suggest that baseball's core market will be in relative decline. MLB has wisely prepared for this possibility by offering a range of more expensive products that provide its most intensive fans the opportunity to spend more money and by creating a strategy to further internationalize the game and ultimately generate revenue from new and growing overseas markets.

This challenge could lead big league baseball to changes of the kind described in the previous chapter that will fundamentally remake MLB. The corporate brand will not change, as MLB ultimately is whatever MLB says it is. However, major changes could disrupt the continuity of MLB that defines it for many fans. If that happens, thirty years from now, MLB could be much smaller, much more international, or more of a hybrid of league, tournament, and exhibition play. Ultimately, whether that constitutes survival is a subjective question.

NOTES

PREFACE

1. Because of tensions between the two leagues, no World Series took place in 1904.

2. Brett Smiley, "'Baseball Is Dying': A 100-Year History of Doomsday Proclamations," *Fox Sports*, March 12, 2015, available at http://www.foxsports.com/buzzer/story/baseball-is-dying-proclamations-031215.

3. Hal Sheridan, "Tennis Is Now Threatening Baseball," *Pittsburg Press*, May 19, 1915.

4. Dorothy Seymour and Harold Seymour, *Baseball: The People's Game* (Oxford: Oxford University Press, 1991), Kindle edition, chap. 6.

5. Bernard DeVoto, *Mark Twain: Letters from the Earth* (New York: Harper and Row, 1962), 70–71. This passage was brought to my attention by Henri Gueron, a noted French American observer of the game.

6. Alistair Cooke, "Loss of Sportsmanship," *Letter from America*, BBC, July 1, 1977.

7. Quoted in 'Duk, "Jim Rice Criticizes Jeter in Same Breath as Manny and A-Rod," *Big League Stew*, available at http://sports.yahoo.com/mlb/blog/big_league_stew/post/Jim-Rice-criticizes-Jeter-in-same-breath-as-Mann?urn=mlb,184442.

8. John Kass, "Baseball Isn't America's Game Perfect Game Anymore—and No One Is Surprised," *Chicago Tribune*, August 4, 2013, available at http://articles.chicagotribune.com/2013-08-04/news/ct-met-kass-0804-20130804_1_perfect-game-baseball-moment-playing-field.

9. See, for example, Dan Kedmey, "It's Official: Soccer Is Bigger Than Basketball, Baseball," *Time*, June 24, 2014, available at http://time.com/2917615/

world-cup-2014-soccer-ratings; Roger Bennett, "MLS Equals MLB in Popularity with Kids," *ESPNFC*, available at http://www.espnfc.com/major-league-soccer/story/1740529/mls-catches-mlb-in-popularity-with-kids-says-espn-poll; Chris Chase, "Kids Like European Soccer More than the World Series?" *For the Win*, October 31, 2013, available at http://ftw.usatoday.com/2013/10/world-se ries-ratings-children.

CHAPTER 1

1. "Average Salaries in Major League Baseball 1967–2009," Major League Baseball Player Association, available at http://hosted.ap.org/specials/interac tives/_sports/baseball08/documents/bbo_average_salary2009.pdf.

2. Ronald Blum, "Dodgers Top Spender, Ending Yanks' 15-Year Streak," *AP Top Story*, March 26, 2014, available at http://bigstory.ap.org/article/dodgers-top-spender-ending-yanks-15-year-streak.

3. This information is drawn from the Play Index at www.baseballreference.com.

4. Ibid.

5. Roger Angell, *Five Seasons: A Baseball Companion* (New York: Simon and Schuster, 1977), 85–86.

6. David A. Kaplan, "Exclusive: Bud Selig: The Baseball Commissioner's Exit Interview," *Reuters*, January 7, 2015, available at http://news.yahoo.com/exclu sive-bud-selig-baseball-commissioners-exit-interview-124124894—mlb.html.

7. "1994 Strike Was a Low Point for Baseball," *Associated Press/ESPN*, August 10, 2004, available at http://sports.espn.go.com/mlb/news/story?id=1856626.

8. Gary Smith, "Big Swingers Mark McGwire and Sammy Sosa Treated the Nation to a Home Run Race That Was as Refreshing as a Day at the Beach," *Sports Illustrated*, December 21, 1998.

9. Shaun Assail and Peter Keating, "Who Knew?" *ESPN The Magazine*, November 9, 2005, available at http://sports.espn.go.com/espn/eticket/story?-page=steroids&num=8.

10. Mike Bauman, "Under Selig, Game Continues to Flourish," MLB.com, December 31, 2013, available at http://mlb.mlb.com/news/article/mlb/mike-bauman-under-commissioner-bud-selig-game-continues-to-flourish?ymd =20131230&content_id=66244686&vkey=news_mlb.

11. Past attendance figures are from www.ballparksofbaseball.com.

12. Maury Brown, "Major League Baseball Sees Record $9 Billion in Rev-enues for 2014," *Forbes*, December 10, 2014, available at http://www.forbes .com/sites/maurybrown/2014/12/10/major-league-baseball-sees-record-9-billion-in-revenues-for-2014/.

13. The box score and other details from this game were found through retrosheet.org.

14. Paulsen, "MLB Postseason TV Ratings: ESPN Sets Wild Card Record in Playoff Return," *Sports Media Watch*, October 2, 2014, available at http://www .sportsmediawatch.com/2014/10/mlb-postseason-tv-ratings-giants-pirates-espn-wild-card-most-watched-ever/.

15. *Sports Media Watch*, available at http://www.sportsmediawatch.com/tag/mlb-ratings/.

16. "Game 7 Seen by 23.5 Million Viewers," *Associated Press/ESPN*, October 30, 2014, available at http://espn.go.com/mlb/playoffs/2014/story/_/id/11792338/world-series-game-7-san-francisco-giants-kansas-city-royals-seen-235-million-viewers.

17. Bill Chappell, "U.S. Women Shatter TV Ratings for Soccer with World Cup Win," *NPR*, July 6, 2015, available at http://www.npr.org/sections/thetwo-way/2015/07/06/420514899/what-people-are-saying-about-the-u-s-women-s-world-cup-win.

18. According to baseballreference.com, between 2009, its first year of use, and 2014, attendance at the new Yankee Stadium ranged from 3.2 million to 3.7 million each year, good enough to rank first in the AL for each of those six years. In 2015, this number fell to just under 3.2 million but still led the AL.

19. Chappell, "U.S. Women Shatter TV Ratings for Soccer with World Cup Win."

20. "Yankees Rookie Nervously Tells A-Rod How Much He Used to Hate Him as a Kid," *The Onion*, February 27, 2015, available at http://www.theonion.com/article/yankees-rookie-nervously-tells-a-rod-how-much-he-u-38117.

21. Scott Simkus, *Outsider Baseball: The Weird World of Hardball on the Fringe 1876–1950* (Chicago: Chicago Review Press, 2014).

22. During interleague play, the DH is used in AL parks, but not in NL parks. Between 1973 and 1975, the DH was not used in the World Series. From 1976 to 1985, the DH was used in even-numbered years in the World Series. Beginning in 1986, the DH has been used in the games played in the AL parks, but not in the NL parks.

CHAPTER 2

1. See, for example, Richard Leutzinger, "Lefty O'Doul and the Development of Japanese Baseball," *National Pastime* 12 (1992): 30–34; Joseph A. Reaves, *Taking in a Game: A History of Baseball in Asia* (Lincoln: University of Nebraska Press, 2004); or Robert Whiting, *You Gotta Have Wa* (New York: Vintage Books, 2002).

2. Dennis Snelling, *The Greatest Minor League: A History of the Pacific Coast League, 1903–1957* (Jefferson, NC: McFarland, 2012), Kindle edition 3779.

3. Michael Shapiro, *Bottom of the Ninth: Branch Rickey, Casey Stengel, and the Daring Scheme to Save Baseball from Itself* (New York: Holt, 2009), 35.

4. John M. Rosenburg, *The Story of Baseball* (New York: Random House, 1975), 65.

5. Samuel A. Alito Jr., "The Origin of the Baseball Antitrust Exemption," *Baseball Research Journal* 38, no. 2 (2009): 86–93.

6. Federal Baseball Club v. National League, 259 U.S. 200 (1922).

7. Permission to reprint granted by Chuck Brodsky.

8. Adrian Burgos Jr., "Latinos and Baseball's Integration," in *Beisbol*, edited by Ilan Stevens (Santa Barbara, CA: Greenwood, 2012), 37.

9. Neil Lanctot, *Negro League Baseball: The Rise and Ruin of a Black Institution* (Philadelphia: University of Pennsylvania Press, 2004), 317.

10. Snelling, *The Greatest Minor League*, 37.

11. Simkus, *Outsider Baseball*, Kindle edition, chap. 5.

12. Ibid. When each league had only eight teams, the term "first division" referred to the top four teams in each league.

13. *Seinfeld*, Season 6, "The Label Maker."

14. MiLB.com, available at http://www.milb.com/milb/stats/stats.jsp?y=2014&t=l_att&lid=117&sid=l117.

15. Ian Gordon, "Inside Major League Baseball's Dominican Sweatshop System," *Mother Jones*, March/April 2013, available at http://www.motherjones.com/politics/2013/03/baseball-dominican-system-yewri-guillen.

16. Jorge Ortiz, "In Suing MLB, Minor Leaguers Want Minimum Wage for Maximum Effort," *USA Today*, April 22, 2015, available at http://www.usatoday.com/story/sports/mlb/2015/04/22/minor-league-baseball-players-lawsuit-mlb-major-league-baseball-minimum-wage/26179605/.

17. John Virtue, *South of the Color Barrier: How Jorge Pasquel and the Mexican League Pushed Baseball toward Racial Integration* (Jefferson, NC: McFarland, 2008), 205–206.

18. Ibid., 132.

19. Ibid., 158–162; italics in original.

CHAPTER 3

1. Gia Kemoklidze, interview with author, June 22, 2015.

2. FIP, according to fangraphs.com, "measures what a player's ERA would look like over a given period of time if the pitcher were to have experienced league average results on balls in play and league average timing." ERA+ is ERA normalized so that it can be more easily compared across time and ballparks.

3. The Hall of Fame requires candidates to receive votes from 75 percent of voters. Voters can list up to ten candidates on their ballots.

4. A related and even better trivia question is who has the most wins of any left-handed Jewish pitcher. The answer is Ken Holtzman, not Sandy Koufax.

5. Robert Fitts, *Mashi: The Unfulfilled Baseball Dreams of Masanori Murakami, the First Japanese Major Leaguer* (Lincoln: University of Nebraska Press, 2015), Kindle edition.

6. For an entertaining and detailed description of that famous trip, see Robert Fitts, *Banzai Babe Ruth: Baseball, Espionage, and Assassination during the 1934 Tour of Japan* (Lincoln: University of Nebraska Press, 2012).

7. Brian McKenna, "Lefty O'Doul," SABR Baseball Biography Project, undated, available at http://sabr.org/bioproj/person/b820a06c.

8. Nicholas Davidoff's *The Catcher Was a Spy: The Mysterious Life of Moe Berg* (New York: Vintage, 1994) is probably the best biography of Berg and describes this event, and Berg's other wartime exploits, in some detail.

9. Fitts, *Banzai Babe Ruth*, Kindle edition, chap. 15.

10. Joseph A. Reaves, *Taking in a Game: A History of Baseball in Asia* (Lincoln: University of Nebraska Press, 2004), 114.

11. Ibid., 116.

12. Adrian Burgos Jr., *Playing America's Game: Baseball, Latinos, and the Color Line* (Berkeley: University of California Press, 2007), 4.

13. Noel Busch, "Joe DiMaggio," *Life*, April 30, 1939, 64. It is notable that his preference for Chinese food over Italian food somehow made him more American, but DiMaggio was a San Franciscan too.

14. Baseball Reference, www.baseballreference.com.

15. Jeff Katz, *Split Season: 1981* (New York: St. Martin's Press, 2015), Kindle edition, chap. 3.

16. Sadaharu Oh and David Falkner, *Sadaharu Oh: A Zen Way of Baseball* (New York: Vintage, 1985), 268–275.

17. Robert Fitts, *Wally Yonamine: The Man Who Changed Japanese Baseball* (Lincoln: University of Nebraska Press, 2009), 193.

18. Zachary D. Ryner, "Are Opening MLB Series Abroad a Good Thing for Teams, Baseball?" *Bleacher Report*, March 21, 2014, available at http://bleacher report.com/articles/1999310-are-opening-mlb-series-abroad-a-good-thing-for-teams-baseball.

19. Kemoklidze interview.

20. "World Baseball Classic Rules and Regulations," World Baseball Classic, available at http://web.worldbaseballclassic.com/wbc/2013/about/rules.jsp# eligibility.

CHAPTER 4

1. LOOGY is an acronym that stands for "left-handed one-out guy." The term refers to left-handed relief specialists who are brought in to pitch in key situations to get the opponent's top left-handed hitter out. Graeme Lloyd, Javier Lopez, and Mike Myers are contemporary or recent LOOGYs. Perhaps the best-known LOOGY of all time is Jesse Orosco, who pitched for nine different teams over the course of twenty-four years, but for the last thirteen of those years never pitched as many as sixty innings.

2. Maury Brown, "Major League Baseball Sees Record $9 Billion in Revenues for 2014," *Forbes*, December 10, 2014, available at http://www.forbes.com/sites/maurybrown/2014/12/10/major-league-baseball-sees-record-9-billion-in-revenues-for-2014/.

3. Jon Pessah, *The Game: Inside the Secret World of Major League Baseball's Power Brokers* (New York: Little Brown, 2015), iBook edition.

4. The A's played eighty-one home games in 1974, but because they played five double-headers, they only had seventy-six home dates.

5. Bill Pennington, *Billy Martin: Baseball's Flawed Genius* (New York: Houghton Mifflin Harcourt, 2015), iBook edition.

6. Ibid.

7. Baseball Almanac, available at http://www.baseball-almanac.com/ws/wstv.shtml.

8. "Facts: Sports, Activity and Children," Aspen Institute: Project Play, available at http://www.aspenprojectplay.org/the-facts.

9. "Pediatric Overuse Injuries Increase Due to Year-Round, One-Sport Training," *Orthopedics Today*, July 2014, available at http://www.healio.com/orthopedics/pediatrics/news/print/orthopedics-today/%7Bd50c170e-85cb-438d-8c24-1ab35d60d06f%7D/pediatric-overuse-injuries-increase-due-to-year-round-one-sport-training.

10. Carrie Armstrong, "AAP Releases Recommendations on Overuse Injuries and Overtraining in Child Athletes," *American Family Physician* 76, no. 11 (2007): 1725.

11. Quoted in "The Benefits of Playing Multiple Sports: A Conversation with David Epstein," *TrueSport*, available at http://truesport.org/benefits-playing-multiple-sports-conversation-david-epstein/.

12. David Epstein, "Sports Should Be Child's Play," *New York Times*, June 10, 2014, available at http://www.nytimes.com/2014/06/11/opinion/sports-should-be-childs-play.html.

13. Fred Engh, *Why Johnny Hates Sports* (Garden City Park, NY: Square One, 2002), 135.

14. Interview with author, November 16, 2015.

15. Interview with author, December 29, 2015.

16. Brian Costa, "Why Children Are Abandoning Baseball," *Wall Street Journal*, May 20, 2015, available at http://www.wsj.com/articles/why-baseball-is-losing-children-1432136172.

17. Kelly Balfour, "Life in the Stands: The Experiences of Female Major League Baseball Fans" (Ph.D. diss., University of Tennessee, 2012).

18. Derek Thompson, "Which Sports Have the Whitest/Richest/Oldest Fans?" *The Atlantic*, February 10, 2014, available at http://www.theatlantic.com/business/archive/2014/02/which-sports-have-the-whitest-richest-oldest-fans/283626/.

19. Jennifer Ring, *A Game of Their Own: Voices of Contemporary Women in Baseball* (Lincoln: University of Nebraska Press, 2015), xxvii–xxviii.

20. Ibid., 191.

21. Ibid., 17.

22. Dorothy Seymour and Harold Seymour, *Baseball: The People's Game* (Oxford: Oxford University Press, 1991), Kindle edition, chap. 23

23. Albert Spalding, *America's National Game: Historic Facts Concerning the Beginning, Evolution, Development and Popularity of Base Ball, with Personal Reminiscences of Its Vicissitudes, Its Victories and Its Votaries* (New York: American Sports Publishing, 1911), 10–11.

24. Ira Boudway, "Fixing Baseball's Old-People Problem," *Bloomberg*, April 1, 2014, available at http://www.bloomberg.com/bw/articles/2014-04-01/fixing-baseballs-old-people-problem-with-merchandise-highlights.

25. J. C. R. Licklider, "Televistas: Looking Ahead through Side Windows,"

in *Public Television, A Program for Action: The Report and Recommendations of the Carnegie Commission on Educational Television* (New York: Harper and Row, 1967), 212.

26. Rob Peters, *The Social Media Marketing Handbook—Everything You Need to Know about Social Media Marketing* (Aspley, Australia: Emereo, 2012), 779.

27. Christine Rosen, "The Age of Egocasting," *New Atlantis* (Winter 2004–2005): 51–72.

28. GIDP is the number of times a player grounds into a double play.

29. Ingrid K. Williams, "Japanese Baseball: Root, Root, Root and Buy Me Some Eel," *New York Times*, July 1, 2009, available at http://www.nytimes.com/2009/07/05/travel/05journeys.html?_r=0.

30. Joseph A. Reaves, *Taking in a Game: A History of Baseball in Asia* (Lincoln: University of Nebraska Press, 2004), 156.

31. Chris Rock, "Chris Rock's Take on Blacks in Baseball: Real Sports (HBO)," YouTube video, 7:09, posted by HBO, April 22, 2015, https://www.youtube.com/watch?v=oFFQkQ6Va3A.

32. Maury Brown, "In-Market Streaming of MLB Games Could Hinge on Allowing MLB.TV to Co-Stream," *Forbes*, March 9, 2015, available at http://www.forbes.com/sites/maurybrown/2015/03/09/in-market-streaming-of-mlb-games-could-hinge-on-allowing-mlb-tv-to-co-stream/.

CHAPTER 5

1. Jeff Pearlman, "At Full Blast Shooting Outrageously from the Lip, Braves Closer John Rocker Bangs Away at His Favorite Targets: The Mets, Their Fans, Their City and Just about Everyone in It," *Sports Illustrated*, December 27, 1999, 64–68.

2. Curt Smith, *America's Dizzy Dean* (St. Louis: Bethany Press, 1978), 117–118.

3. James R. Walker and Robert V. Bellamy, *Centerfield Shot: A History of Baseball on Television* (Lincoln: University of Nebraska Press, 2008), 193.

4. Ibid., 198.

5. Victor Luckerson, "Fewer People Than Ever Are Watching TV," *Time*, December 3, 2014, available at http://time.com/3615387/tv-viewership-declining-nielsen/.

6. "Are Young People Watching Less TV? (Updated—Q1 2015 Data)," MarketingCharts, June 30, 2015, available at http://www.marketingcharts.com/television/are-young-people-watching-less-tv-24817/.

7. Jim Edwards, "Brutal: 50% Decline in TV Viewership Shows Why Your Cable Bill Is So High," *Business Insider*, January 31, 2013, available at http://www.businessinsider.com/brutal-50-decline-in-tv-viewership-shows-why-your-cable-bill-is-so-high-2013-1.

8. Edmund Lee, "TV Subscriptions Fall for First Time as Viewers Cut the Cord," *Bloomberg News*, March 19, 2014.

9. Luckerson, "Fewer People Than Ever Are Watching TV."

10. Pulkit Chandna, "Streaming to Blame as Decline in U.S. Live TV Viewership Accelerates," *TechHive*, February 6, 2015, available at http://www.techhive.com/article/2880051/streaming-to-blame-as-decline-in-u-s-live-tv-viewership-accelerates.html.

11. Ibid.

12. Cecilia Kang, "TV Is Increasingly for Old People," *Washington Post*, September 5, 2014, available at http://www.washingtonpost.com/news/business/wp/2014/09/05/tv-is-increasingly-for-old-people/.

13. Marshall Smelser, *The Life That Ruth Built* (New York: Quadrangle, 1975), 167–168.

14. The Baseball Almanac, available at http://www.baseball-almanac.com/quotes/quomatt.shtml.

15. Leigh Montville, *The Big Bam: The Life and Times of Babe Ruth* (New York: Doubleday, 2006), 13–14.

16. Murray Schumach, "Babe Ruth, Baseball's Great Star and Idol of Children, Had a Career Both Dramatic and Bizarre," *New York Times*, August 17, 1948.

17. Joe DiMaggio, *Lucky to Be a Yankee* (1949; repr., New York: Grosset and Dunlap, 1971), 194.

18. Tom Meany, *The Magnificent Yankees* (New York: Grosset and Dunlap, 1963), x.

19. Jim Bouton, *Ball Four* (Cleveland: World Publishing, 1970), 85.

20. Dick Young, quoted in Jim Bouton, *I'm Glad You Didn't Take It Personally* (New York: William Morrow, 1971), 3.

21. Ibid., 12.

22. Dan Epstein, *Big Hair and Plastic Grass: A Funky Ride through Baseball and American in the Swinging '70s* (New York: St. Martin's Press, 2012), 3.

23. Murray Chass, "On Baseball: Was Silence Better for Steve Carlton?" *New York Times*, April 14, 1994.

24. Mike Oz, "Derek Jeter's No. 2 Is Baseball's Top-Selling Jersey of All Time," *Yahoo! Sports*, September 23, 2014, available at http://sports.yahoo.com/blogs/mlb-big-league-stew/derek-jeter-s-no--2-is-baseball-s-top-selling-jersey-of-all-time-233941388.html.

25. Drew Gold, "Derek Jeter Most Popular Current Baseball Player," St. Leo University Polling Institute, March 28, 2014, available at http://polls.saintleo.edu/derek-jeter-most-popular-current-baseball-player/.

26. Ben Lindbergh, "The Tragedy of Derek Jeter's Defense," *Grantland*, August 27, 2013, available at http://grantland.com/features/the-tragedy-derek-jeter-defense/.

27. David Lariviere, "ESPN Should Be Ashamed by Keith Olbermann's Rant about Derek Jeter," *Forbes*, September 24, 2014, available at http://www.forbes.com/sites/davidlariviere/2014/09/24/espn-should-be-ashamed-by-keith-olbermanns-rant-about-derek-jeter/.

28. Michael Gray, "Derek Jeter Has Made This Season an Ego-Driven Circus," *New York Post*, May 17, 2014, available at http://nypost.com/2014/05/17/how-derek-jeter-has-turned-this-season-into-an-ego-driven-circus/.

29. Tom Mechin, "Derek Jeter: A Legend or Overrated?" *Bleacher Report*, April 6, 2011, available at http://bleacherreport.com/articles/656875-derek-jeter-a-legend-or-overrated.

30. Mark Lelinwalla, "Sports Illustrated Players Poll Names Derek Jeter Baseball's Most Overrated," *New York Daily News*, June 19, 2008, available at http://www.nydailynews.com/sports/baseball/yankees/sports-illustrated-players-poll-names-derek-jeter-baseball-overrated-article-1.293992.

31. Howard Megdal, "The Indisputable Selfishness of Derek Jeter," *Bleacher Report*, September 2, 2014, available at http://www.sbnation.com/mlb/2014/9/2/6097443/derek-jeter-batting-order-team-player-joe-girardi-lou-gehrig.

32. Richard Justice, "Jeter Deserving of Place among Yankees' Legends," MLB.com, February 12, 2014, available at http://m.mlb.com/news/article/67700502/richard-justice-derek-jeter-deserving-of-place-among-yankees-legends.

33. Mike Bauman, "Baseball Will Miss Jeter's Class, Humility Most." MLB.com, August 27, 2014, available at http://m.mlb.com/news/article/91754550/mike-bauman-baseball-will-miss-derek-jeters-class-humility-most.

34. Trent C. Rosencrans, "Al Kaline Calls Mike Trout 'An Outstanding Player,' Compares Him to Mickey Mantle," *CBS Sports*, July 17, 2012, available at http://www.cbssports.com/mlb/eye-on-baseball/19601463/al-kaline-compares-mike-trout-to-mickey-mantle.

35. Jake O'Donnell, "Fact: John Rocker Should Not Be Allowed to Tweet Anymore," *Sportsgrid*, November 30, 2013, available at http://www.sportsgrid.com/mlb/fact-john-rocker-should-not-be-allowed-to-tweet-anymore/.

36. Jonathan Lehman, "Chipper Jones and the Ignorant Side of Athlete Twitter Sharing," *New York Post*, February 10, 2015, available at http://nypost.com/2015/02/10/chipper-jones-and-the-ignorant-side-of-athlete-twitter-sharing/.

37. Doug Short, "The Median Household Income Little Changed in July," *Advisor Perspectives*, September 11, 2015, available at http://www.advisorperspectives.com/dshort/updates/Median-Household-Income-Update.php.

38. "Business of Baseball Downloadable Data and Documents," SABR, available at http://roadsidephotos.sabr.org/baseball/data.htm#data.

CHAPTER 6

1. Baseball America, available at http://www.baseballamerica.com/online/leagues/mlb/yankees/top10archive.html.

2. When presented in that format, those three numbers refer to batting average, on-base percentage and slugging percentage.

3. Bruce Jenkins, "Giants Coach Hensley Meulens a True Man of the World," *San Francisco Chronicle*, March 27, 2014, available at http://www.sfgate.com/giants/jenkins/article/Giants-coach-Hensley-Meulens-a-true-man-of-the-5347584.php.

4. Serge F. Kovaleski and David Waldstein, "Madoff Had Wide Role in Mets' Finances," *New York Times*, February 1, 2011, available at http://www.nytimes.com/2011/02/02/sports/baseball/02mets.html?_r=1; and Richard Sandomir and Ken Belson, "Mets' Owners Agree to Settle Madoff Suit for $162 Million," *New York Times*, March 19, 2012, available at http://www.nytimes.com/2012/03/20/sports/baseball/mets-owners-pay-162-million-to-settle-madoff-suit.html.

5. Jared Diamond, *Collapse: How Societies Choose to Fail or Succeed* (New York: Viking, 2005), 421.

6. Harris Interactive, "Football's Still Doing the Touchdown Dance All Over Baseball's Home Plate," January 21, 2015, available at http://www.theharrispoll.com/sports/Footballs_Doing_The_Touchdown_Dance.html.

7. The New York Yankees cleverly riffed on this annoying trope by making a T-shirt that says, "Why is it called the World Series if it is played in the Bronx every year?"

8. Interview with the author, October 1, 2015.

9. Darren Rovell, "Rob Manfred: 154 Games Possible," ESPN.com, February 24, 2015, available at http://espn.go.com/mlb/story/_/id/12370390/rob-manfred-says-consider-shortening-season-there-was-interest.

10. The greater Tokyo-based teams are the Yakult Swallows, the Yomiuri Giants, the Chiba Lotte Marines, the Saitama Seibu Lions, and the Yokohama DeNA BayStars.

11. Jon Michaud, "How to Fix the World Baseball Classic," *New Yorker*, February 28, 2013, available at http://www.newyorker.com/news/sporting-scene/how-to-fix-the-world-baseball-classic.

12. Ibid.

13. Jayson Stark, "The Stark Plan Will Give WBC Big Boost," ESPN.com, March 20, 2009, available at http://sports.espn.go.com/mlb/worldclassic2009/columns/story?id=3999459.

14. Interview with the author, October 1, 2015.

15. Joseph A. Reaves, *Taking in a Game: A History of Baseball in Asia* (Lincoln: University of Nebraska Press, 2004), 68; italics in original.

16. For an overview of the contraction discussion, see David Schoenfeld, "Still 30 Teams: Contraction Timeline," ESPN.com, February 5, 2002, available at http://assets.espn.go.com/mlb/s/2002/0205/1323230.html.

17. "Muhammed Ali: The Ultimate Fighter," BBC, July 27, 2012, available at http://www.bbc.co.uk/timelines/zy3hycw.

18. "Harris Poll: NFL Remains King among U.S. Adults, But Gap with Baseball Closer," *Sports Business Daily*, January 28, 2015.

CHAPTER 7

1. The other contender for this admittedly obscure title is former Reds star Mario Soto.

2. Phil Elderkin, "Joaquin Andujar: A Colorful Character and a Top Pitcher," *Christian Science Monitor*, May 16, 1983, available at http://www.csmonitor.com/1983/0516/051634.html.

3. George Vecsey, "Sports of the Times: 'One Tough Dominican,'" *New York Times*, October 21, 1982, available at http://www.nytimes.com/1982/10/21/sports/sports-of-the-times-one-tough-dominican.html.

4. Michael Eisenbath, *The Cardinals Encyclopedia* (Philadelphia: Temple University Press, 1999), 130.

5. Lincoln Mitchell, "How Good a Player Was Jackie Robinson?" *Huffington Post*, April 17, 2013, available at http://www.huffingtonpost.com/lincoln-mitchell/how-good-a-player-was-jac_b_3099879.html.

6. Ronald Reagan, "Remarks at the Presentation Ceremony for the Presidential Medal of Freedom," March 18, 1984, available at https://reaganlibrary.archives.gov/archives/speeches/1984/32684a.htm.

7. Michael Beschloss, "Jackie Robinson and Nixon: Life and Death of a Political Friendship," *New York Times*, June 6, 2014, available at http://www.nytimes.com/2014/06/07/upshot/jackie-robinson-and-nixon-life-and-death-of-a-political-friendship.html?abt=0002&abg=0.

8. Richard Nixon, "Statement on the Death of Jackie Robinson," October 24, 1972, available at http://www.presidency.ucsb.edu/ws/?pid=3651.

9. Arnold Rampersad, *Jackie Robinson: A Biography* (New York: Ballantine, 1997), 160.

10. Martin Kohout, "Hal Chase," SABR Baseball Biography Project, available at http://sabr.org/bioproj/person/aab1d59b.

11. Jacob Pomrenke, "Gambling in the Deadfall Era," National Pastime Museum, available at http://www.thenationalpastimemuseum.com/article/gambling-deadball-era.

12. Frank Hobbs and Nicole Stoops, "Demographic Trends in the Twentieth Century," Census.gov, November 2000, available at https://www.census.gov/prod/2002pubs/censr-4.pdf 33, accessed September 24, 2015.

13. Ibid.

14. Ibid.

15. See www.baseballreference.com.

16. David Ritz, *The Man Who Brought the Dodgers Back to Brooklyn* (New York: Simon and Schuster, 1981), 286.

17. Permission to reprint granted by Dan Bern.

18. "Shoot O'Malley twice" is the punch line to an old Brooklyn joke dating to shortly after the Dodgers left. The setup is "What would you do if you were in a room with Hitler, Stalin, and Walter O'Malley and had a gun but only two bullets?" *Shoot O'Malley Twice* is also the title of a 2011 play by Jon Brooks.

19. Albert McKeon, "Companies Building CRM Strategies Can Learn from How Major League Baseball Uses Social Media to Connect with Fans," *TechTarget*, July 2012, available at http://searchcrm.techtarget.com/feature/MLB-Teams-Batting-a-Thousand-with-Social-CRM.

20. Walker and Bellamy, *Centerfield Shot*, 179, 185.

21. See, for example, Jose Canseco, *Juiced: Wild Times, Rampant 'Roids, Smash Hits, and How Baseball Got Big* (New York: Regan Books, 2005); Mark Fainaru-Wada and Lance Williams, *Game of Shadows: Barry Bonds, BALCO, and the Steroids Scandal That Rocked Professional Sports* (New York: Gotham, 2006); George

Mitchell, *Report to the Commissioner of Baseball of an Independent Investigation into the Illegal Use of Steroids and Other Performance Enhancing Substances by Players in Major League Baseball* (2007); or Jon Pessah, *The Game: Inside the Secret World of Major League Baseball's Power Brokers* (New York: Little, Brown, 2015).

22. Michael S. Schmidt, "Selig Says Steroid Era Is Basically Over," *New York Times*, January 11, 2010, available at http://www.nytimes.com/2010/01/12/sports/baseball/12steroids.html.

23. David Sheinin, "Baseball Moves to Strengthen Its Drug Policy," *Washington Post*, January 14, 2005, available at http://www.washingtonpost.com/wp-dyn/articles/A6921-2005Jan13.html.

24. "Selig Hints Aaron Still Baseball's HR King," April 8, 2014, Associated Press, available at http://www.usatoday.com/story/sports/mlb/2014/04/08/selig-hints-aaron-still-baseballs-home-run-king/7483779/.

INDEX

Negro Leagues, 15, 18, 20–22, 24–26, 31, 58, 159, 161, 176
Netflix, 114, 116
Netherlands, 3, 8, 51, 67–68, 70, 73, 143, 161
Nettles, Graig, 122
New Atlantis, 99
Newcombe, Don, 5
Newhouser, Hal, 41
Newman, Jeff, 79
New York City, 6, 20, 22, 28, 30, 34–37, 41, 45, 49, 52, 60, 66, 77–79, 82, 109–110, 120, 122, 128–129, 142, 151, 157, 159, 179–180, 184
New York Daily News, 124
New York Giants, 17, 22, 26, 30–34, 40, 55, 110–111, 179–180
New York Mets, 6, 22, 104, 109, 117, 125, 145
New York Post, 130
New York Times, 118
New York World-Telegram, 152
New York Yankees, 11, 20, 27, 29, 55, 65, 118, 142
NFL (National Football League), 14–16, 155
Nielsen ratings, 10, 93, 114
Nilsson, Dave, 67
Nippon Professional Baseball (NPB), 56–57, 62, 64, 159, 164
Nixon, Richard, 125; comments on death of Jackie Robinson, 175
NL. *See* National League
Nomo, Hideo, 62–66
North Beach, 60
Norton, Ken, 169
NPB (Nippon Professional Baseball Organization), 56–57, 62, 64, 159, 164

Oakland A's, 34, 35
Oakland Oaks, 27–28
Oates, Johnny, 141
O'Brien, Eddie, 123
O'Doul Lefty, 19–20, 23, 27, 29, 55
Office of Strategic Services (OSS), 56

Oh, Sadaharu, 42, 56, 64–65, 124
Ohio State University, 87
Olbermann, Keith, 130
Olympics, 16, 70–71, 154, 165
O'Malley, Walter, 180
Onion, The, 13
OPS+ (on-base plus slugging), 19
Ortiz, David, 24, 45, 51, 127
Osaka, 153, 155
OSS (Office of Strategic Services), 56
Ott, Mel, 5, 130
Owen, Mickey, 40–41, 164

Pacific Coast League (PCL), 18–20, 27–29, 31–32, 38, 159–160, 179
Pagan, Angel, 71
Paige, Satchel, 21, 23, 36, 41
Palmeiro, Rafael, 127
Palmer, Jim, 50
Panama, 2–3, 44–45, 61, 70, 156
Pan American Games, 70
Park, Chan Ho, 66, 160
Pasquel, Jorge, 41–42, 164
Pavlas, Dave, 3
PCL (Pacific Coast League), 18–20, 27–29, 31–32, 38, 159–160, 179
Pearlman, Jeff, 109
PEDs (performance-enhancing drugs), 1–2, 7–8, 35, 63, 126–129, 146, 168–170, 182–184
Pennington, Bill, 81
Peralta, Jhonny, 183
Perez, Juan, 27
Performance-enhancing drugs (PEDs), 1–2, 7–8, 35, 63, 126–129, 146, 168–170, 182–184
Perry, Gaylord, 52
Pessah, Jon, 76
Peters, Rob, 99
Pettitte, Andy, 127
Philadelphia Athletics, 30–31
Philadelphia Magazine, 127
Philadelphia Phillies, 30–31, 76, 151
Piazza, Mike, 19
Pittsburgh Pirates, 28, 30, 61, 63, 76, 78–79, 141, 166

Lincoln A. Mitchell is a scholar and writer based in New York City. He was on the faculty of Columbia University for many years and has contributed to numerous publications, including the *Washington Quarterly,* the *American Interest, World Affairs Journal,* the *Washington Post,* and the *New York Times.* Visit him online at www.lincolnmitchell.com.